Spirited Waters

Spirited Waters

Soloing

South

Through

The Inside

Passage

Jennifer Hahn

THE
MOUNTAINEERS
BOOKS

For David Arthur Hahn,
journeyer, magician,
heyoka, and brother,
buried at sea.

Published by
The Mountaineers Books
1001 SW Klickitat Way, Suite 201
Seattle, WA 98134

© 2001 by Jennifer Hahn

First edition, 2001

The Brandy Tree (Otter's Song), words and music by Gordon Bok. Copyright 1967. Reprinted courtesy of Timberhead Music.

Published simultaneously in Great Britain by Cordee, 3a DeMontfort Street, Leicester, England, LE1 7HD

Manufactured in Canada

Project Editor: Christine Ummel Hosler
Copyeditor: Brenda Pittsley
Cover and book design and layout: Mayumi Thompson
Cartographer and illustrator: Jennifer Hahn
Cover photograph: *Sea kayak on beach at sunset.* © Ron Watts/CORBIS

Library of Congress Cataloging-in-Publication Data
Hahn, Jennifer, 1958-
  Spirited waters : soloing south through the Inside Passage / Jennifer Hahn.— 1st ed.
    p. cm.
Includes bibliographical references (p.   ).
  ISBN 0-89886-744-4 (cloth)
  1. Sea kayaking—Inside Passage. 2. Inside Passage—Description and travel.
  3. Hahn, Jennifer, 1958—Journeys—Inside Passage. I. Title.
  GV776.115 .H34 2001
  797.1'224'092—dc21
                                                                    2001001904

Contents

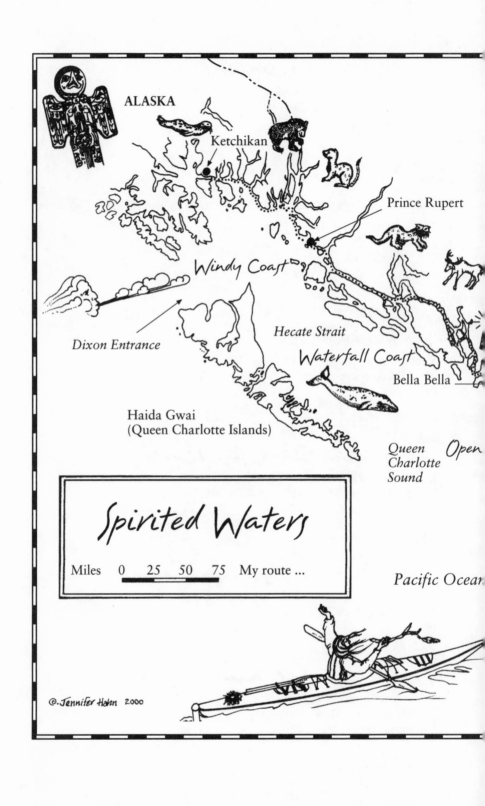

ALASKA

Ketchikan

Prince Rupert

Windy Coast

Dixon Entrance

Hecate Strait

Waterfall Coast

Bella Bella

Haida Gwai
(Queen Charlotte Islands)

*Queen
Charlotte
Sound*

Open

Spirited Waters

Miles   0   25   50   75   My route ...

Pacific Ocean

©.Jennifer Hahn 2000

ALASKA

CANADA

WASHINGTON

BRITISH COLUMBIA

Namu

Salish Sea Coast

Vancouver

Komo Kulshan
10,778'

Johnstone Strait

*Big Island
Coast*

Bellingham

Vancouver Island

Victoria

Strait of Juan de Fuca

Seattle

Mt. Tahoma
14,410'

WASHINGTON

Foreword

It begins with a whisper, writes Jennifer Hahn, of her seafaring solo vision of kayaking the Inside Passage south from Alaska to Bellingham, Washington. Hahn listens not only to the still, small voice within but also to the whispers of waves and whirlpools, "humpbacked whale trees," and eagle's scree. And on her first plunge into the Inside Passage, she hears this: *You must return here and kayak alone.*

In many of the Native peoples' stories of our Pacific Northwest, there are those who can listen and journey between worlds, of land and sea, human and animal. There are those of us still in the twenty-first century who listen to the Sound, to the heart-shaped blows and bass rumbles of whales, to the sonorous, violet mists that make meditative islands of us, hidden even in our own homes. Our natural world and all her animals are always speaking to us; it is we who often have lost the art of listening, of hearing ourselves called into companionship with forces much greater than we.

Attuning her senses and strengths, her fears and hopes to the spirited waters that will carry her home, Hahn accepts the true offering of the Water Way wilderness adventure—and that is not conquest, but true humility. *With all my skills, I still surrender to a greater body of water.* Perhaps here is also a more feminine form of the hero's journey into the very heart of nature. There is no heroic boast—*I will do this! I will make my mark!*

Water, unlike a mountain peak, cannot be claimed or summitted. Staying afloat, horizontal with the waves, not rising above but paddling in perfect synch with the currents, navigating the certainties of tide, the vagaries of weather—these are the skills of a seafarer. And though Hahn has these survival skills honed from years of running her own kayaking company, there is no ambition in her hope to kayak the Inside Passage. There is, instead, fear, some admitted foolhardiness, and much spirit.

Naming her kayak after the Yoruba ocean goddess *Yemaya*, Hahn's own passage is a spirit quest, complete with terror, adventure, and even the "woman's touch" of a few surprising recipes. While contemplating a near-capsize in a storm off Slate Island, Hahn seeks several days of island solitary shelter. Here she follows a weasel along the wind-battered beach to search out sea algae— from rabbit-eared *fucus* (popweed) to make sea Cheetos to dessert delicacies of *Gigartina* (Turkish towel) to make chocolate ocean pudding.

Spirited Waters is a journey initiated and at last fulfilled by ocean storms. At the end of her two springs and summers of solo kayaking, Hahn writes, "My courage and competence in storms had grown like the rings of an old fir tree. I was stronger in my heartwood and exterior."

She has also expanded her range of hearing. In home waters at last, Hahn rejoices with the storm "shape-shifting Rosario Strait" and listens to the "rushing, whooshing energy passing through" a three-story alder tree, discovering "a river inside a tree." Realizing that the trees, like the river, like the ocean, were a "hollow conduit for sound waves to travel," Hahn at last understands why her solo journey was not lonely. For all along the way she had been in communion with living beings—water, trees, sky, and animals.

She asks us to contemplate with her what we humans have lost by not listening. "We must talk with many things," she concludes. "Seals and eagles. Water and wind. Columbine flowers and spruce trees. By broadening our idea of companions, we discover we don't so much experience solitude, as multitude."

So even on our solo and wild journeys, we are never alone.

Brenda Peterson,
author of *Living by Water* and *Singing to the Sound*

Acknowledgments

It takes a community to write a book and keep your marbles. Oceans of thanks to my wanderlust father, Warren "Bud" Hahn, who showed me Volkswagens float. His simple advice still compasses me: "Do what makes you happy—outside." Hugs to Chris Moench, my life partner, who made the dream of a writer's life reality and who, heart and soul, is in it for the long haul. Thanks to my step-mom Marian Stewart Hahn, a fine writer in her own right, who led by example. Eternal gratitude to my mom, Maryjane Peterson Hahn, for the first ocean cradle.

Applause for the heartfelt support of wizardess and agent Anne Depue, who is as hard-working as she is kind. Chocolate-smothered thanks to my gracious, spunky editors, Cassandra Conyers, Christine Hosler, and Kathleen Cubley, four-star publicist Alison Koop, visionary eye Mayumi Thompson, and all the wonderful folks behind the scenes at The Mountaineers Books, including Margaret Foster for bringing me "on board." Brenda Pittsley—for gutsy and glorious editing—Bravo!

For "a room of one's own" and surrogate family between travels—wild banshee trills over still water to Leslie Clark and "the boys." A heart-spun thanks to Nancy Simmerman for a cozy island cabin, fresh hen's eggs, and editorial feedback these last months of writing. Thanks to *Audubon* magazine mentor Rox Sayre for telling me the earth needs more women nature writers. Belated thanks to writing gurus Don McLeod and Annie Dillard, whose wise teachings sprout beyond classroom walls.

Gene Meyers, blessings bow and stern for the gift of a homemade kayak years ago. Dee Anderson, for fortitude and a million-dollar laugh and C.J. Seitz for guiding—mucho kudos. To the new owners of Elakah!—Rob Seckinger and Ina Clark—three cheers for your support as I navigated words and waters. Gratitude to Roger VanStelle whose generous resources and labor got the Elakah! dream floating and who shared survival skills on early kayak voyages, like gaffing a 75-pound halibut from a kayak and baking a pineapple-upside-down cake in 60-knot winds.

Humble thanks to the many editorial "eagle eyes" that scrutinized this manuscript in its early and later forms: Krista Hunter, Katy Beck, Ginger Oppenheimer (who retrieved many a draft from her midnight porch), my women writing books circle—Dana Jack and Ara Taylor (who urged, "write wildly— the wilder the better!"), and my dear mom-in-law Sarah Moench. Thanks to Fay Fenske at the Bellingham Public Library, the Western Washington University library, and the Royal Museum of British Columbia. Thanks to Lisa Beck, Dave Castor, David Scherrer, Sandy Jilton, Rod Burton, Frank James, Erin Merenda, Josh Kramer, Mark Miller, and "Seal Woman" in Ashton, Oregon.

A high five to the lightkeepers of the Inside Passage: the Rose family for taking a soaked waif in as family; Andy and his wife at Boat Bluff, as well as Barb and Bob of the "Boat Bluff Home Brewery." Thanks for Coast Guard-strength duct tape and kindness from Addenbroke Island's lightkeepers, Barry and Grant. To "Fil" of Driad Point—your memory is a trellis of roses.

"Puddle stomps" to the Widness clan and Southeast Exposure in Ketchikan. Gratitude to my women's group who "sent me off" with a ritual launch and talismans for the journey: Ingella Abbott, Leslie Clark, Margaret Currin, Nancy Friedman, Rose LaBelle, Elaine Wibbey, and Carolyn Matthews. Chris Kress and the Anderson clan, your photos sparked hazy memory.

Thanks to the First Nations people—the elders at Klemtu, the Speck Family, and the fishers en route—who hold land and sea sacred. May we all. Gratitude to the biologists and stewards of the watershed world: Rick M. Harbo, Jane Watson, Joe Scott at Northwest Ecosystems Alliance, Steve Seymour, Wendy Scherrer of Nooksack Salmon Enhancement Association, Shannon Moore, Clare Fogelsong, and Mike Featherstone. Thanks to the crews of *Dancer*, *Freya*, and *Tatoosh*.

For the rose on my kayak bow—a reminder to "love myself out there"— Whitebear—yes! Marj Meyer—for magic and mother love after my own mom's (your sister's) death—infinite blessings.

Thanks to Clyde Ford for believing and Chris Martin for music. Raised paddles to Maya Gauvreau, Peter Hahn, Jessica Hahn, Chris Myatt, Bob Moench, Yarrow Moench, North Moench, Sally Fairbanks—family all. "Yahoo!" Unc' Bill and Barb for champagne enthusiasm over my wild-hair ventures. One big hug of thanks to my tribe of beloved friends in Bellingham and on Lopez and Lummi Islands who tolerated many a turned-down invitation to hike, sail, kayak, and ski while I holed up writing. Here's to umpteen adventures ahead!

In the chapters to follow, some people's names have been changed to respect their privacy.

Prologue

You are about to embark on an account of my solo adventure kayaking the Inside Passage from Ketchikan, Alaska, to Bellingham, Washington.

It is not a linear story. It was a journey of waterways, but also of mind, spirit, and emotion. It is the story of my own inside passage amid the animals, plants, people, and oceanography of the Inside Passage. I set out on this journey and no other because I wanted to live in nature. I wanted the ocean, tides, trees, and sea stars to be my teachers. I'd done my time at a university studying natural history and ecology, and now I wanted to have rooted, winged, furred, and feathered teachers. I wanted to live wildly, to be an apprentice to the ocean. I knew there would be lessons to learn and that they'd unfold along the way. There would be hardships, too—dark nights filled with fear of attack. But I wanted to learn to grapple with my fears, not cave in to them.

Georgia O'Keefe said it beautifully: "I've been absolutely terrified every moment of my life and I've never let it keep me from doing a single thing I wanted to do." More than anything in the world, I wanted to take this solo journey.

My plan was to solo paddle the Inside Passage, but I didn't have time to complete it in one fell swoop. So I did it in chunks as time allowed. This adventure encompassed two springs and two summers between 1992 and 1996— 750 miles in seventy days.

In writing this book, I organized the story geographically north to south by coasts, though my actual travel was less exact. During the time I paddled the Inside Passage, I also owned a sea kayak touring company that led natural history trips in Washington State and Alaska in summer and fall, and in Baja, Mexico, in winter and spring. Running a business precluded taking time off to do one long paddle. Yet, I reasoned I could paddle a couple hundred miles in a month.

So off I went in the spring of 1992 on my first journey, which became "The Waterfall Coast: Bella Bella to Prince Rupert, British Columbia," traveling 29 days and 230 miles. I bowed out in 1993 and 1994, however. I had a debilitating case of tendonitis in my forearms, and chose to rest between guiding seasons for fear that I would not be able to work if I risked further injury.

I returned to the Inside Passage in the spring and summer of 1995 and paddled between Ketchikan and Bellingham, but skipped the book sections titled "The Waterfall Coast" and "The Open Coast: Queen Charlotte Sound and Cape Caution." The latter stretch had been on my itinerary for that trip, but was socked in by storms and I was lucky to hitchhike on a sailboat through the worst of it to Vancouver Island. After a brief break on Vancouver Island to rejuvenate my storm-flogged spirit, I returned to complete the southern part of the journey, covering "The Big Island Coast: South Along Vancouver Island" and "The Salish Sea Coast: Strait of Georgia and San Juan Islands."

Perhaps it would have been fine to leave things there. But the next summer, I felt "The Open Coast" calling and returned in 1996 to complete the final leg.

Kayaking is my passion. A kayak gives me access to the sea, whom I've loved since I was six. A kayak sets me intimately within, yet atop and apart from, the sea's body. From that low vantage, I can watch the goings on of animals and plant life moving about in her great, blue-gray belly. A kayak sets me close to danger, too—the fifty-degree water, storms, tide rips. And in a visceral way, I love that too. It keeps me awake—and humble.

Taking off alone in the Inside Passage for chunks of time allowed me to sink into the rhythm of the waves, tides, moon, and weather systems. Solitude breeds a kind of hunger pang of loneliness that expands your idea of companionship. A weasel, a stone, the ocean herself become fine company. Each time I set out, I quickly became lost in the mythic realms. Camping, harvesting wild edibles, sleeping, and breathing within the great cradle of the mother ocean, I was a child again. The ocean rocks me eternally. I am her beloved daughter.

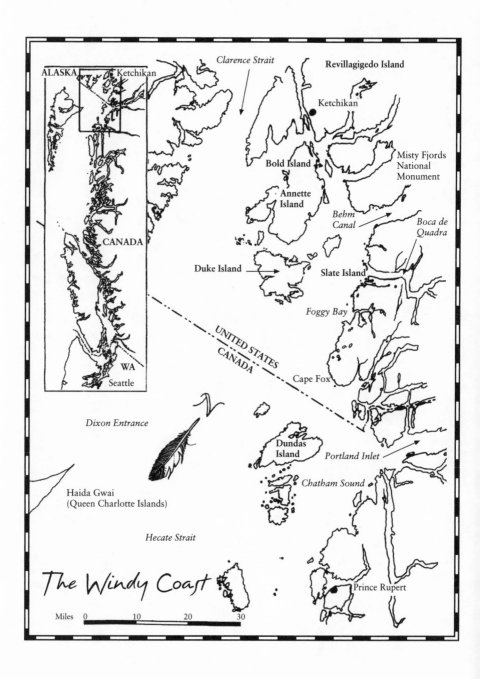

ALASKA · Ketchikan

Clarence Strait

Revillagigedo Island

Ketchikan

Misty Fjords
National
Monument

Bold Island

Annette
Island

Behm
Canal

Boca de
Quadra

CANADA

Duke Island

Slate Island

Foggy Bay

UNITED STATES
CANADA

WA
Seattle

Cape Fox

Dixon Entrance

Dundas
Island

Portland Inlet

Chatham Sound

Haida Gwai
(Queen Charlotte Islands)

Hecate Strait

The Windy Coast

Prince Rupert

Miles   0   10   20   30

Part 1

The Windy Coast: Ketchikan, Alaska, to Prince Rupert, British Columbia

Early spring, 103 miles, 7 days

Please know that I am aware of the hazards.
I want to do it because I want to do it.

—Amelia Earhart

1 Volkswagens Float, Don't They?

When I reach back in time, looking for the path that led me to sea kayak the Inside Passage alone, I always find water.

To begin with, there was the summer of 1962 when my father lashed a twelve-person army surplus tent to the bumper of our VW microbus, then drove our family of five two thousand miles—from the rolling hills of Eastern Wisconsin to the rainforests of Western Washington. My older brothers and sister traced the highlighted route on the AAA TripTik. I was only four and working hard to stop sucking my thumb before kindergarten. We stopped the bus only to get gas, pee, or camp in a national park. For three days we ate nothing but sandwiches—peanut butter and jelly, egg salad, liver sausage, or salami—washed down with lemonade.

It was the first big road trip since my mother's death in an auto accident three summers earlier. We'd been driving home from a camping vacation when a semi-trailer truck driver asleep at the wheel rear-ended our VW bus. It rolled and caught fire. My mother died, and we four kids, age fifteen to nine months, were delivered into the hands of our overwhelmed but adventurous father.

I'll never forget the sight of our huge canvas tent set up in the Hoh Rainforest on Washington's Olympic Peninsula. It looked like a tiny mushroom squatting under Goliathan trees. To mark the occasion, my father, the king of posed vacation photography, attempted to snap a photo of us four kids encircling a giant cedar trunk in a downpour. It was the biggest living thing we had ever seen. We were dressed in baggy rain slickers that smelled of new plastic and still showed creases from being unfolded. But no matter how we stretched our hands out, we couldn't quite reach around the tree. Our mother's arms would have completed the circle.

I was too young to fathom my mother's absence. Instead, I recall trotting off to stand perfectly still by myself in the forest. Thumb in mouth, I listened curiously to the hollow scutter of rain on a skunk cabbage leaf umbrella. The air smelled of skunk and rain-soaked earth. Feathery ferns dripped one . . . two . . . three pearls. Rain sparkled like emeralds on the woolly trunks. I didn't have the words for it yet, but I felt something wonderful fluttering inside my small body. I now realize it was an enchantment. In that rain-drenched moment, nature baptized a wild spirit that I carry with me to this day.

Water also flowed through another family trip two summers later. This time it was saltwater ebbing from a bay at Acadia National Park in Maine. Tides are astonishing to a six-year-old girl from the Great Lakes. The horseshoe bay magically emptied each day, revealing rocky pools of strange animals. Sticky-tipped anemones, grinning blue mussels, a whip-tailed skate soft as wet soap. Then around dinnertime, when my brother would plunk lobsters into a bubbling pot on the Coleman stove, the water crept back, gurgling over rocks, swallowing the creatures, transforming a wondrous playground into a shining lake reflecting the night sky.

"Travel," our father always said, "is without a doubt the best education I can give you kids." Embarking on family trips every other summer was a rhythm as regular as the tides. After my mother's death, Dad snagged a job that was in sync with school vacations. September through June he taught welding at the Milwaukee Area Technical College. During alternate summers, he raised money for the following year's travel fund by working as a welder at an oil refinery in Joliet, Illinois, commuting 110 miles each way.

He once confided, "Jenny, you wouldn't believe it. A guy could retire at forty on the salary a pipe welder's paid!" And in the next breath, his blue eyes sparkling, he asked, "What do you think of going to Mexico and Central America?"

And so, in 1968, off we chugged on another family venture—a cross-country marathon to the Gulf of Mexico. My brothers were now grown and vagabonding on their own, so our dwindling family downsized to a VW bug. South of the border, an event unfolded that forever sealed my taste for adventure travel.

Dad had located a "shortcut" on the map of Guatemala. Our route followed one of those dotted-line roads instead of a solid one. "Two dotted inches on the map," he calculated, "will save us hundreds of miles driving through Guatemalan jungles." Two days later the mud road, which was still under construction, halted abruptly at a riverbank. Bridges would come later, we guessed. The rutted road resumed one hundred feet away on the other side of the river.

So the family patriarch mused the infamous words: "Well girls, Volkswagens float, don't they?" Who were we—my sister Maya, eighteen, and me, nine—to know better?

Our father waded out into the gray-green current with his khaki pant legs rolled up. He told my sister to back up the bug as far to the upstream side of the road as possible without getting stuck in the vegetation. He was planning ahead to overcome river drift. Next, he knotted a rope to the front bumper, then looped the free end around his waist.

"Okay, easy does it, Maya," he called, waving her forward to the river.

My sister piloted while my father pulled, straining forward like a mule tethered to a Mississippi freight barge. Only this was not a tame canal. It was a jungle river, unpredictable and wild. I remember the python green current sliding coolly around my ankles as I rode the running board. We did float to the other side. The VW landed on target, its exhaust pipe still sputtering. From that day forward any miracle seemed possible.

Twenty-seven years later, I was alone aboard an Alaska ferry humming north up Tongass Narrows amid sheets of blowing rain. I tried to focus on the last of my packing and not on the storm revving up around me. Stuffing handfuls of warm sleeping bag into a waterproof sack, I could hear rain sluicing in sheets off the solarium's eaves. It splat on the nylon tents pitched on the ferry's open-air deck. Puddles rolled and jumped with the ferry's deceleration as it prepared to enter a slip at the Ketchikan terminal.

It was 6 A.M. The change in the boat's vibrations sent me vibrating as well, though maybe it was merely the fear and excitement of taking the first step—or first paddle, as it were. After docking in Ketchikan, I was given five minutes of the Alaska Marine Highway captain's time to get a weather printout showing the high and low pressure storms brewing offshore. This would add to the limited verbal report broadcast on my VHF weather radio-telephone. The weather in Southeast Alaska resembles a rugby scrum with two teams—the advancing summer high and the retreating Aleutian low—battling for control of the eastern Pacific Basin. An average of three to five lows passes close to the Southeast Alaska coast each month. Reluctantly, the ferry purser unchained the "No Admittance" sign blocking a stairwell and led me up the narrow stairs to the captain's quarters.

The captain, a white-shirted chap polished as a brass button, was clearly not impressed with the ambitions for my journey. His owl-eyed stare suggested he thought I was a ninny interrupting his time off, or, worse, a Pollyanna kayaker just waiting to be a Coast Guard rescue statistic. "Have you *ever* done anything like this before?" he asked in a bruising tone.

"Kayaking is how I make my living. I own a kayak touring company," I told him reassuringly. But inside my jacket I was sweating under his fatherly scrutiny.

"Then you must know what you're up against," the captain concluded, softening a little. He scanned the weather report on the fax printer and wagged his head ominously. Before handing me news of the stormy forecast, he launched a question that would plague me for weeks. "Tell me something . . .why are you paddling from north to south? Don't you know the dominant winds in Alaska blow out of the south?"

"You're kidding!" I wanted to say, but I felt too foolish to admit this grave oversight. Instead, I was stunned speechless. Half-formed thoughts banged and sparked inside my head like bumper cars at a state fair. *Yikes! . . . Is this my fatal oversight? How come no one told . . . ? Headwinds . . . hundreds of miles . . . sounds like hell . . . damn . . . should have bought an* Alaska Coast Pilot . . . *even if it does cost thirty dollars and weighs as much as a city phone book . . . .*

"Well, you see, Captain," I said, regaining my composure, "I wish to paddle toward home."

Disembarking foot passengers trudged up the metal drawbridge into the downpour. Some disappeared into taxis and waiting cars. A Swedish couple cranked up the incline on newly assembled mountain bikes, fluorescent yellow panniers bulging. They looked such a cheerful sight, I wished I were riding with them. Instead, I waited alone with kayak in tow on the far side of the ship's gaping door. I was content to chat with the crew while the main traffic cleared. I was in no particular hurry to head into the storm just yet, especially since the wind, as if to prove the captain's point, was blowing the rain horizontally.

The first mate, a dimple-faced fellow wearing a Navy jacket and holding a handheld radio, yelled over the din of off-loading cars and trucks, "Where you headed?"

"South to Prince Rupert."

"Should have been here three weeks ago. Sunny skies. No wind."

"Yeah, now it's hard out of the south," I said with newfound authority.

"You got that right. Storm blew out of there a day ago. Supposed to last a while."

"Any boat launches nearby?" I asked, looking out to the riprap shoreline.

"Not really, mostly private wharves. There's a public launch miles north of here. Another a ways south."

Oh gosh. I hadn't planned on that either.

The first mate must have read the dismayed look on my face, because he turned to me with earnest concern and said, "Don't worry. If you get in a pinch, my house is right next to a launch. I get off work in a couple of hours, and I'll give you a ride if you haven't left by then."

"Hey, thanks," I told him, smiling for the first time all morning. The kind gesture warmed me just enough that I tightened my hood against the storm and marched up the ramp with my kayak into Alaska.

Tugging a 250-pound kayak on lawn-mower wheels up a thirty-degree washboard proved to be no graceful matter. Every few yards the laden wheels of my home-welded carrier jammed on the toothed grate. A fierce tug loosened it but caused the stern to skitter sideways. Before I was halfway along, the kayak jackknifed and blocked a lane of off-loading cars, campers, and trucks. I set the heavy bow down and jogged back to realign the stern. I'd wanted to heave this carrier overboard ever since the wheels fell off and rolled away as I boarded the ferry in Bellingham three days before. But I couldn't; the load was far too heavy for me to shoulder alone.

Above and behind me, passengers hooded against the rain in slickers lined the railings to watch the mayhem. Some held blowing umbrellas. By the time I got to the terminal only fifty yards away, my long johns were soaked in sweat. Standing at the edge of the parking lot in swirling rain, I tried not to feel sorry for myself. Better to focus on logistics. So I tried to imagine myself carrying the boat down the forty-five-degree riprap of boulders . . . .

"Can't navigate in this chowder," shouted a well-humored geologist I'd befriended on the ferry. Chuck leaned his capped head out an open truck window as he jounced through the puddled parking lot, windshield wipers slapping.

Then, "Need a paid job until the storm clears?" he asked. "I'm desperate. Field partner can't fly in 'cause of the fog."

Chuck was desperate, all right. And I was a forlorn and gullible grunt ready to jump at the chance to put off launching in a rainstorm.

"Are you serious? What about my kayak?"

Chuck had it all figured out. "Throw it on my roof rack and we can lock it in my storage unit."

"How many days you need a schlep?"

"Two. And I'll pay you 180 bucks."

"I'll do it!" I yelled, laughing out loud at my amazing good fortune.

"There are spirits who protect holy fools," an Alaska Native man once told me. Standing at the edge of the Tongass Narrows in Ketchikan, clapping sulfurous mud from my rubber boots and about to shove off into the unknown, I had the urge to pray. I needed to mark the moment with a small ceremony, the threshold over which another holy fool was about to pass.

In a few moments, I would step into a sixteen-foot hydrodynamic suitcase—bulging with one month of food, a plethora of high-tech camping equipment, forty PowerBars, two pounds of chocolate, a *Marine Atlas*, a VHF radio, and poet Mary Oliver's *American Primitive*—and launch southward into the Pacific. What could I possibly say to calm my heart and gain the favor of the universe before starting the first leg of a 750-mile Inside Passage journey? Beginning on this day and encompassing the next few years, I ultimately planned to paddle from Ketchikan, Alaska, through Canadian waters to Bellingham, Washington.

Turning south, the direction my bow pointed, I looked on snow-crusted mountains heaved straight up from the far shore. Annette and Revillagigedo Islands hunched before me like giant gatekeepers. Between them, Revillagigedo Channel, my route through the Alaska Southeast, wound out of sight like an indigo thread. Twenty-some miles beyond that the channel knotted into Dixon Entrance. Dixon Entrance, it's been said, is the punching bag of the wide open Pacific.

Before leaving home on this trip, I often lay on my bedroom floor mesmerized by an ink-blue water trail cascading the length of a ten-foot map of the Inside Passage tacked to the wall. The northwest-southeast waterway descended seven latitudinal degrees between Ketchikan and Puget Sound. It would carry me through hundreds of straits, sounds, channels, bays, and pinched passes. As I imagined paddling that serpentine route, four waterways jumped out from the pack. In these four places the Inside Passage was either exposed to the Pacific Ocean or narrowed to a bottleneck.

Dixon Entrance loomed as the first of the four challenging "thresholds"— as I decided to call them—that I'd encounter on my journey. The other three were Queen Charlotte Sound (sixty miles of unprotected coastline north of Vancouver Island), Seymour Narrows (where the middle of Vancouver Island bulges east to create a boa constrictor kink in the passage; it is famed for whirlpools and overfalls), and Boundary Pass (a shipping lane between Canada and the United States choked with freighter traffic and stadium-size tide rips).

Standing ready to launch into the lovely blue waterway that I'd been dreaming about, reality set in and raised incipient doubts. The local coast guard weather report carried news of a second storm rumbling off the Southeast Alaska coast. This was worrisome news, but it wouldn't hit for another twenty-four to thirty-six hours. I reasoned that I'd waited nearly a week already. Why wait to get socked in by another storm? I was excited and impatient to get moving. I figured I could make twenty to twenty-five miles in the calm window in between.

But still I stood there terrified to push off! Suddenly I couldn't *believe* I'd blabbered to my family and dearest friends—strangers, too—that I was going to paddle alone from Alaska to Bellingham. It was the kind of thing a girl raised by a wanderlust father who floated a VW bug across a jungle river might think is a sensible thing to do. But I was a woman. You'd think I'd have outgrown my girlish wild-hairs.

"You must give the kayak a blessing," a voice inside me murmured. It seemed so obvious. My kayak was like a ship about to break from the shackles of the shipyard—only I had no champagne. Perhaps this was another one of my mind's tricks to procrastinate the inevitable. I stared at my loaded kayak. We'd been together for two years and she'd proved to be a seaworthy boat. She packed a lot of gear and was moderately swift and stable. Her name was *Yemaya*. It means ocean goddess. *Yemaya* was made of fiberglass, white with turquoise hatches, cockpit, and seam. Atop the spare paddle lashed with a bungee on her stern was a cedar branch I'd cut from a tree outside my home on Puget Sound. I'd toted it north with no clear idea why. Now that spontaneous clipping made sense. I loosened the branch. The pungent needles held the scent of home.

"You can make this journey safely . . . you really can," I told myself. Hundreds of miles from home, I tried to remember what it was like to be strong. I half wanted to ask the plucky person standing in my boots, "Hey, remind me again, why are we here?"

It took years for me to come to this place, about to launch a dream that had a long gestation. The notion first whispered to me in the summer of 1983 from the deep, translucent waters of the Octopus Islands off the coast of British Columbia. It was my first plunge into the far reaches of the Inside Passage—the waterway that stretches from Skagway, Alaska, to Olympia, Washington, snaking its way through nearly one thousand miles of islands. Four friends and I had traveled north on a homemade trimaran sailboat with two kayaks strapped to the pontoons.

One morning, we woke early and motored at slack tide through British Columbia's famed Hole in the Wall. The cliff-faced canyon is fabled for churning up a thirty-foot whirlpool at maximum tides. Our vessel, *Leucothea,* measured nineteen feet from her bow to her stern. On the other side of the black hole, as we called it, something changed. We had unwittingly slipped into a time before time. The Coke-bottle-green water turned lucid as glass. Fish, seals, and river otters swam about freely and as visible to our eyes as if there were no water at all between us.

Eager to jump in the water and look around ourselves, we stretched on wetsuits, fins, masks, and snorkels and plunged into the icy elixir. For equal buoyancy, we swam to an island and filled our wetsuits with rocks. Then we sank down into a world of underwater cliffs—vertical forests of feathery anemones and sea-breathing creatures. Fanning in the soft current, the plants and animals moved as if animated. We plucked a basketball-size sea urchin off the wall. Like otters, we floated to the surface and cracked it open. We ate our first gooey urchin roe for supper.

At sundown, when the sky flamed abalone-shell pink, I slid a kayak off the sailboat's pontoon. Paddling through the labyrinth of islets, looking down into the translucent water, is when I heard the whisper.

You must return here and kayak alone.

I was still a greenhorn back then, at sea kayaking and at navigating a wilderness coast by chart and compass. But kayaking was my newfound passion. I loved how it set me low above the water so I could look out from an otter's eye view. But under my boyfriend's wise tutelage—he worked as a naturalist and sea kayak guide on weekends—I learned how to navigate in currents and winds, decipher tide and current tables, read a chart, identify water hazards such as tide rips and eddylines, and harvest edible wild plants.

Over the years, I continued to take long kayak trips with friends to Alaska, the Queen Charlotte Islands, and Baja, Mexico, and eventually I found myself teaching new friends. With the help of my boyfriend, I started my own kayak touring business and named it Elakah!, which means otter in Chinook jargon, a pidgin trade language of the North Pacific coast. Teaching outdoor skills as an adult was a natural offshoot of my years camping and traveling as a kid. One life had blended seamlessly into the other.

Beware the power of whispers and dreams. They might pester you into doing something—even if it scares you! In your waking hours you might gasp, *but I'm not ready . . . why, I could die doing that!* That's what I said when I heard the whisper in the Octopus Islands. All at once, however, I felt mesmerized by the possibility of such a fantastic dream actually happening. Maybe, if I put my mind to it, I could develop the skills to undertake a solo kayak expedition.

Dreams, I've learned, have the patience of Job. Like mushroom mycelium, they can live underground for years, laying a vast framework while awaiting an opportune rainstorm to waggle their fruits. Unbeknownst to me, such a storm was approaching as I strode into my early thirties. Along about the time I turned thirty-two, a terrible, fatalistic shudder passed through me. *There may not be much time left.* At some insidious level, I couldn't help remembering that neither my mom nor my eldest brother made it past their thirty-sixth year.

My mother died during that fateful family vacation. At age thirty-two, my oldest brother, David, was captaining his own tanker ship between Belize and Norfolk, Virginia, when he drowned in a salvage diving accident. My family consoled ourselves with the knowledge that my mom and brother died doing what they loved. They were living their dreams. They were happy. Whatever dreams lay sleeping inside me, my intuition said I'd better roust them ASAP. For all I knew, like my adventurous mom and brother, I might not live past my mid-thirties either.

The following January, amid the logistical frenzy of packing the kayak trailer and van for the winter guiding season in Mexico, I heard the whisper again. This time it spoke in the dark of night. From a fathomless sleep, I surfaced abruptly, aware of something watching me. It was the luminous face of the full moon! She shone into my bedroom window so brightly I was awakened by the light on the walls. I turned and looked out on Chuckanut Bay.

The moon climbed the south shoulder of Lummi Island. Below, Puget Sound swelled with high tide and poured itself north. Where the current surged through Hale Passage, a zigzag of silver stretch marks lit the sea's black belly. It looked so beautiful, so tragically beautiful. Staring out at the moonlit sea, I heard the whisper.

It is time. You have the skills to survive now.

I jolted awake. I felt shaken out of my fool senses. I knew exactly what the whisper was talking about. Even though years had passed, I hadn't forgotten. And the little voice was right when it acknowledged that I knew about wilderness survival. I also understood the dangers. I could reel off a fearsome list in a wink—grizzly bears, capsizing, hypothermia, tide rips, whirlpools, surf, crashing headlands, and violent storms. I'd be sure to meet fishers, loggers, hermits, and other travelers. Would they be kind? I knew I was ready, but God I was terrified, and that seemed like a wise response. It made me think carefully about how to deal with each turn of danger, to plan, to take calculated risks. After all, second to the dream to go, I wanted to survive, to come home and tell about it.

That night, as I watched the stars smoke over with the rising moon, I wanted to release myself from the crazy dream to kayak the Inside Passage alone. I wanted to wake with the dawn over Chuckanut Mountain, finish packing the kayak trailer, and vamoose for sunny Mexico. I wanted to bury this whisper beneath the cool underside of my pillow. But it was too late to close my ears now. I lay in the moonlit bedroom, afraid, but equally enchanted. I wanted to live wildly, to be an apprentice to the ocean.

The whisper was right. I had the skills. I also had the time. I could carve out a month or more between Mexico and the summer guiding season in the San Juan Islands. I could begin. I had no idea how far I'd get, but I could pick up again where I left off. And that is what I did, for seventy days spread over two springs and two summers.

Standing at the waterline in Ketchikan, I dipped the cedar bough into the sea and brushed *Yemaya* with saltwater, starting at the stern and working my way to the bow. As I brushed, I envisioned a safe journey home. As I dipped the branch a second time to brush my paddle, my mind caught the image of salmon. Salmon recognize their homeland by smell. Subtle changes in scent cue them to stay on course. Perhaps the aromatic cedar would tell the kayak and paddle where to go, as when a stream calls home a chinook salmon pregnant with harvest-moon eggs.

In an additional hopeful gesture, I tossed a stick wrapped with yarn, a grass blade, and a feather into Tongass Narrows. It splashed down on the inverted reflection of a storm cloud. A Native friend had suggested I do this. "Tell the sea your dream. It will carry it outwards before you." I liked that. It rang of optimism and old wisdom that I knew better than to question.

I cradled the boat's heavy stern and pushed with both hands. The kayak slid over the mud until she floated on the still lid of the sea. I stepped in, fastened the neoprene spray skirt, and pushed off. Ripples circled out in all directions. West. North. East. Home.

Ketchikan, with its rows of gas-heated houses, twenty-four-hour grocery stores, souvenir shops, and quaint courthouse, slipped away. Something began to change, slowly at first, then growing into a thick silence. A silence punctuated by wind and water. Only elemental sounds remained.

A bold sense of freedom seeped into my lungs and heart, but it was mixed with lingering apprehension. I wasn't worried that I'd forgotten something vital. I'd combed over the gear list—at the last minute I'd even added three more weighty but essential pieces: rubber boots, a plastic ground cloth, and the *Coast Pilot 8: Pacific Coast Alaska, Dixon Entrance to Cape Spencer*. My supplies seemed beyond cushy when I thought of John Muir with his sack of oatmeal and a wool blanket. In fact I was excited by what a self-sufficient little island I had become.

No, the dread, both thrilling and loathsome, came from the awareness that I now had very little control over circumstances. I had no idea where I'd sleep. No conception of when the wind might hurl whitecaps across the calm channel where I nosed along at three miles per hour. I couldn't know what would happen even an hour from now. Or five minutes. All I had was the rhythm of the paddle singing *plop-shush, plop-shush, plop-shush*. And the simplicity was utterly intoxicating.

To kayak through the Inside Passage is to travel through long and open-ended coastal valleys scooped by the toes of glaciers, then flooded by an ocean of melting ice. Naturalist John Muir traveled the Inside Passage in 1879. An inquisitive amateur geologist and botanist, Muir recognized the massive footprints of glaciers that once blanketed the region.

"All the islands, great and small, as well as the headlands and promontories of the mainland, are seen to have a rounded, over-rubbed appearance produced by the over-sweeping ice-flood . . . during the great glacial winter just now drawing to a close."

The wonder of kayak travel is that it allows you to see all those islands, headlands, and promontories at a walking pace. That's about three miles per hour if there's no wind or current. I figure if human senses—seeing, hearing, smelling, and so on—evolved to work at their utmost saturation when a person is moving at the speed of natural locomotion, then kayaking offers a traveler one of the most holistic and sensual rides.

Passing Mountain Point at the south end of Tongass Narrows, a totemic spruce wafted citron sap. Sunlight trembled off the sea's mirror across the fifty-foot trunk. High in the bottle-brush limbs, spider gossamers shivered rainbows. A bald eagle with a head bright as a snowball watched me slip by far below. If I had zipped past this same tree in a motorboat, the eagle might have attracted attention, but the luminous spider garlands wouldn't have. In a glass-enclosed ferry cabin stale with cheap coffee and auto fumes, aromatic sap is a moot point. If I'd hopped in a float plane and zoomed down the Narrows, my spruce tree would have been lost in a tapestry of mountains, valleys, and islands. I wouldn't see trees so much as forested watersheds. But from the water the coast transformed into a sensual smorgasbord. Grooving on these delicious minutiae, I was already drunk with pleasure my first day out.

I paddled out Tongass Narrows and into the silver chop of Revillagigedo Channel. My Ketchikan friends call it "Revi" for short. I liked the nickname. It fit. I was *revi-ing* up. An eagle hooded in hemlock boughs stared out to sea from Bold Island. Clouds clipped the summit of Black Mountain. Fourteen miles south of Tongass Narrows at Point Alava, I turned up Behm Canal looking for a beach on which to pee. Unzipping the Farmer-John wetsuit, balancing with one foot in the boat, one on a slick, seaweed-covered rock, I remembered what a challenge it is to seek relief on steep shorelines.

Floating once again, I inhaled a bagel, cheese, and avocado. At 7 P.M. the sea lay smooth as a mirror off Alava and I was reluctant to stop. I charged across two-mile-wide Behm Canal to beach *Yemaya* on the far shoreline in pursuit of my first campsite. As I stepped one foot from the kayak to shore, I suddenly heard a crunching sound. And it wasn't the sound of *my* foot stepping on shore rocks. Instinctively I sat back into the boat, tightened my grip on the paddle, and pushed off. Safely afloat, I turned back toward the noise. Seventy yards distant inside a wreath of boulders stood two ba-ba-bears! The mother looked shaggy and thin from winter hibernation. Fur hung loose about her belly and heavy flanks like a coat one size too large. She was black with a tan muzzle. Her magnificent rump and side faced toward me. Rotund and fluffy as if freshly shampooed, a cub stood a few feet from its mom.

I floated offshore watching as she overturned an intertidal rock with one flip of her paw. The hole underneath formed a perfect chowder dish of crustaceans. She slurped them up with her efficient tongue.

Bear see, bear do. The cub poked a muzzle into its mom's beach excavation, sniffed, then sat back on its haunches as if bewildered about the purpose of the exercise. I supposed it was still nursing and hadn't yet tasted its first purple shore crab. It waited patiently for the sow to upend a second rock and sniffed again.

How lucky could I be? Neither bear suspected my presence. Silent as a feather I floated back into Behm Canal.

2 Bearanoia

The three things I feared more than anything before I set off on my solo journey were bears, drowning, and harmful men. Darkness was a close fourth—I'd do just fine if I didn't need to sleep.

Daylight began to fade from Revi Channel as I paddled on about twenty-six miles south of Ketchikan, and my enthusiasm for traveling solo faded with it. The sun dropped into a haze of yellow stratus tilted like Saturn's rings over Annette Island on the western horizon. The mainland mountains grew tarnished and dull. A leaden gloom mantled the water, land, and me. No two ways about it, as darkness fell in bear country my mind jumped like a line-hooked halibut and dove for the murky bottom. Even before this trip I had a track record for "bearanoia," of which I was not proud. Shaggy stumps sprouted limbs. Bushes jumped.

Scanning ahead through binoculars, I spotted a promising camp on Black Island a half-mile south. A long paddle on that first day had aggravated an old injury and my arms already burned with tendonitis. So I paddled toward the island's northern terminus with a hopeful heart. I wanted an island camp. In a five-minute stroll I could inventory the entire neighborhood from root to tree crown. Not that bears don't find islands attractive, too. In spring, moms and cubs often swim to islands to keep out of big daddy bruin's path. But, compared to the bear-abundant mainland, I was willing to hedge my bets with an island. I'd sleep better surrounded by water, not forest.

The nightmares had started two weeks before I left home. Bears tramped through my dreams—dragging me from flimsy shelters, gnawing my hands and arms. To heighten the nocturnal terror, I confess to having done a stupid thing. I'd lollygagged in a bookstore and consumed half the spine-tingling stories in *Alaska Bear Tales* and *More Alaska Bear Tales*. The well-known books need no subtitle. But if they had one, it could be "101 Ways for a Bear to Maim, Scalp, Crush, Disembowel, and Eat You Alive."

Before starting this journey, whenever I mentioned my plan to solo kayak in Alaska and British Columbia, well-meaning people often suggested, "You're taking a gun, aren't you?"

My answer—"No, I'm carrying pepper spray"—drew open-mouthed looks of disbelief, like I was clearly out of my gourd. I received two offers for free shooting lessons. I had the same response when my college friend, Charlotte

McKay, and I decided to spend a summer hiking the Pacific Crest Trail. We didn't carry a gun. But the third night on the trail, in the Marble Mountains of California, we found ourselves sleeping in shifts and constantly feeding a bonfire to scare off a four-hundred-pound black bear.

This time, because I knew I'd be alone, I had sincerely considered the gun option. I borrowed a friend's 12-gauge shotgun. The black barrel and pump-action stock made me feel like a *Rambo* extra. I took it to the Whatcom County Parks Rifle Range for target practice. The first time I fired the gun—with bird shot, mind you—I was knocked backward two feet. A short, athletic woman in her fifties two stations down set aside her handgun to wave me over. "Honey, you gotta scrunch low. Bend those knees. Pretend someone's tossing you a fifty-pound sack of potatoes."

I practiced the stance. I stalked my Labrador mutts through the vegetable garden as if they were menacing bears. I timed myself loading and unloading ammunition in daylight and dark. I learned to clean and oil the sucker. But I never felt wholly confident.

Finally, after lying awake another night paralyzed with fear at the horrific image of an eight-hundred-pound grizzly dragging me from my tent while I'm still zipped in my mummy bag, I decided to seek different advice. I called the Alaska Department of Fish and Game. A biologist there told me to consider myself lucky to see a bear. They are beautiful, powerful creatures. "If you should find yourself in a close encounter," he said, "capsicum pepper spray has been used with good success repelling bears in the Tongass National Forest. You can buy a can at a sporting goods store. And stay away from *Alaska Bear Tales*. It's meant to scare you. Find a copy of Stephen Herrero's *Bear Attacks: Their Causes and Avoidance.*"

Herrero is an authority on bear behavior. I liked his slant immediately when I read, "Your best weapon to minimize the risk of bear attack is your brain." Although Herrero carries a gun in bear country, he also says, "To kill a charging grizzly bear in order to defend yourself you must be capable of shooting to kill an object hurtling at you, perhaps through dense brush, at speeds of up to forty-four feet per second. If you aren't expert enough to do this, then you may be better off without a firearm . . . ."

Given a few more months of target practice at the shooting range, I might have reached a skill level where I wouldn't jump like the Cowardly Lion every time I heard the rifle blast. Or I'd learn to withstand the shotgun's land-me-on-my-ass recoil. But my previous gun experience was limited to squirt guns fired at squirrels raiding bird feeders in the Milwaukee 'burbs where I grew up. So, with only two weeks of practice, I felt dangerously incompetent. I imagined that if I stood directly in the path of a charging bear, I might just shoot the animal in the foot before it clawed me to pieces like a hapless stick in the blades of a John Deere lawn mower.

Herrero's recommended defense in place of guns is making loud noises to avoid surprising a bear. A few tinkling sleigh bells such as I had once carried while hiking in Yellowstone aren't enough. In powerful winds, near rushing rivers, or in thick woods, bells and human voices don't travel far. Low frequency sounds carry farther through trees.

If he finds himself in a forest with only his voice for protection, Herrero says he makes "deep guttural sounds combined with a yodel and a short, explosive high-pitched sound at the end." People may deem you nuts or paranoid, he said, but leave them to their opinions.

Herrero also recommends handheld boat horns as probably the most impressive noise a person can make without firing a gun. I already carried an air horn in my dry box to alert other vessels of my whereabouts during foggy channel crossings.

Floating offshore of my first island camp, I pressed the horn's trigger. *WHOOONK. WHOOONK.* I yelled toward the dark woods, "Heyyyy, beaaaarrrrs. Any beaarrs here?" I waited . . . I listened . . . I watched. When nothing alerted suspicion, I beached the kayak and hobbled stiffly up the beach, gripping the pepper spray.

Who Lives on This Little Island?

River otter (front paws)

"Pigeon-toe" gate of unidentified gull

Heart-shaped Sitka black-tail deer track

One hand long!

Heron and deer recently ambled by.

Otter's hind track often shows inner toe reaching "sidewards"

Great blue heron's outer two toes are webbed

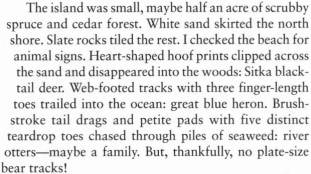

The island was small, maybe half an acre of scrubby spruce and cedar forest. White sand skirted the north shore. Slate rocks tiled the rest. I checked the beach for animal signs. Heart-shaped hoof prints clipped across the sand and disappeared into the woods: Sitka black-tail deer. Web-footed tracks with three finger-length toes trailed into the ocean: great blue heron. Brush-stroke tail drags and petite pads with five distinct teardrop toes chased through piles of seaweed: river otters—maybe a family. But, thankfully, no plate-size bear tracks!

Next I bushwhacked straight into the island's middle, thwacking through wild huckleberry and rose under spruce and cedar boughs. I sang whatever jumped into my scared mind, punctuated with toots from the air horn.

THE BEAR WENT OVER THE MOUNTAIN,
THE BEAR WENT OVER THE MOUUUUNNNTAAAIN,
WHOOONK! WHOOONK!
AND LEFT THE KAYAKER ALONE . . . .

The point was to make clamorous pandemonium. Herrero also warns campers to look for signs of recent bear activity such as bedding places with wisps of fur; pits where bears have foraged for corms, roots, or rhizomes; tree trunks with claw scars marking territory; sheets of bark pulled loose where bears have fed on succulent cambium; and scat piles laced with crab shells, grass, vegetation, berries, or animal fur. I discovered none of these.

I returned to the kayak and noticed two bald eagles watching me quizzically from a snag. "Eagles," I said, "since you are the only ones around, is it okay if I camp here?" I was so focused on looking up, I nearly missed the feather at my feet. A fifteen-inch primary poked up from the beach sand like an arrow. Was this a sign? The eagles didn't wait to tell me. They flapped away toward the mainland. I collected the lovely talisman and determined to erect my tent right there.

Making camp with other people is a cinch. You carry the heavy kayak above the waterline together. One person sets up the tent while someone else starts dinner and gathers wood. Whoever didn't cook washes the dishes afterward. Everyone helps hang the food and other smellies. Now I had to do the chores alone.

These tasks seemed especially daunting after twenty-six miles of butt-numbing paddling. First, in order to lighten the kayak enough to haul it to high ground by myself, I emptied *Yemaya* of all the gear except for the pump, rescue float, sponge, and cedar bough. I knelt down, grabbed inside the cockpit, and curled the craft up to my knee. Barnacles nipped at the hull. Powdery white gel coat formed into little cones of sawdust as if from termites on the low-tide rocks. A little jump, and I was upright, though precariously, holding *Yemaya*, now lightened to fifty-two pounds. My grasp too far aft in the cockpit caused the bow to thump the ground like a see-saw. The two of us teetered into the forest like a giant two-legged clam.

Driftwood makes a spiffy beach smoother. After raking a log over lumpy beach sand just as one might use a board to level freshly poured concrete, I pitched the tent on ground as luxuriously flat as a putting green. Into the tent's open flap went sleeping bag, pad, clothing dry bag, water bottle, and dry box. I inflated the mattress, fluffed the synthetic-fill bag, strung a cheery candle lantern, and unsnapped the lid on the dry box. Here's where things deviated from kayak camping trips in the San Juan Islands of home.

Alongside the sleeping bag I laid three self-defense items: knife, pepper spray, flare gun. My greatest bugaboo was being attacked by an *Ursus arctos horribilis* while asleep. The way I figured it, if a bear clawed through the tent, I'd shoot it with pepper spray and slash a new door out the far side with the knife. If it followed, I'd pop a flare straight at it.

For all the thousands of tree limbs on this island, few were equal to handling fifty pounds of food bags without snapping. I'd already broken two. I tossed the pulley and rope over a third stocky limb. It was lower to the ground than I'd guessed. After I heaved and *HEAVED,* the mass lifted only seven feet before topping out at the pulley. Curious about how bear-proof it was, I climbed a nearby log and swiped a hand toward the forty-day supply of food. *Whack!* At this height, I'd constructed a festive bear piñata. Tired and irritable, I left it swinging.

Coming out of the woods, I stopped in my tracks—a dark hump was swimming in the water south of the island. I'd once heard a frightening tale about two kayakers who'd paddled three miles offshore to camp on a bearless island. After dinner they were relaxing on the beach when they spotted a black dot moving toward them. It was too big for a deer. One of the kayakers looked through binoculars and recognized a grizzly. Panicked, they stockpiled beach rocks. When the bear came within shooting range, they lobbed the rocks rapid fire. The bear slowed its pace, but kept coming. Eventually, it gave up and swam back to the mainland.

I didn't know whether to grab a rock or run for binoculars. So I did both. By the time I returned, the object hadn't budged. Was it waiting? I squatted by the forest and raised the binoculars. A furry, oblong boulder peered back through a mop of seaweed. To be sure, I checked the *Marine Atlas* and discovered a rock awash marked by a star south of the island. Whew.

Night folded its raven wings. Shivering, exhausted, I poked the last coals of the fire. The tide had long since pulled the plug in the channel separating my island from the far shore. Shoulders of rock and broadening beaches glowed faintly under the dull moonlight. A bear bridge was forming. Soon an inviting trail would appear that a hungry Yogi could scamper across. If not for a sniff of my smoked salmon and rice dinner, then perhaps just to scratch the itch of curiosity. Herrero had noted that "Young adult grizzly bears are particularly curious."

Two black shapes appeared on the darkening shore. Every few minutes, I'd catch myself checking their progress on the far beach. Eventually, I took a seat on a log facing the now unseeable shore. Squinting into the inky darkness, I spooned salmon and rice from the pot without looking down. How far away can a bear's nose capture a waft? Given a favorable wind, I imagined savory food smells could wend the woods for miles. What if a bear did amble across the shred of channel? What if it found my tent? I was too spooked to sleep.

How do you reach inside and calm the winds of fear? I had to remind myself that I was choosing to be afraid. At any moment, I could navigate away from this Mobius strip of bearanoia. Or I could sit on a chill log late into the night, growing tired and hypothermic while a cyclone of terror rolled over my sensibilities.

I mean, I *like* bears. Really, I do. John Muir said it wonderfully. "Bears are made of the same dust as we, breathe the same winds and drink of the same waters . . . ." Bears are remarkably like us. They belch from upset stomachs, bawl from pain, and growl when angry. Cubs cry when hurt and hum when suckling. Bears can sit upright like a person in a chair or stand and walk on two legs, if only for a few steps. They hold grudges and are able to recognize uniforms and vehicles. Their dexterity lets them open screw-top jars and door latches.

Bears are playful. They engage in games similar to our own. They like to wrestle, shadow box, pounce, nibble, and play tug of war and hide and seek. Bears can make snowballs, hang upside down, and slide downhill on their rumps and tummies. They love to wallow in pools to soak, splash, cool off, and relieve itching. They swim, not just to fish, but for pleasure, too. Like us, they are creatures of habit, often following the same trails for years. And when the cubs misbehave, mom spanks them—a key to their survival. Bears have been around for almost forty million years since the early Oligocene Epoch, when, according to Gary Brown in *The Great Bear Almanac*, they evolved from small tree-climbing carnivores.

I'm afraid of being mauled by a carnivorous *Ursus*, but I'm also deeply drawn to wild nature precisely because of the unpredictable, powerful predators that can chuck me off the highest rung of the food ladder with one paw swipe. Bears humble me.

I carried the empty pot to the shore, filled it with seawater, tossed in beach sand, and whirled the water. Bioluminescent plankton spun neon green threads. I sloshed the magical nightlights over the half-submerged rocks, watching as the sparkles drained away and snuffed out. I looked up. Twinkling through torn clouds, Ursa Major and Ursa Minor cast familiar cheer. It was a beautiful night. If I didn't squelch my obsession with bears soon, fear would swallow the pleasure of this night and all the nights to come. I turned my unguarded back to the channel and ducked into the tent.

At 2 A.M. I woke to hear food bags being shredded outside my tent. My heart flew like a terrified bird against my ribcage. Surely it beat loud enough to give away my hiding spot. When the ravenous beast hunched outside my nylon tent finally paused its noisome chewing, it would surely hear my little grouse heart wuffing and decide I was juicier game. The carnivore would thrash its way through the flimsy tent and eat me whole.

I wanted to yell, but I couldn't eke out a whisper. My mind blurred fast-forward for solutions. I grabbed the VHF radio and cranked the volume. Any loud noise would do! At least now if it dragged me out of the tent, I could make an emergency call on the VHF radio from the hole it buried me in.

The shell beach crunched under a paw step. A rock went skipping. I died a thousand deaths with every breath. I made it perfectly clear with the powers that be that I *wasn't* seeking death-defying moments to write about later. I didn't want to die or even come close. I pushed the lock off the bear spray and aimed at the door. I was ready to fight!

A long minute passed. I wondered why nothing was crashing through the tent. I squelched the radio and tuned my ears out into the darkness. Branches scudded along the fly, wind sucked the tent walls, waves slapped the shore. Something rumbled and shook like plastic bags. A storm must be galloping up Revi Channel. And then I thought, "My food bags are forty yards down the beach and in the woods. Why would a bear drag plastic-lined food duffels here, to my tent, to open them?" It didn't measure up. So what was making that frightful noise?

I flashed on my headlamp, boldly unzipped the tent, and peered into the branches above. Hanging like a ghost, a white bag lifted and quaked against the wind-rattled branches. Aha! The tent bag liner flapped where I'd hung it to dry hours ago.

More shells clacked. Another rock slipped. I turned to see a long furry face, wet black nose, and watery eyes staring unblinking—like a deer in a headlamp. The animal stood tall as the tent—four feet high. Its glossy, muscular body and long legs were the color of cedar. It stood perfectly still, looking at me, ears spread horizontal. Relaxed but alert. I remained quiet until the deer turned away to meander down the beach, black tail swishing. I wadded up the fool bag.

But who was the fool? I began to feel stupid, even selfish and self-indulgent. I had to get a grip on my fear.

I stood beside the tent, thinking, holding the plastic bag as the wind rocked me and ruffed the tent. In the dim moonlight, the Alaskan mainland rose from the ocean like an indigo wave. I imagined how many bears might be ambling in those woods, digging corms, suckling cubs. The Tongass Forest and The Great Bear Rainforest (from the Alaska border south to the north end of Vancouver Island) host populations of grizzly bears and black bears that are among the largest in the world. These two areas are the last strongholds of the North American rainforest. Pristine and rugged, they guard the heartland of the wild bear.

I reminded myself that grizzlies used to roam all of North America. In the twenty-first century, they hang on to ten percent of their former range. What if bears, as some scientists foretell, disappear in the next forty years? It's not impossible. Grizzlies don't have protected status under Canadian law as they do in the United States. The same bears amble back and forth across the forty-ninth parallel, given sanctuary on one side, gunshot on the other.

Instead of being afraid *of* the bears, I knew I should be afraid *for* them. Empathy filled my whole being. Love flowed from the same heart that had pounded in fear so recently. I knew that logging companies were punching roads into and around these untrammeled areas daily. Roads and logging are two of the worst assaults on bears. Logging decimates salmon streams and strips the land of shelter. Roads, besides cutting up the grazing, hunting, sleeping, hibernating, and birthing areas, are a welcome mat to poachers.

The Vancouver-based Western Canada Wilderness Committee estimates that forty thousand black bears alone have been poached in North America for their meat, paws, skin, teeth, and gallbladders. An international trade in bear parts supports the slaughter. Bear-paw soup goes for a hundred dollars a bowl in some Asian restaurants. The slimy gallbladders are sold for up to three thousand dollars apiece as aphrodisiacs and for use in Asian medicine.

Long ago, the Kwakiutl people also used bear gall to treat certain maladies. Ethnographer Franz Boas wrote that a person with ailing kidneys "takes the dried gall of a black bear and bursts it open. Then he puts the gall in a cup and pours water on so that the cup is full. When the water and gall are mixed, he holds the cup and prays, 'O Supernatural One, you are the supernatural power of the black bear . . . now come into me, please set my insides right. Go on, please, make me well . . . you, Long-Life-Maker . . . clear out the sickness of my kidneys . . .' Then the sick person drinks the potion and the kidney pain generally stops at once."

You see, it actually works. Bear bile slams a medicinal punch. A chemical called tauroursosdesoxycholic acid (note the tauro-urso in its name) is capable of treating liver diseases, cardiovascular problems, and fevers. A fresh gallbladder is brilliant green and jiggly as a water balloon. Dried it becomes a prune-like sack. The acid forms into tiny crystals. The bitter powder is then scraped out and stirred into juice, water, or tea. Today, the active chemical is made in a lab with exact chemistry, yet traffic in bear parts continues.

It goes on even though the science of nature tells us that our health and that of the bears are one. If we eliminate bears to preserve people, whether we do it for timber or bile—when we *have* alternatives—what kind of medicine is that? Ecological diversity is the medicine of a healthy ecosystem. The bear is wilderness medicine and physician. We can be thankful and duplicate it in the lab, or we can kill the physician. What sane patient kills the physician? What would the world be like bereft of bears?

"Bears," I whispered into the wind, "I hope you feast well tonight." I turned slowly in a circle, facing south toward British Columbia, then toward the island's center. Finally, I faced north where I'd seen the black bear digging crabs. Facing all 360 degrees, I silently sent out a message of love. I imagined a quilt of protective light flickering over all of us. Feeling stronger than before, I turned away from the channel, the dark shapes, the seaweed-covered rocks, and crawled into the tent. Before zipping the door, I carefully placed the eagle feather in the sand—for the bigger vision.

3   The Storm

The "Inside Passage" isn't all inside. There are places, such as Dixon Entrance, which I was approaching, and Queen Charlotte Sound, where the chain of islands protecting boaters from the open ocean disappears. Kayaking through these stretches is dicey. Who would drag me onto the kayak's fiberglass deck if I bowled over on the green shoulders of ocean swells, or if my Eskimo roll failed?

So after breaking camp on Black Island, I tucked the eagle feather I'd found the day before under the bow's bungee cord as a kind of talisman for vigilance. Like eagle, I thought, *I must be watchful.* I said the words again as I stuffed the tent, tarp, and clothing duffels into the kayak's front hatch. Zipping on my flotation vest and clipping the VHF marine radio into a carabiner on the vest's armhole, I repeated the line once more: *I must be watchful.*

It would be my mantra as I struck out toward the open waters of the windy border country beyond Revi Channel.

Just before takeoff, I squatted on the gravel beach beside the packed kayak listening to the morning weather update on the radio: *Dixon Entrance, storm warnings. Showers. Winds south 35 to 45 knots . . . .*

Forty-five knots! In a rough calculation, 45 knots times 1.13 (the variable used to calculate miles per hour) meant winds blasting over 50 mph.

Suddenly my stomach felt like I'd swallowed thistles. A visceral memory loomed of the last time I camped along the Pacific Coast in a storm. A friend and I were stranded for four days on Spring Island in Kyoquot Sound, British Columbia, with twenty-foot seas lashing surf against our tent door. We'd gotten into trouble when our radio reception was cut off by mountains flanking a fjord we paddled across. When the fjord opened to the sea, we didn't stop to check the weather. Instead, we hightailed it to Spring Island, a mile off the coast, enchanted by rumors of a beautiful beach there. The 60-mph storm slammed into us at midnight.

Asleep in the tent, buffered by the hood of my synthetic bag, at first I was only vaguely aware of a far-off booming sound. But soon I realized it was the wind's nightstick clobbering the tent. The noise was so loud it sounded like a prankster catapulting melons—Thub! Thub! Thub!—against the nylon. I flashed on my light. Roger lay awake. We watched the tent's walls jump like a punching bag springing upright after each gust passed. Only the weight of our bodies kept the tent down. How long would it hold? Then we heard a deafening crash. The surf was thundering up the gravel, groping for the stakes.

Springing from the tent into a searing horizontal rain we each grabbed two corners of the tent and sailed up the beach like a kite dragging two human tails. We repitched behind a grandfather-size log, an old cedar three feet tall on its side. To fortify the tent ends, we stacked driftwood hip high and chinked the gaps with seaweed. Then we lashed a tarp over the whole heap. By 4 A.M. surf frothed against our log fortress. Amazingly, thankfully, the ancient trunk didn't roll.

Alone on Black Island, aware that a storm roared somewhere over the horizon, I was thankful for having had the experience of Kyoquot Sound. This would be the first storm I'd ever faced alone, a daunting but powerful thought. Leonardo da Vinci said it well: *When you're all alone, everything belongs to you, and when a companion is present, only half belongs to you.*

This storm would be all mine.

Looking around, however, the ocean didn't look especially risky. Out in Revi Channel there was one-foot chop, but no whitecaps. Between Black Island and the mainland the passage appeared only restless and gray, like the fur on a deer mouse back. Not too worrisome. Along the coast, north and south, fat skeins of stratus wrapped the summits of Behm and Backbone Mountains like a cat's cradle. The low cloud ceiling hid the sawtoothed crests rising straight from sea level to 2500-foot summits. From where I stood, the coast appeared to be flanked by gentle receding blue mesas. A soft wind blew suggestively, beckoning, "It's a fine morning to travel."

Without the weather report, I wouldn't have been concerned at all. There was a time when I couldn't afford a radio. Back then, I didn't know much of anything about shoals, tidal rapids, williwaws, katabatic winds, or storms. I was a greenhorn kayaker who navigated by whim and whatever enchanted me hither. Sure, I sometimes got into minor trouble. But now, equipped with my *Coast Pilot*, NOAA charts, and a *Marine Atlas*, not to mention a VHF radio, I was scared crapless well before anything ever happened.

Erring on the side of conservatism, I opened the *Marine Atlas* to study the lay of the coast and plot a short route. I was nearing the intersection of two great bodies of water, Dixon Entrance and Hecate Strait, both wide open to the rigors of the Pacific.

Knowing a storm was approaching, but seeing no sign of it, I decided to travel six miles south to Kah Shakes Cove, named after a Tlingit chief. I read that there had been a native settlement at Kah Shakes Cove as late as 1883, complete with a fish weir and a dam in the stream. The weir was likely gone, but remnants of the dam might remain. It seemed like the kind of place where I could gain a sense of the people who plied these waters before me in dugout canoes. As an additional plus, a few nearby islands might offer a restful night's sleep.

Once on my way, the kayak seemed to fly, passing over reflections of inverted spruce trees like a snow goose leading a V-shaped white wake of imaginary honkers. Despite some shoulder pain and numbness in my right wrist, I was thrilled with my progress. But within an hour, the water mirror crumpled and I was bucking headwinds. My forearms burned from tendonitis. Bobbing in the waves, I popped two ibuprofen tablets and rubbed on arnica gel to minimize swelling.

Squinting down-coast I saw a forested peninsula jutting southwest with white shell beaches spilling out in three places—Kah Shakes Point. Four peaks rose above it. The highest, South Quadra Mountain, wore a crown of clouds. To reach the white beaches, I first had to cross Boca de Quadra fjord. Named for the sixteenth century Spanish explorer, the fjord has the outline of a four-pronged elk's antler. At the butt end where I floated it measures two miles across. I calculated that in calm weather it might take me forty minutes to sprint to the far shore. But what if the wind kicked up? Part of me questioned the prudence of entering open water and trying to outrun a storm.

I could also see a cluster of four islands floating like sentries at the opening of Boca de Quadra's mouth. The atlas mentioned that on August 7, 1793, Captain George Vancouver and his crew rowed to these islands and found "It being one entire quarry of slate . . . ." Vancouver named them accordingly. At that moment, Slate Island seemed to beckon me. I thought, "Why go farther? Why take a chance?" A white shell beach offered a perfect landing and camp.

But I didn't listen. I was overcome by a restlessness to keep moving south. A bigger part of me was hell-bent on pushing as many miles under my hull as possible before the storm froze my progress. After all, I'd only crawled four miles down the chart that morning.

Before nosing the kayak into open water, I took the customary precautions. I inflated the rescue float halfway, secured the deck gear—pump, chart, fishing hand line, spare paddle, and kayak wheels—and powered up with a handful of gorp. If the storm caught me halfway across, I'd need to about-face and run for shore. Scanning the fjord's banks, I looked for a safe haul-out. Boulders the size of tree stumps fortified the edges. No room for mistakes.

Next, I surveyed the sea in all directions. Colors and textures are the hieroglyphics of navigation. One indication of a storm's proximity and strength is a darkening wind line. An azure horizon on sterling seas, for example, could mean 15 mph winds approaching. Observing a bruised, blue-black horizon, however, I'd be fortunate to have the grace of minutes for evacuation to terra firma. But from my bow to the sky's hem I saw only even gray chop. No problem. So I arrowed the kayak bow on a snag silhouetted above Kah Shakes Point and glanced at my wrist watch. In twenty minutes I would be halfway there.

A half-mile offshore, a chill wind galloped over the surface, shading the water alder-bark gray. The sea shifted, hunching itself into rhythmic hills. The sudden change gave me pause. Yet, I knew what to do in seas like this. I leaned forward, paddling with shorter, faster strokes. Each brief pass of the paddle through the sea acts as an outrigger by stabilizing the boat on the stroke side. In choppy seas, the more strokes, the more stability. I breathed deeply with long exhalations and punched the blade into the wind like a slow-motion boxer. This posture increased the kayak's force against oncoming waves. It also signaled my brain to feel alert and calm.

I must be watchful.

The hull rose skyward, dove into a wave's trough, then bounced up again, like a dirt bike bumping over liquid hillocks. First the hillocks measured shoulder high, then a head higher. Their increasing stature reminded me of a passage I'd read in the *Coast Pilot:* "Storms entering Dixon Entrance build from the southeast and push swells into nearby passages, which break on shoals or against shorelines, and are heavy at times." These were ocean swells! Dixon Entrance was snorting swells while Hecate Strait herded gale winds up to meet them. Only a dangerously close storm could steer swells into Revi Channel.

A kernel of fear began to swell in my throat. The calm pragmatist in me wanted to ignore it and continue on. Don't let a speck of fear become a mountain, I reasoned, think only calm thoughts now. Looking out across the jumping water, I told myself that the white shell beaches at Kah Shakes Cove were visibly closer. But I couldn't be sure how much, since the headwind was also increasing.

How I longed for another voice to tell me what to do. Ahead of me: the deadly seriousness of being alone in a rough crossing. Behind me: Slate Island. Inside me: the self-doubt that came from having no one to concur or offer a second opinion. Overcome by questions, I stopped paddling altogether. Carouseling up and down in the swells, trying to think fast what to do, I felt like a minuscule plankton about to be swallowed by a whale of a storm.

That's when my alter-ego, a mutinous, brazen-faced character, took command.

"Don't let fear paralyze you," she said. "You're wasting time with indecision, you could be paddling across the channel. *Go for it!* Before the waves build! She who hesitates is lost!"

It was the Against-All-Odds Adventurer part of me—the one who will not give up. Her reasoning is cunning in its flattery, for she assumes I am invincible.

Unfortunately, she's not always right, but this time I believed her. I grabbed my paddle and scolded myself for indecision, *"Daamnittttt. Moovve!* Don't just *sit here!"* I stroked hard into a gust of wind. But as soon as I bucked into a white-cap wave, another voice countered the first.

"She who hesitates does so for a good reason. Fetch the binoculars. Look at the horizon. You'll see why." What cryptic voice said that? Suddenly I was aware there weren't just two, but three of us, possibly more, in that cockpit: the Adventurer, a watchful Mother, and me.

I raised binoculars toward Dixon Entrance, but I couldn't believe what I saw. A horizon sharp-toothed as a bow saw. *Holy Crow!* There was no more time to hesitate. Only action. I dashed up the paddle and heaved south toward Kah Shakes.

Leading me thither was the Adventurer. Her logical commands kept my mind focused on the present. "Quick! Glance behind your shoulder. Size the trees on the far shore. Now compare them to the forest on Kah Shakes Point. You must be a third of the way," she calculated. "Just thirty more minutes, forty if the wind doesn't pick up."

"*If* the wind doesn't pick up?" said another voice. "That's an optimistic

mind game. A kayaker sitting two feet tall in her kayak can only see [
half miles to a flat horizon. That storm's charging forty to fifty mile[
It'll mow over you in ten to fifteen minutes."

"Who's that curmudgeon?" the Adventurer wondered. The voice continued, whether I listened or not.

"Fighting headwind, crawling one mile per hour, you'll only make it to
mid-channel when the storm hits. Remember trying to roll in surf at Long
Beach? You didn't fare too well. Remember how it felt to capsize then, with
friends around? You'll be too tuckered to roll or to yank yourself back in if you
fail. Turn around now and you'll still be surfing out of control. And to where?
A boulder shore? Who the hell do you think you are paddling in these conditions?" It was the voice of Prudence.

But the Adventurer wasn't listening one iota. She kept the kayak on course.
"White Reef is directly west. It marks the halfway point across Boca de Quadra
and you're almost even with the reef. You're almost halfway," she said with
assurance.

I stared at the waves pummeling White Reef as if I wasn't in my body at
all, but watching a catastrophic weather review on television. Swells slammed
the rocks. *Klup-Fheww!* King-size sheets of seawater sailed into the air. The
Adventurer reminded me that reefs always look scary in big seas because the
waves bottom out, rise up on tiptoe, and curl white. "It's just the waves talking
to the rock," she said. Listening to her voice, I remained calm and detached.

But the Mother was yelling, *"Turn back! What if you dump out here in
ten-foot, breaking seas?"*

Another fifty yards and the waves steepened into tightly spaced ridges. Every sixth or seventh wave was capped in white froth. These rollers plowed into
me, washed around my waist in a wreath of effervescent sea foam, then poured
off. I saw countless whitecaps, which told me it must be blowing thirty knots.

The Mother recalled every time I'd ever been caught in rough water and
now recounted those knee-quivering images in adrenaline-inducing detail.
Rosario Strait: slalom surfing out of control in a tide rip, thirty-knot winds,
five-foot rollers, hull torqued sideways to the waves. Sea of Cortez: humping
over sixteen-foot swells when one wave crested unexpectedly, frothing white
and pouring ice water into my spray skirt, and taking me down in a wash of
blue-green. Lake Michigan: sudden tornado warning, wind lifted the paddle
right out of my hands. Boca de Quadra: . . .

"*—Breathe! BREATHE!*" the Adventurer interrupted, coaching me along.
"Punch into the waves. Here comes a big one . . . *PUNCH!*"

The bow sliced into the sharp fin of a five-foot wave, plunged down, and
slammed over the top of the next wall of translucent gray-green. Seawater shot
out like white wings. For a moment, I marveled at *Yemaya*'s skill. Hers is an
ancient Inuit design wedded to twentieth-century fiberglass technology. The
bow corked up from each breaking wave like a storm petrel and stayed on
course. I was reminded that this boat was made for open coasts. Then I remembered that open-coast waves come in sets. Here, every seventh one is the

biggest. Now I counted them . . . one . . . three . . . six . . . and exploded with speed into the seventh one.

I flashed my eyes down to my wrist watch. Twenty-five minutes of paddling. Come on, you can make it, I reassured myself. But doubt crept insidiously. I kept jerking my head down to look at my watch, then up to the far, storm-darkened horizon. Questions plagued me. *How fast is the storm traveling? Will I make it to Kah Shakes without flipping? Should I turn back? Where do I aim if I do? Can I surf safely to Slate Island? What dark angel drove me here? Have I lost my senses?* My mind was flooded with visions of my capsized boat, awash in the surf, gear floating away, me frantically trying to upright the swamped kayak a mile from shore.

Just then a ferocious white-capped wave burst over the bow, rose to my chest, and poured icy rivulets down my neck and shoulders. The frostiness shocked me into a panic. Whatever courage or determination I'd scraped together minutes before now heaved from me like a scream. On the next wave crest I wheeled around down the wave's face so fast that the kayak skittered sideways like a stick. To keep from log-rolling and dumping, I slammed my blade like a beaver tail into the rising curl. I pushed hard away from the wall and, surprisingly, recovered facing north. A successful 180-degree turn, except that now I was surfing too fast and fizzing with adrenaline or fear. Or both.

Winging across the waves, paddle flailing like a soaked cormorant that can't take off, I was two-hundred percent alert. Looking up and down the channel to measure my progress, I noticed a small white fishing boat plugging up the inlet. Three fluorescent orange floats glowed from the port deck. I headed for it.

"Paddle like hell," I told myself, "then decide what to do next. This little boat is your only chance for help if you go down." I realized the nearest landable coast was two miles away at Slate Island. These people were a mile closer than the islands. How I longed to be aboard with them.

Paddling furiously and closing in, out of breath, I waved. I was surprised when no one waved back. As I drew closer I noticed a half dozen fishers in forest green Helly Hansen raincoats. Each man was focused on his rod and line, mug of coffee, or anything but me. Seated in my kayak, surging up and down in the waves, I tried to maintain a veneer of calm, though inside I was scared shitless.

"Any luck?" I shouted by way of introduction, still twenty yards off.

One man shook his head, cupping his ear as if to mime, "Too windy . . . I can't hear you. . . ."

I paddled closer around to the lee side of the fishing boat. Bouncing up and down in swells, I paddled in place to keep from blowing off.

"I SAID, YOU CATCHING ANY FISH? . . . ANY LUCK?"

"Only bad," shook one head, grimacing downward.

From the unfriendly stare his two neighbors cast my way, I suddenly saw what they thought: a dumb-ass kayaker—and a *woman* at that—out in a storm meant for 95-horsepower Evinrudes. So I got to the point.

"Say, is the captain around? I'd like to get a second weather check on this storm that's coming in."

A blond, sun-chiseled face poked up from the wheelhouse.

"You don't want to know," he growled, biting his cigarette.

"I do," I laughed, uncomfortably. "My VHF radio reports 45-knot winds."

The captain inhaled impatiently on his cigarette and yelled, "You got it right." Then he wagged his head, "This is miserable weather to camp in. You ought to head to Mink Bay Lodge . . . hole up there 'til the storm rides out."

I was hoping he'd offer me a dry hitch. But nothing was mentioned, so I shouted back, matter-of-factly, "How do I get to Mink Bay?"

He pointed up Boca de Quadra Channel as if we could see the lodge. I squinted past his finger to where the Quadra turned and disappeared into a forested fjord.

"Just go down this channel, take a right, then a left . . . then . . . ."

I continued looking past his pointed finger, but I was no longer listening. Mink Bay Lodge, no matter how cozy, was too far. The captain was giving directions as if I were a motor boat. A quick check of my chart showed it to be at least thirteen miles. It would take half a day to paddle there, never mind the cost of a wilderness hotel. Suddenly, Slate Island sounded real good.

"Thanks," I shouted, "I'll think about it."

"Where you coming from?" another blank, unshaven face yelled from cupped hands.

"Ketchikan."

"Where you headed?"

"Bellingham, Washington."

More heads turned to look. Now I wished I hadn't told the truth. I felt suddenly vulnerable until one fellow actually smiled and shouted enthusiastically, "No kiddin'! All by yourself? Why, good luck there to you, Miss." His eyes shone with fatherly approval.

I waved good-bye, turned *Yemaya* away, and surfed furiously toward Slate Island. There were times during the mile-long crossing when my eyes ached to fill with tears. It would have felt so good to cry just to relieve the overwhelming stress of my predicament. But I couldn't afford to blur my vision now. I needed to see every nuance of change in the boat's angle and speed as it crashed through the waves. Fifteen wild minutes later, soaked and shaking, my hull touched down on the white shell beach that had beckoned me earlier.

Slate Island felt immovably solid beneath my feet. A fence of towering spruce blocked the wind's roar. Standing in dark somber robes, the ancient evergreens appeared as monks offering refuge in their quiet arbor. Walking up the shell beach carrying my bowline, I felt almost stupid, even embarrassed, in their wise presence. If I'd heeded caution and turned toward Slate Island earlier instead of bounding across Boca de Quadra's roughening seas, I wouldn't be sandbagged by remorse now.

The booming voice that drove me past this island hours ago had acqui-esced. Now, as I set foot on the island, not by choice but by being defeated, I was stung with the obvious truth—second-guessing my assessment of the con-ditions could have cost me my life. I hitched the bowline over a driftwood log. A short distance away the charter fishing boat sped across Revi Channel and disappeared. I envied the fishers motoring home to Duke or Annette Island, to propane-heated lodge rooms, steaming baths, and a hot dinner. I'd wanted to ask if they'd take me along. But pride held me back. Now I felt utterly alone. Inside my chest, the guttering candle of hope snuffed out.

I leaned against the trunk of a spruce tree and watched as the storm whipped up the sea. White battalions of waves ushered from Dixon Entrance into Revi Channel. Fields of six-foot, then ten-foot, and finally what I guessed were sixteen-foot rollers blew past the island. Spindrift spewed off their tops. Foam streamers rode up their steep faces, crashing down in an avalanche of surf. Viewed altogether, the field of waves was both mesmerizing and terrifying—endless caravans of gray hills rising, sharpening, cresting, falling. The horizon turned ghostly white with condensed spray. I felt numb with uncertainty and cold. If I tarried any longer, I might never leave this tree.

I walked once around the island scrambling over hummocks of slate that opened onto stretches of white shell beach, then more slate lumped up and covered with seaweed that popped underfoot. I told myself I was looking for a camp, but really I was restless and confused about why I'd imagined it was a good idea for me to take a solo trip on the storm-beaten Alaskan coast in the first place. It was hard to believe it was only the second day.

Just trying to walk the beach in a straight line in the heavy winds was nearly impossible. I was pushed right, then left, then backward, as if two play-ground bullies were heaving me back and forth. My hat flew off and cartwheeled down the beach. My hair whipped in high circles as I chased the hat to a tide pool where it floated upside down.

On the southern point of the island the wind heaved the spruce and west-ern hemlocks so vigorously they danced like marionettes. The entire island was dancing—the trees, salal bushes, and flapping ribbons of seaweed tethered to the slate rocks. Occasionally a sprig of spruce broke free and tumbled through the wet air, somersaulting to shore.

On the Beaufort Scale—a system for estimating wind speed devised by Sir Francis Beaufort, a nineteenth-century British admiral—twigs snapping loose means winds rocking along at up to 46 mph. "A fresh gale," Sir Beaufort might have quipped. But walking back I stepped over a recently downed, paddle-length branch that caused me to upgrade the storm to "strong gale" with winds up to 50 mph.

To escape the relentless din, I bushwhacked toward the island's center. Wading through thickets of vetch, trundling over fallen trees, I didn't even think about bears. Soon I found myself stooped under a broken-off spruce ogling at great splotches of guano. Just six feet above my head, staring down from a ragged mattress of sticks, glared a bald eagle.

Never in my life had I witnessed an eagle's nest so low. I could practically jump up and touch it. The realization washed over me that few humans had set foot on its island kingdom. Vividly distressed at my nearness, cream-feathered crown arced my way, white eye watching from under a shadowed brow, hooked bill opening, it whistled, then lifted off the nest in a great spread of wings and circled back around. Did the eagle want me to follow? I quickly moved away.

A short distance farther into the island's center, the air felt substantially calmer. The wind no longer luffed by my ears. I could hear my breath again. And in that still sanctuary I looked down to discover the most amazing sight. A bouquet of red and gold blossoms—each one hovering on a slender stalk and nodding five spurs of bright plumage. I knelt in the duff to admire these hanging lanterns of the forest. Fifty yards to the south, waves cannonballed the shore. Wind-blown rain soared in sheets. The air rumbled like a freight train. Black and white tones dominated the seascape. Yet here in the island's heart columbine flowers knew such peace. How grateful I was for a moment of tranquility. If I could have crawled inside those red petals to be rocked, I would have.

I do not know what Juan Diego felt in 1536 when, walking alone up a desert hillside, he discovered a bouquet of red roses blooming impossibly in winter. Nor what words he spoke to Our Lady of Guadalupe who appeared to him with folded hands and a star-spangled robe. But surely, even 460 years later, I must believe in the smallest of signs. I faced a storm and found refuge. Now, like a spring flower, I must rise from the ashes of self-doubt and travel on. *Thank you, Columbine*, I said, standing up and brushing off my knees.

On the island's leeward side, I smoothed a swatch of beach gravel for my campsite under a three-foot-wide spruce. So much of the day had been out of my control that it felt good to do something familiar. I tied out a tarp, set a cookpot at the tarp's lowest corner to catch the rain for drinking water, and pounded tent stakes. For as long as I can remember, a weather-proof camp is something I love creating. I love selecting the perfect quartet of trees to tie my tarp to, hiding the tent behind beach logs so it's out of the wind and out of sight of anyone passing by, and finding a wide log for a kitchen counter. It's like playing Little House in the Wilderness. I've done it so often—working in sun, downpours, wind, lightning, and hail—that it takes me less than an hour.

Running back down to the beached kayak one more time, I heard *sploosh! ker-sploosh!* Four bowling-ball heads bobbed in the swells not far offshore. Harbor seals! Up to their whiskers in surging waves. The seals tossed and somersaulted in the breakers. I laughed at their shining, round faces and they came closer. Seems I was the main attraction. I heaved the white kayak onto my shoulder and trudged up the beach to stash it beside a clump of purple vetch. I tied the bowline to a new log and headed back to camp. The seals followed my land route by water.

Soon I discovered that wherever I walked, the seals pursued me, swimming along the island's perimeter, dunking under the curling surf, popping up again after a wave passed to see where I'd moved. They trailed me like devoted dogs. Like Artemis the Huntress and her hunting hounds, I mused. When I stopped to admire a moon snail shell, they stopped too. So I tried an experiment. When a wave curled again and they dove, I hid behind a driftwood log. When I poked my head up, four heads were watching. Next, I walked toward them to see what they'd do. I walked slowly, hoping to keep their trust. I began to sing a sweet sea shanty called "The Brandy Tree (Otter's Song)."

I go down to the windy sea
And the little gray seal will play with me
Slide on the rock and dive in the bay
And sleep on the ledge at night

I couldn't be sure if the seals heard me over the crash of breakers, but I like to think they did, as they seemed to mirror my curiosity by drifting closer. I sang another verse.

But the seal don't try to tell me how
To fish in the windy blue
Seal's been fishing for a thousand years
And he knows that I have too. . . .

Three heads stopped, while the fourth drifted closer yet. I sat down on a rock at the water's edge and waited. Harbor seals have an insatiable curiosity. How many times had I paddled along imagining I was alone, then jumped from a *ka-ploosh!* behind my rudder? If I glanced quick I often caught the mottled back of a seal diving behind me. But why should this wild creature trust a human? I know stories that suggest they would be better not to trust.

For example, there's a beach on San Juan Island in Puget Sound that some local boys call the squishing beach. They roar their all-terrain vehicles over napping seal pups hauled out on the gravel. Wolf Hollow, an animal recovery center, knows who the culprits are, but the glitch is they have to catch the idiots in the act. And I've talked to an angry fisherman who every spring shoots pups on sight because otherwise they'd grow up to compete for "his" salmon. Over the years I've pulled my kayak up to half a dozen seals floating dead with bullet holes.

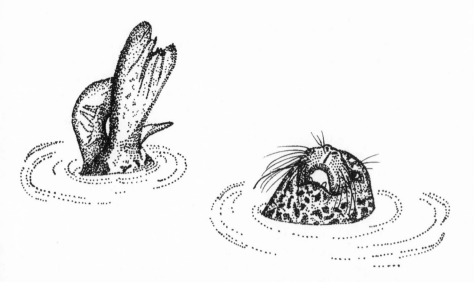

Given recent history, it's astounding that a seal dared to play with me. Perhaps a seal's instinct is to turn the other cheek.

Through the raindrops, far above the beach, the eagle hovered in its black gloves, wind riffling its head and wing feathers, white tail fan ruddering to adjust for the gusts. It was too rough for fishing so it must have been riding the updrafts along the island's edge just for fun. The eagle glided west toward Dixon Entrance, banked, then slid back over the island, shuttling back and forth through the rain, never making a wing beat.

A black surf scoter plunged its carnival-orange-and-white striped bill headfirst into a breaker, corked up, shook off, and dove again. "Animals teach you how to live in the moment," a Menominee man told me before I left on this journey. This island's animals seemed to thrive in storms and enjoyed playing in the intense uproar of waves. How much I had to learn.

Nightfall. The last smudge of light over Dixon Entrance was as soft as down, but the wind was still howling forty-plus knots. Snapped branches littered the beach. I wondered about the chance of one clobbering my tent.

After dinner, I carried a mug of chamomile tea to the calmer north point. Sitting on a boulder promontory, I mended an old tear in the kayak's neoprene hatch cover. Looping a needle threaded with mint floss up through the neoprene, then sealing the stitching with a seam of barge cement, I remembered how my father's eternal tinkering—sharpening the lawnmower, troweling wet cement, welding a crack in a motorcycle frame—always gifted him with a handsome sense of pride. He had supported this solo trip wholeheartedly. Remembering his enthusiasm over the phone right before I left, I felt confidence returning. I held up my finished hatch cover for admiration, and smiled. The torn edge of fear was mending.

On the darkening ocean, whitecaps surged like an infinite school of dolphins homing north. The booming sound of surf and the pungent aroma of iodine were everywhere. Overhead, the sky faded from deep lilac to gray to soot. Stumbling across wet slate in the dark, I was welcomed at the forest's edge by the citrusy loam of spruce needles and earth. I crawled into the tent, lit a candle lantern, and flicked on the weather radio.

This is Prince Rupert Coast Guard Continuous Broadcast at 23:45 Saturday . . . A low over the Queen Charlottes will move north into the Gulf of Alaska . . . Dixon Entrance storm warnings, winds 35–45, easing to 35. Outlook, strong southerlies . . . Lighthouse reports. . . .

Barometric pressure was falling everywhere down the coast. But just the presence of another voice at all, no matter what weather it foreshadowed, felt comforting. Like a kid at bedtime, I flipped to another channel just to enjoy the soothing quality of being read to aloud.

Outside the tent, the wind moaned like the haunted song of a troubadour. Inside, I did sit-ups to break the chill in my limbs. I peeled off damp clothes. Then, remembering that I had only two more dry sets, I put them back on. They'll dry while I sleep, I told myself.

Pleasantly cocooned from the storm, lying in my tent reading the *Coast Pilot*, I fell asleep to the *shhhhh* of rain on the tarp. The cookpot by the tarp's low corner sang *Gloop! Tup! Ploop! Good for you!* like a raindrop lullaby. But not long after I dropped my head into the folded pile jacket, a strange sound startled me awake.

I sat bolt upright as a boat engine passed at some immeasurable distance between the islands. After a few seconds, I woke enough to recognize the whine of a horsefly buzzing in and out of earshot around my camp.

Later, after I was dreaming again, I startled to hear a deep growl. Lying motionless while the wind in the treetops roared like a jet engine, I waited for the sound to repeat. Then I recognized it. A far-off wave, crashing in a line down the beach mimicked a deep growl. I laughed out loud. But my hand reached out to check that the pepper spray was still a short grab away.

4 Feasting on Flotsam

Unzipping the tent door the next morning I surprised a ruddy weasel slinking through camp. Underneath, from chin to belly, it glowed from one long brushstroke of white. Delicate ears lay flat against its almond head like small shells. It stopped, glanced over its muscular shoulder, and echoed my stare. But it quickly turned away, trotting down the open beach to the tide pools on the rocky point, its black-tipped tail sticking straight out behind.

Going hunting, I supposed.

Wholly carnivorous, short-tailed weasels range from the tideline to heather-filled mountain meadows preying on voles, mice, crickets, beetles, crabs, sculpin fish, snails, and urchins. Like their mustelid cousins the river otters, they can swim, but would rather not. Thirty feet away, this short-tailed weasel again froze in its tracks peering skyward and nosing the air, then dashed for the beach rocks. I looked up, surveying the branches for winged silhouettes, but saw no obvious signature of eagle, only the sudden rush of ten thousand leaves in a burst of wild stadium applause. The storm was still far from puffing itself out.

Out across the water, whitecaps catapulted upward as far as my eyes could see. The horizon, now completely erased by blowing spindrift, smoked white as after a great fire. And the stratus-quilted sky seemed to carry the weight of eternity.

Guess I'm staying here today.

So following weasel's cue and trying to make the best of my island strand-ing, I pulled on boots and rain jacket and ventured toward the windy point, wondering what gifts the storm heaved up the night before.

Unlike weasel, who sneaks up on her prey, my boots noisily popped and crackled like intertidal fireworks over the seaweed-covered slate. Popweed or fucus, a warty, green sea algae with rabbit-ear floats, is easily recognizable by its sound. I knelt down and pinched a bulbous float between two fingers. It popped, then oozed a clear gelatinous fluid as viscous as an ovulating woman's mucus. Because of this, I'd long called this slick substance "fucus mucus."

In *Seaweeds at Ebb Tide,* my all-time favorite beachcomber book, Dr. Muriel Guberlet explains the reason scientists hesitate to classify certain marine algae such as fucus as "plants." Some seaweed species ride the fence between two kingdoms. These enigmatic life-forms look like plants. They have leaves, stems, chlorophyll, and holdfasts that anchor them to rocks. But when it comes to reproducing, they behave more like animals. For instance, Dr. Guberlet says, "Fucus has sixty-four sperms in the male organ and eight eggs in the female organ, the egg being as much as thirty thousand times larger than the sperm. During ebb tide, the small motile sperms and motionless eggs of fucus are discharged into the water. While the eggs float, swimming sperms congregate near them, attach themselves, and spin around at the point of attachment. One sperm fertilizes the egg and the others disappear. The fertilized egg immediately begins to develop. Fucus produces eggs and sperms throughout the year. Of course, this process cannot be seen with the naked eye."

However one classifies this puzzling life-form that sends its children hitchhiking south on the out-going tide, the gel inside its floats may hide apothecarial secrets. Used like aloe, fucus juice seems to soothe skin and heal mild sunburns. In a foot bath with hot water, it comforts sore feet. In past times it was routinely rubbed on corns and skin tumors. Brewed into a tea, it's a lung tonic.

An ethnobotanist friend, Mac Smith, whose passion is kayaking to remote coastal islands and living off the roots of his ancient wisdom and the luck of his hand line, is a culinary star with popweed. Mac simply scissors off the floats, spreads them over a cookie sheet, and oven bakes them on low heat. The gelatin puffs up into a whitish fiber with a slight crunch. Mac tosses the pops while they're still hot with powdered cheddar, and—voila!—sea Cheetos.

Lacking an oven on many journeys, I learned another secret from Mac. Fucus that has been tossed up by high-tide storms and sundried is equally flavorful. You need only snap off a small handful of cinnabar floats and crunch them alongside your sandwich. I like to hunker down and graze a few sea Cheetos whenever the ocean and sun give the opportunity. But it was too damp after the previous night's downpour. However, fucus has another use that would have suited the stormy weather just fine. The Quillayute Natives who lived in Washington State used to harvest and burn seaweed when a strong wind was blowing. They believed the acrid-smelling smoke could drive the wind away.

A clam's throw from the ocean's breakers, I leaned into the gusting wind and poked through a one-hundred-foot-long drift of tangled seaweeds looking for species I knew. Wading into these knee-deep piles was like walking into a boat hold filled with slippery cod that skittered under boot and invited me to skate in place, feeling momentarily triumphant before landing smack on my slimy butt. And all just to yard out a few interesting varieties or perhaps a delicious leaf for lunch.

Collecting, drying, and cooking with seaweeds was not something I adapted to casually. At age eleven, pushing my breakfast tray along a buffet line in a Japanese youth hostel, I was horrified when a cheery cook spooned up a bowl of seaweed soup, one raw egg, and rice, and slid it toward me. The seaweed, let alone the raw egg, was enough to make me swear to survive on rice and soy sauce until I returned to the oceanless 'burbs of Wisconsin. Years later, Marine Biology 101 taught me to mount and dry delicate fronds of seaweed on stationery paper so they became translucent, dancing-Shiva leaves. That was the beginning of my zealous appreciation.

These days, when guiding sea kayaking trips, I am more like the cheery Japanese cook, pushing my homemade kelp chowder toward skeptical guests who politely wave their hands across the empty bowls saying, "Ah . . . just a spoonful, please." I now know that cooked seaweeds—diced and stirred into soups, stir-fry, and casseroles—are as innocuous and mellow as zucchini or asparagus. Yet the untamed part of me always savors the wild wonder of grazing on nori or sea lettuce right from a tide pool. Fresh from the sea, these leaves taste like the primordial soup they come from: wet, salty, and full of vitamins and trace minerals.

In truth, seaweed is so renowned for its ability to siphon trace minerals from the ocean that some dietitians contribute the low incidence of premenstrual syndrome among Japanese women to a diet high in sea vegetables. Since sea algae has no roots—only a holdfast cements it to the sea floor—the plant's entire surface—leaf, stem or stipe, and holdfast—absorbs the ocean's nutrients. "If you think about it," Mac once said, "all the mountain ranges, rivers, and plains that transport water eventually deposit every known mineral into the ocean."

In the high-tide rack surrounding my boots, the feather-shaped wing kelp was the most profuse algae. I tugged and tugged, eventually pulling loose a long sheet. Its hefty length makes perfect sense. Wing kelp grow prolifically in the winter—up to one inch in a day—whereas other seaweed species die back to the holdfast each fall. Come spring, the boa-length leaves of wing kelp are easily torn loose by storm waves and tossed onto beaches. Meanwhile, its neighbors are just beginning to leaf out.

I call wing kelp the "asparagus of the sea," because it cooks up tender like asparagus in soups. It's easy to identify, even when it's swaying five feet below your kayak, by the yellow mid-vein rib running up the leaf's center. Divers see the plant as a long, undulating golden feather. In Alaska, these giant sea feathers can stretch as long as two single kayaks placed end to end. But the leaf in my hands was relatively small, about five feet I estimated by raising it from my boot to my shoulder. I sliced the top foot off and pocketed it for that day's lunch—cream of kelp chowder.

Another fine soup ingredient, though less prolific in the drift, is sea lettuce—a chartreuse seaweed that resembles a wilted head of leaf lettuce. *Ulva* thrives on rocks that are covered and uncovered with the tide, where it dries into taut, shiny cellophane at low tide. Eaten raw like parsley it's loaded with vitamin C. Chopped into confetti, sea lettuce adds a colorful dash to soups, casseroles, and potato salad. I removed a handful from a nearby rock for the chowder, careful to press my thumb against the tiny holdfast before tearing off the leaves. It's important to leave the holdfast attached to the rock to allow this perennial to regenerate each spring.

Next from the pile I untangled a stiff, leathery leaf thick as a lasagna noodle and as long as my leg. Two parallel rows of seersucker rumpled the blade's midline. To fully identify it, I took a little bite. Slippery, sweet mucus oozed over my tongue. Probably the most notable quality of *Laminaria saccharina*, or sugar wrack as it's also called, is the sugar alcohol (mannitol) it produces. The Japanese slice and dry sugar wrack into strips for a tasty candy. I would stir some into my soup for its honey-like flavoring.

Another puckered leaf, egg-shaped in outline, lay under the sugar wrack. This leaf is solid seersucker, as if blistered, hence the common name of seersucker. Seersucker grows prolifically on wood pier pilings and can cover a sunken wood boat in less than two months. Though I'd never eaten it, I knew it was edible.

No sea algae in the Pacific Northwest will kill you. Only one type, *Desmerestia,* nicknamed the "color changer," contains a mild acid that can upset your stomach. Color changer turns from brown to green when it's removed from the water. Toss a leaf into a plastic bag with other sea algae, and it bleaches its neighbors white. If in doubt about what you're collecting, bite into raw color changer to encounter an eye-squinting bitterness. I've heard of ingenious home canners who use it to make a brine for kelp pickles.

By far the most coveted treasure I excavated from the high-tide rack was a palm-size, wine-red blade of Turkish towel or *Gigartina*. Red-colored seaweed is rarer for beachcombers to find because it grows at great depths. Only with a storm to heave the leaves from their dark home could I hope to discover them in abundance. Green and brown algae, on the other hand, grow in shallower waters and wash up with great frequency.

Turkish towel's nubby texture is unmistakable and also highly useful. Hundreds of upraised nipples make it an abrasive pot scrubber or loofah-quality washcloth. But even better, within its walls it hides a bounty of carrageen—a natural thickener used commercially in ice cream, pudding, chocolate milk, yogurt, cake icing, lotion, and shampoo, as well as a clarifying agent for beer. My favorite high-tide dessert using carrageen-rich Turkish towel is chocolate ocean pudding.

I could barely keep myself from dashing back to camp to begin. But the first step in making a thick seaweed pudding is harvesting enough fresh Turkish towel blades. I continued to search the drift for two more dark red ones. They had to feel dense and leathery to the touch, not thin and floppy. Blotchy pink and white leaves were too rain soaked and already leaching the thickener I coveted. But the carrageen-rich leaves are most likely to be found washed ashore in late summer after a long growing season, so on this day in early spring I'd be happy if I ended up with a chocolate ocean milkshake. Trotting back to camp, trailing streamers of golden leaves, coat pockets bulging with Turkish towel and sea lettuce, I startled the short-tailed weasel chawing on sculpin fish at the lip of a tide pool.

"Look, weasel," I whispered, shaking the ribbons toward her stare, "thanks to you and this storm, I'm feasting on flotsam today."

At camp I spread my treasures across a rock, then stood back to admire their luminous colors and sundry shapes: burgundy, copper, and chlorophyll green; feather, lettuce, spade, and ovoid; puckered, leathery, nubby, and smooth. I selected the best ones for chowder and pudding, then went to work.

Slicing up kelp leaves that are as long as my outstretched arms without dragging them through the sand requires an artful technique. The neatest way

I know is to first roll the kelp leaf into a loose column. Then press it down with the flat of your hand and cut pasta-size strips from the curved side. *Whop! Whop! Whop!* They fell into stacks of pudgy linguine. I also chopped up potatoes, onion, garlic, carrots, zucchini, and cabbage, exhausting half the fresh vegetables I had with me.

My recipe for cream of kelp chowder evolved over years of kayak cookery and from the help of many a culinary guide, though Mac's seaweed broth was my original inspiration. Yemaya's Chowder is the fond nickname I've given it.

Yemaya's Chowder
Serves 4

4 red potatoes, cut in ½-inch cubes
¼ red onion, diced
2 carrots, cut in thin rounds
1 tablespoon basil
½ teaspoon fennel
pinch of cayenne
2–3 cloves garlic, diced
2 chicken-flavored bouillon cubes
1 cup wing kelp or ribbon kelp, sliced in ¼-by-2-inch strips
2 zucchinis, cut in half moons
½ cup red cabbage, chopped
¼ cup sweet red pepper, chopped
½ cup dry milk powder, mixed according to package instructions, or 1
*   12-ounce can evaporated milk*
sea lettuce, minced for garnish

I diced the vegetables and tossed potatoes, onion, carrots, and spices into my fire-blackened cookpot. My goal was a thick broth, so I limited the amount of water, barely covering the vegetables. When the potatoes were nearly soft, I used a fork to mush half of them against the inside of the pot to thicken the broth. Next I threw in the quick-cooking vegetables: kelp, zucchini, and red cabbage.

Now came the fun part when the soup starts to resemble Mardi Gras confetti. Even the wing kelp briefly masquerades in a bright, kelly green color. Heat causes the brown kelp's chloroplasts to burst out chlorophyll, but the expended kelp turns brown again after a few minutes.

When the kelp leaves felt as tender as well-cooked asparagus and could be squished against my tongue, I dumped in a cup of premixed, extra-thick powdered milk and the red pepper. A sprinkle of minced sea lettuce for garnish would be the last step. But first, on to dessert.

Chocolate ocean pudding is a chemistry experiment worth the effort. First I wadded three Turkish towel leaves in the center of a clean bandana, brought the corners together, and tied the bundle. I covered the bundle with fresh water in a small cookpot, covered it with a lid, and brought the water to a boil. After

Laundry Line and Sea Algae

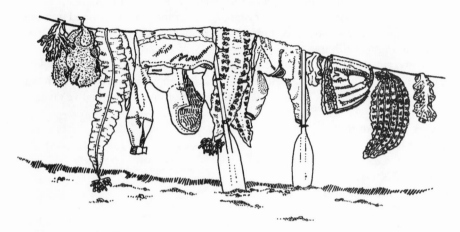

"After the storm" (left to right): Bladder wrack, Turkish towel, wing kelp, skanorak, sugar wrack, pile jacket, sea lettuce, float vest, seersucker, dulse.

fifteen or twenty minutes, I turned the heat to low and squeezed out the bandana to collect every bit of carrageen.

Last, I stirred in one cup of premixed instant milk (you can also use a 12-ounce can of evaporated milk), several heaping spoonfuls of instant hot cocoa mix, and a crumbled-up dark chocolate bar.

As soon as the chocolate melted I dug a hole in the beach gravel low enough so that it filled with cool seawater, and set my covered pot inside. This cools it down to speed the jelling—and eating—process. If there had been a creek, I'd have snugged it inside a slow eddy wreathed by rocks with a hefty stone on its lid.

As I scooped beach gravel back around the buried pudding pot, something *ker-plooshed* out past the low-tide rocks. I squinted across the turbulent water and spied four frolicking seals. Each one was proclaiming the sun on top of its polished, eight-ball head. Suddenly I realized that the storm clouds were subsiding. Sunlight, glorious sunlight, was falling through billowing cumulus. White spears descended to platinum-blue water. Forty-knot winds still blasted out of the south, whitecaps flashed everywhere, but *sun*. Drying, warming, welcome *SUN!*

Back at camp, I slung a drying line across driftwood logs and propped it skyward with paddles

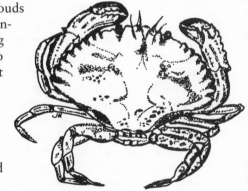

and more driftwood crutches before dragging the damp sleeping bag, pad, and rain-soaked clothes from the tent. It was comforting to watch the sea algae fluttering in the sun between my clothes, to watch the steam puff-puffing from the chowder pot.

I unclipped my dry bag and hauled out pencils, pen, and sketch pad. But before I curved my back to a log, I emptied the final beach-combings from my coat pockets—one moon snail plump as a goose egg and nippled at the apex; two butter clams with holes drilled by a predatory snail; one whirled triton shell with a window broken through; and a red rock crab molt light as a pencil.

Sketching these treasures, I realized I'd finally become comfortable on my journey. Appreciating beauty was a sign of that change. So was the centered feeling that accompanies eating a wild-harvested meal. Something had shifted inside. I didn't know if it was lasting, but I was more kicked back. The unknown was becoming familiar.

Suddenly—*Ssztreet! Ssztreet!*—what's that noise? My goddess, an unexpected blessing! A male Anna's Hummingbird, head red as first-day menstrual blood, whirred past, banked, and paused beside my left ear, hum, hum, humming. I sat as still as the log, my breath light as hummingbird breath. The whirring wings receded, then became a red ribbon zinging past my eyes and burning a fiery trail like a sparkler at night. This time the tiny bird zipped to my right ear. Again, the soft rush of wing feathers humming, humming.

Next the thumb-size bird hissed into front view and hovered before my sunglasses. Sunlight sparkled in its black, moccasin-bead eyes. Suddenly, it burst forward and stitched in and out of the floral patterns on the fuchsia bandana I'd knotted around my neck to keep out the chill. He was "sucking" the nectar from my pink bandana!

After three storm-bound days on Slate Island, the seas grew calmer—for a few hours at a time anyway. At first light on the fourth day, I unzipped the tent door. Wind was down! Instead of fifteen-foot swells mashing the rocky southern tip, two-foot waves clupped the shore. The coast guard report announced, *high pressure system moving in, winds south 15-25 knots.* I guessed it was blowing seven to eight knots. I would try to press on two miles to Kah Shakes, then five more to Foggy Bay, before the waves reared up. Restless and excited to see new sights, I heaved gear out of the tent. In its place, I left a shell filled with clippings from *Yemaya*'s cedar bough in an offering of thanks to Slate Island. *Yippee!* I shouted, pushing off from the beach that had cradled *Yemaya* and me through the wild storm.

Tide ebbed out the mouth of Boca de Quadra as *Yemaya* and I bolted across. A rising ten-knot wind blowing in from the open ocean smacked against the current. A few whitecaps laced the channel. A quarter-mile west, White Reef rose up like dark fingers into vaporous spume. I rounded Kah Shakes Point bouncing and bucking like a mechanical bull until I reached the protection of Kah Shakes Cove. It was so pleasant to be out of chaotic water, I thought, "Why not wait until flood tide, when wind and tide move in sync? The sea might iron out more. Maybe I could find the old fish dam I read about."

Moon snails and sea stars tiled the shallows. The *Marine Atlas* showed Kah Shakes as a cluster of lagoons. I paddled deeper into the labyrinth. The water was clear as a swimming pool. A moon snail plowed through the delicious mud snuffling for clams. Its past success was apparent from the many white clam shell halves punctured with miniscule drill holes. The cove felt perfectly magical. A Lilliputian world lived right beneath my hull. I floated on the ceiling of a twelve-inch-tall room.

Fifty yards west, a beach opened out invitingly. Rivulets of water braided down a dark mud plateau. I landed on the slick surface and walked the beach, checking for bear tracks. All I found were fresh Vibram boot prints. I looked in the woods. No camps. I was alone. The sun felt warm against my back and shoulders. I unzipped the wetsuit, squatted on the beach, and peed. Out of nowhere gun shots ripped through the forest behind me. BOOM! BOOM! They thundered and echoed through the lagoons. I jumped up and jerked on the wetsuit.

BOOM! BOOM! BOOM! A second wave of explosive shots tore across

Butter Clam

Showing bore hole from a predatory Lewis's moonsnail—who chows one clam every 4 days! Slate Island, Alaska.

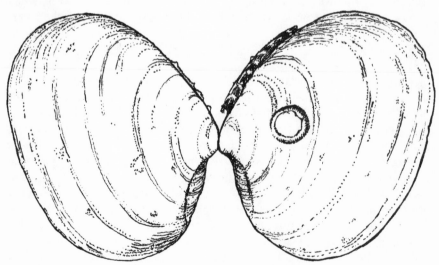

the still water. *What lunatic is shooting out here? A poacher? Someone doing target practice? An unpredictable derelict?* I didn't want to linger and find out. I was better off with ocean waves than waves of buckshot! I grabbed the kayak's bow and heaved. But the boat was suctioned into the mud. BOOM! BOOM! BOOM! The blasts were coming from just over the rocky headland. I yanked HARDER. *Come ON Yemaya!* I couldn't believe I couldn't lift her out. I heaved one last time using my whole body. *Whuck!* The mud released its grip.

I immediately headed into open water. The seas hadn't ironed out after all. Instead, the wind had picked up a notch. Flood tide and south wind pushed against me. Waves rolled over the bow, chart bag, and pump. Foam spun around the waist on my spray skirt. Wind spattered salt spray on my glasses. I aimed south, turning into steeper head-on waves. This time I did not care.

"Focus," I told myself. "You will be all right," I promised. "If you paddle for three miles you'll reach Foggy Bay. You can rest there. Just get the hell out of Kah Shakes."

At Foggy Bay, I had to make a left turn and travel vulnerably sideways in steep curling waves. Kirk Point—the northern terminus of Foggy Bay—is where I got slammed. I was glancing sideways, sizing up a beach inside the headland. Could I portage over that beach and skip the treacherous surf off Kirk Point altogether? It would be better than flipping—WHAM! I didn't see the gray wall coming. It pushed *Yemaya* into a breech. We went skittering down the frothing wave's face. My paddle blade braced instantaneously atop the white mane of thunder. It held us upright. The wave surfed *Yemaya* sideways for twenty feet then let her go as it petered out. I steered toward the beach I'd seen moments before. Avoiding Kirk Point was unquestionably worth a portage now.

If I'd flipped, I thought, at least I'd have had a short swim. Boat and gear would have blown in. We surfed right up the grainy white sand. I jumped out fast and tugged the boat up higher before a wave could haul her backwards. Land beneath my boots! I would have loved to stand still and rest, but the tide was rising fast. My mission was to climb up the nearest rock promontory and take a gander into Foggy Bay.

Five miles long and one mile wide, the bay offered only a few small beaches. Through binoculars, each one bristled with thick, scrubby forest on the up-lands. The tide might rise to meet the lowest branches, I reasoned. I'd have to hack out a tent site. The thought of being camped in an enclosure of bushes in bear country made me feel too vulnerable. I wanted to be able to look out a ways from the tent door. I wanted an island. I yanked the chart bag off the deck and ducked behind a boulder out of the wind. Looking at the *Marine Atlas*, I figured the best option was Very Inlet at Foggy Bay's south end. Earlier, in Ketchikan, I'd stopped in at Southeast Exposure, a kayak outfitter, to ask about camping spots. They knew of a state trooper cabin beside a creek near Very Inlet. It wouldn't be available to sleep in they said, but it would have fresh water. I was down to one gallon. It was Very Inlet or bust!

Oh, but the wind was tiring. My spirit was plunging. After portaging, then punching into wind and waves for two hours, I turned east away from the open sea and surfed through a narrow entrance toward Very Inlet. Within minutes, the wind died to nothing. To my surprise two sailboats and two cabin cruisers swung on anchor lines in the lee of one of the islands. I was delighted for the company! An outdoorsy older couple absorbed in a newspaper were settled in lounge chairs aboard their cheery boat. Laundry dried on a line. A middle-aged couple tinkered with sailboat rigging on another vessel. Two furry dogs sporting yellow bow ties looked on. A third boat wafted charcoal-broiled meat from a grill. All at once, I forgot about finding the stream and decided it would be much easier to just ask for three gallons of fresh water.

But what a sight I made. I hadn't brushed my mussy hair in five days. Salt stains crusted my face and sunglasses. For all I knew I still had seaweed in my teeth! I felt like bedraggled flotsam tossed into civilization by the storm. I needed a few minutes to transform back into a human. *Yemaya* and I slipped unnoticed into a side inlet. I pulled off my mirrored sunglasses, rubbed sunscreen over the crust on my face, ripped a brush through my matted locks, and put on my lucky feather earrings. The shape-change reminded me of myths where the trickster Raven transforms into a human to obtain the sun, moon, and stars from a chief. As it worked for Raven, it worked for me.

Soon, two different boats were offering fresh water. I paddled up to one just as the couple on the other countered with, "Hey, come on over here, we'll give you a bed with clean sheets and a shower." The first boat, piloted by the older folks, rejoined, "We can do that too, *and* we'll give you a ride back to Ketchikan if you want."

"Roasted chicken and Caesar salad for dinner over here. . . ."

And so it went until I paddled toward the boat with the chicken dinner and the hosts who also offered a ride to Prince Rupert. I wasn't sure if I'd take them up on the hitch, but at least they were going south.

Ed and Nancy Graham worked as high school teachers in Alaska's outback. They were bound for Seattle to sell their gorgeous, eighty-foot wood sailboat, *Freya*. After years of hoisting canvas, they were tired and wanted a cabin cruiser. When *Freya*'s weather radio predicted high winds over the next three days, they again offered to give me a hitch through Dixon Entrance to Prince Rupert.

"Why stay here?" Ed prodded. "The only dry, flat camp spot is the police cabin site, and ol' Mrs. Bear and her two cubs have moved in there. You can't even get to the creek for water."

"It could be half a week before you get out. Maybe longer. If you head out to Dixon alone, you might get stuck in some hole-in-the-wall beach off the cape. Sounds miserable."

I'd read enough about Dixon Entrance to realize Ed's words had the ring of truth. In 1886, Professor S.A. Saxman and two Indian workers mysteriously disappeared while canoeing around Kah Shakes Cove and Foggy Bay in search of a new school site. They were assumed drowned. In 1793, Captain George Vancouver's men took refuge from heavy seas in Dixon Entrance by running for Boat Harbor near Cape Fox. On July 30, 1896, the schooner *Hero* piled onto Barren Island while feeling her way through heavy fog. On May 19, 1935, at 3 A.M., the crew and passengers of the steamship *Denali* were shaken awake with the realization that the ship had hit something in Dixon Entrance. The "something" was identified as the rocks off Zayas Island. All forty-two people on board were safely rescued, but the next day, as the ship was pounded by surf, some thirty tons of dynamite onboard blew sky high.

The next morning I felt relieved and disappointed to be heading toward Prince Rupert, fifty miles away, aboard *Freya*, my kayak lashed to her polished veneer deck. I consoled myself by watching the surf clash up against Foggy Point. Steering south through Dixon, the entire Cape Fox Peninsula, which had been my intended route, rose to our port side like a gray bastion awash in white spray and chaotic rebounding swells. A gusty wind huffed out of the southeast. Nancy and I huddled in the lee of the cabin as Ed piloted.

The ferry captain's question lingered in my mind: *Don't you know the dominant winds blow out of the south in Alaska?* I certainly did now.

We arrived in Prince Rupert the same afternoon and tied into a slip at the public wharf. The *Freya* crew had been very supportive, but I needed to talk with my pals at home. After three calls from a pay phone, the lesson that temporary defeat is okay finally solidified. Friends in Ketchikan reported that the storm had shattered dishes in their seaworthy fishing boat as it was riding home. I was lucky, they said. Later, my globetrotting sister asked, "Why is our family so bent on extraordinary risk-taking? You don't have to be a hero out there. Be safe." Between the lines, she was reminding me of our adventurous brother's untimely death. Why *was* I out there?

In a third phone call, my friend Whitebear helped clarify my muddled thoughts. "You've heard of losing a battle but winning the war?" she asked. *The storm was a good thing for you to experience. Defeat from great things can make you stronger . . . humbler. Your journey isn't about miles. It's about learning to love yourself out there . . . to accept help when you need it.* Because roses are an age-old symbol of love, she suggested I tie one on the bow of the boat. *The rose will be a reminder to love yourself.* Soon after, I fixed a red cloth rose to *Yemaya*'s bow, and it helped set me on a new path.

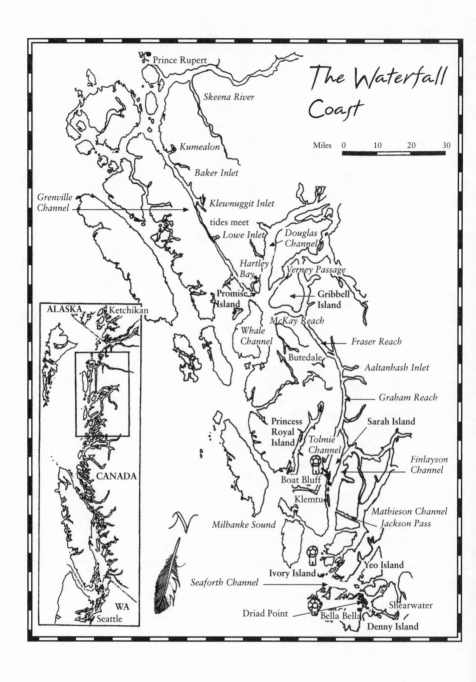

The Waterfall Coast

Prince Rupert
Skeena River
Kumealon
Baker Inlet
Grenville Channel
Klewnuggit Inlet
tides meet
Lowe Inlet
Douglas Channel
Hartley Bay
Verney Passage
Promise Island
Gribbell Island
McKay Reach
Whale Channel
Fraser Reach
Butedale
Aaltanhash Inlet
Graham Reach
Princess Royal Island
Sarah Island
Tolmie Channel
Finlayson Channel
Boat Bluff
Klemtu
Mathieson Channel
Jackson Pass
Yeo Island
Milbanke Sound
Ivory Island
Seaforth Channel
Driad Point
Bella Bella
Shearwater
Denny Island

ALASKA
Ketchikan
CANADA
WA
Seattle

Miles 0 10 20 30

Part 2

The Waterfall Coast: Bella Bella to Prince Rupert, British Columbia

Late spring, 230 miles, 29 days

*Look at me, Old Man, that the weather made by you may spare me;
and pray, protect me that no evil may befall me while I am traveling
on this sea, Old Man, that I may arrive at the place to which I am
going. Great Supernatural One, Old Man.*

—Kwakiutl prayer

5   Sleeping with Otters

It is another spring. To avoid constant head winds, I decided to kayak this leg of my journey in reverse, traveling south to north from Bella Bella to Prince Rupert, British Columbia. I planned to cover 230 miles in approximately one month. At 10 P.M., the B.C. ferry *Queen of the North* chugged into Bella Bella, a remote Heiltsuk Native village on the coast.

We arrived in the midst of preparations for a double potlatch that would take place in two days. As I disembarked, the view was as magical as any I could imagine. A welcome circle had gathered on the wharf to honor an elder visiting from Vancouver Island. A man beat a deerskin hoop drum on the candlelit pier. Red-robed dancers spun and turned, revealing traditional animal designs on their swaying backs. Eagle and Orca. Salmon and Wolf. Five villagers encircling a huge horizontal drum raised a heart-beat rhythm. Abalone headdresses sparkled. Elders chanted an ancient welcome song.

As I stepped from the ferry, people I'd never met took my hand and said, "Welcome! Welcome!" I stood captivated. The river of people moved around me. Everyone was happy. We were all coming home. We smiled and laughed at the sheer joy of it all. When my kayak surfed hand-over-hand down the gang-plank, the crowd oohed and whispered. I briefly worried that the kayak would be mistaken for a potlatch gift, but mostly it felt like a wonderful boat blessing.

Soon the excited potlatchers funneled into waiting cars, and taillights bounced down the washboard of planks and disappeared. I was alone. I searched my end of the darkened wharf for a place to sleep. A Petro Canada shed with a ganglia of capped pipes poking out the back was the only inconspicuous site to sling a tarp. I undid my sleeping bag and crawled in with all my clothes on. I sunk twenty fathoms into sleep. A short while later bike wheels screeched to a halt inches from my nose. Two sneakered feet hit the deck.

"Hey, Mike, look, there's a boat over here!"

My heart beat the *1812 Overture*. The teens didn't know I was under there. Think fast! In my lowest, gruffest male voice I yelled, "HEY! CAN'T A MAN GET ANY SLEEP AROUND HERE?"

"Oooo. Sorry, sir."

The night riders torqued off into the iodine air. Tide was out. I could smell the fucus and the mud. Across the intertidal flats the Heiltsuk Hotel's pool room and bar amped its jukebox with "Oh, baby, baby, it's a wild world."

"That's for sure!" I agreed as I nodded off. Next time I woke, a brilliant light shone through the nylon ceiling. I pulled the tarp aside. Ahh . . . an orange moon floated over the jagged Chinese paper-cut of Hunter Island. "Hellooooo, beauuuutiful mooooon!" I exhaled. She smiled down at me, as moons often do. A fishing boat had moored at the far end of the wharf. In the wheelhouse the captain and two crewmates were pouring through a pile of charts. Their cabin lights reflected gold in the black water.

I remembered docking in Bella Bella years before on a purse seiner called *Homeshore*. Five of us waited out a gale in Hecate Strait while en route to Haida Gwai—the Queen Charlotte Islands—for a three-week kayak trip. To pass the time, we poked about town. It didn't take long to discover a slice of the Heiltsuk people's history. Inside a chicken-wire enclosure, raised on saw-horses, rode a half-finished dugout canoe awash in a drift of pungent cedar chips. The adz marks grooving the canoe's graceful sides hearkened back to a time not so distant when everything was made by hand.

Historically, the Heiltsuk First Nations were hailed as champion canoe carvers. In the mid-nineteenth century, on a boast, they once carved a look-alike *Beaver* steamship from a huge cedar log, complete with portholes and smoke stacks. More recently, the Bella Bella Heiltsuk challenged tribes from Alaska and British Columbia to carve traditional dugouts and "Paddle to Seattle" for the Washington State centennial celebration in 1989.

Maybe my fiberglass kayak threatened the tradition, because the next day an event unfolded that will always be a mystery. A Bella Bella man, eyes burning with anger, hosed the kayak interior full of water while I was off buying a package of sweet rolls at the store. I was totally baffled by his actions. When he saw me waving and approaching, he slipped away. Had we had a misunderstanding? Was he just joking? I decided that such an odd encounter was a signal to leave town. I pumped out the water and headed out.

The first island I selected to eat lunch and pee sheltered oodles of wild edible plants. I had hardly walked twenty paces before stopping to nibble goose tongue leaves growing in bright bouquets in the gravel. The elongated leaves are tastier than romaine lettuce, with celery-like fibers running through the center. I piled them on my cheddar cheese, mustard, and bagel sandwich along with succulent miner's lettuce, growing in the shade of an old log.

A few feet from the log where I leaned my back, "wild sweet potato" sprawled across the beach on red runners. The plant's sawtooth leaves glow white underneath, hence the plant's other name, "silverweed." I pawed beneath the loose beach gravel and pulled out two thin roots. After a good scrubbing in the ocean, the raw roots had a nutty, slightly salty flavor. I dug up a few more for a wild veggie stir-fry for dinner. Fried or boiled, the roots become mildly sweet and starchy. Truthfully, I can't get enough of them! They are as addictive as potato chips. Long ago, the most productive wild sweet potato patches were owned by a chief. The choicest roots were even presented as wedding gifts.

I soon realized that the heavenly two-acre island, which was only a few miles from Bella Bella and within view of a sport fishing resort called Shearwater, was well worth an extended visit. I never expected that two days later I'd still be camped there munching! But that was the wonderful thing about following my friend Whitebear's "lesson of the rose"—I needn't worry about miles, I only had to love myself. In other words, if I was having fun collecting, sketching, and eating wild plants, I would just go with it.

The deserted island woods were mine for the romping. In a half day I stalked out wild onion, salmonberry shoots (peeled, they make great trail snacks), and my all-time favorite—nettles. Stinging nettle flourished in a dense, knee-high patch in the island's center. With my neoprene kayak gloves, I was able to harvest the leaves yet avoid the stinging hairs on stems and leaf tops.

I could go on and on about the loveliness of nettles. Rich in vitamins A and C, as well as minerals such as calcium and iron—nettles are a wild woman's natural multivitamin. But it's important to eat only new growth. Older plants harbor masses of calcium carbonate on their cellulose walls—which irritate the kidneys. If I were at home, I'd make nettle quiche to celebrate this occasion plus dry a couple jars' worth of leaves in my food dehydrator for later use. Instead, I tucked a dozen handfuls of fresh-cut leaves in a plastic bag and carried it back to camp.

A spring initiation ritual I practice each year is to eat a raw nettle leaf. I know this sounds loony, if not masochistic. But a friend taught me a trick: If you roll one of the smaller leaves up so that the top side is folded in (that's where the stinging hairs are) and only the innocuous underside is exposed, insert the little packet in your mouth and chew, you won't get zapped. I can only say the flavor is zippity-green.

Once heated or dried, nettles lose their punch. In a stir-fry they become mild as spinach. I sautéed the pile of leaves with wild yams, goose tongue, wild onion, and salmonberry shoots. Then I sprinkled the colorful medley with a dash of garlic powder and diced wild ginger, and served it steaming over rice.

A couple of days later I realized my VHF radio wasn't working. I suspected the batteries were dead, but the battery pack was jammed. I wiggled and tinkered, and whapped it on a log, but it wouldn't come loose. This was grave news. So before dark I paddled a half-mile to Shearwater Resort, which my *Marine Atlas* said had a marine repair shop. Dave, the Shearwater mechanic, muscled the pack off and showed me where a loose screw had blocked the slider. That fixed, I walked the gravel road behind the resort to stretch my legs and look for new plants. A bog bristled with Labrador tea. I collected a handful of the down-curled leaves with a fuzzy apricot undersides. I was really happy now! Steeped in hot water with spruce branch tips, these would make a lovely, aromatic, and vitamin-C rich tea. I returned to my paradise island and built a fire for tea water. That night, at dark, the unwelcome visitors came by.

With each telltale *pshht* of a beer flip-top opening, the voices from the sport fishers grew louder. They were floating fifty yards offshore moving at a slink. But, thank God, I told myself, at least they're moving. When the guys figured out I was a woman, the whistles started. Head down, I pretended to ignore them while watching every move through my bangs. They gunned the

Wild Ginger
Asarum caudatum

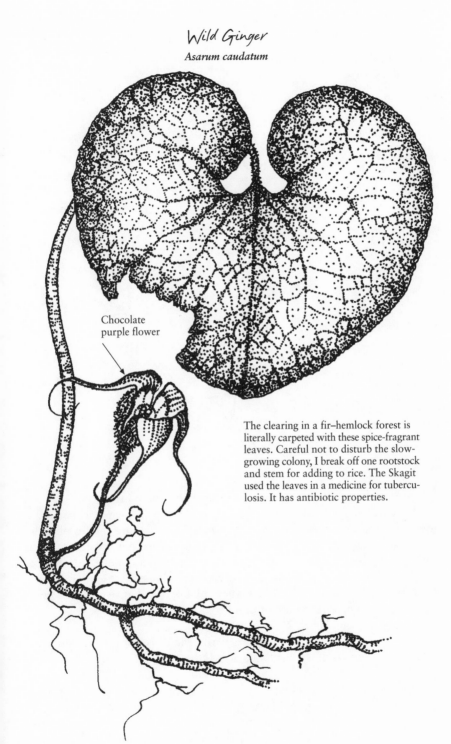

Chocolate
purple flower

The clearing in a fir–hemlock forest is
literally carpeted with these spice-fragrant
leaves. Careful not to disturb the slow-
growing colony, I break off one rootstock
and stem for adding to rice. The Skagit
used the leaves in a medicine for tuberculosis. It has antibiotic properties.

Labrador Tea

Ledum groenlandicum

A handful of dried or freshly picked leaves simmered in 3 cups water = pleasant tea! (Or add leaves to mint tea or black blends.)

Found near peat bog, Denny Island, British Columbia.

Field notes: the edible *Ledum* species shows a fuzzy underside on each leaf. White flowers are also key to distinguishing this plant from "swamp laurel," which sprouts pink flowers and has same habitat and form. (Leaf fuzz is rust-orange on older leaves.)

Medicinal use: indigestion or diarrhea. (May make you sleepy or have to pee a lot.) Drink only weak tea, small amounts!

Evinrude and sped off whooping. As if they had a plan, I thought.

I decided to move camp—even if it was 10:30 P.M. Sleep was beyond me now. I figured it was safer to be near other people in case the drunk fishers came around again. Perhaps it was stupid in retrospect, but I paddled through the darkness back to Shearwater Resort and entered another kind of wilderness—a cafe and bar at midnight. I'd seen a pay phone there earlier.

I dropped in coins and sobbed when my boyfriend answered. All my defenses went down within earshot of a loved one.

"Jen—are you all right?"

"Hon . . . ." I sobbed. I couldn't squeeze the story out for the tightness in my throat. Raucous music throbbed across the smoke-striated barroom, erasing my voice.

"Jen, WHERE ARE YOU?"

"Shearwater," I choked. "Three guys circled my island camp tonight. They were drunk . . . in a skiff. They were so close I could hear beer flip-tops opening. They wolf-whistled and stared, gunned the engine and took off. I was worried they'd return, so I kayaked in the dark to the lights at Shearwater where I knew there'd be other people."

"Where is Shearwater?"

"Three miles from Bella Bella. I came here this afternoon to get my VHF radio fixed. I don't know. Maybe someone got some weird ideas when I paddled off alone." I could barely stop crying to speak. "I'm afraid . . . afraid I'll get raped . . . ."

"Jen, that's not going to happen."

There was a long pause as I took in the truth of his words. Then—"Are there any women there?"

"Yes."

"Talk with them and find out where it's safe to sleep tonight. At first light, get the hell out of there!"

I nodded, tears streaming. I looked back at the half dozen men hunched over bar stools, some playing cards, one lighting a cigarette off the bartender's fag. Two tough-and-tangle local gals drinking coffee and whiskey jawed and chain-smoked at a nearby table. The gal with broomstick blond hair looked my way with a sympathetic smile. Perhaps these women would help.

"Listen to me, okay? This is a temporary situation. The wilderness is safer. You can deal with things out there. You need to GET AWAY FROM CIVILIZATION! Trust that."

He was right. Bears were safer than drunks. Solitude was better than a resort bar with a pay telephone that smelled of cigarette smoke and spilled beer.

"Girl, you need a drink!" said Sue as she pulled out a chair for me to sit down.

"Coffee would be great," I smiled, wiping a stray tear with the back of my hand.

"Coffee and Drambuie," Donna yelled to the bartender.

Donna and Sue listened with sisterly concern to my story about being alone and the boat of whooping men. Sue leaned over and advised, "You watch yourself. Everyone out here's a tad bit loony." Sue worked on a shrimper. Donna's mom kept Shearwater's books.

"Roll your sleeping bag out on the boat tonight," said Sue. "I don't think the captain would mind. He's already asleep anyway." I was ever so grateful.

Lying in the wheelhouse with my head under the captain's stool and my feet against a cat's kibble dish, I hardly slept a wink all night. The shrimp captain snored like a motocross bike. The insomniac cat crunched kibbles. At first light, I tiptoed past the snoring captain who was bunked with Sue. Shuffling toward the door, carrying my wadded sleeping bag and pad, I discovered my exit latched shut. No matter how hard I pushed up on the brass hook, the darn thing wouldn't . . . push . . . push . . . WHAM! The door smacked open.

"HEY! . . . that you, Sue?" the startled captain snorted.

"It's me, Jennifer, Sue's friend," I whispered. "Sorry for the noise."

The captain mumbled something profane under his breath and resumed snoring.

I clambered off the boat to the dock. The predawn air glowed electric blue. Mist settled on my face like cold ash. I reeked of bar smoke. Not a soul was awake yet. *Yemaya* floated sleepily moored a few yards away. I dropped off the sleeping bag, grabbed a couple of empty water sacks, then trotted up the open-air stairs to the resort's second-floor bathrooms. I turned the tap and began filling up.

WHUMPH-WHUMPH-WHUMPH! A combustion engine rumbled awake in the yard. Gasp! I'd triggered the resort generator! Now I hurried to fill the water by cranking harder on the tap. WHUMPH-WHUMPH-WHUMPH! Rushing down the stairs with four gallons of water, I felt like Jack clambering down the beanstalk with the goose that laid golden eggs underarm. I slipped into *Yemaya's* cockpit and pushed off from the wharf. Ahhhh, the kayak felt wonderful. It was home. As I paddled into the mist-veiled islands, the WUMPHING alarm still echoing through the still air, it began to rain. Soft petals at first, then a beautiful, purifying downpour. I wanted to get as far out of Dodge as I could.

Somewhere west of Idol Point on Seaforth Channel, my fear spiked again. Six shotgun blasts—PUCK! PUCK! PUCK!—exploded and echoed across the myriad island channels.

"Jesus Christ!" I jumped in my kayak seat. Wind ricocheted across the water and muffled all but the loudest sounds. Rain fell in fat drops and drummed the kayak deck. I'd been unaware of its approach, but a behemoth Holland America cruise ship, nine stories tall, portholes stippling its polished hull, appeared steaming up channel only seventy yards away to starboard. When the ship got even with my course, I heard someone yell, "PULL!" The ship's guests were flinging skeet pigeons out over the water and firing at the moving targets. PUCK! PUCK! PUCK!

Holland America throbbed past. The gun shots receded up channel. I sank back in the seat, relieved and chagrined.

As I paddled up the north shore of Seaforth Channel, the islands seemed to be raising their walls. I'd seen only three possible campsites all afternoon. A new spot looked promising, but, eyeing the forest that lay behind a mattress-size beach of broken shells, I was again disheartened. Telltale kelp fronds hung like Christmas garlands from the trees' lowest branches. By midnight this lovely pocket beach would be an aquarium.

At least the spring sun is on my side, I told myself soothingly. In these northern latitudes gauzy light can linger in the sky long after sundown. The crepuscular hours, the hours before night swallows the last light, were among my favorites to paddle. On the Inside Passage, the sea was often calmer then. And shy animals—both nocturnal and diurnal—pawed about their business in the wide open. But that night, traveling alone and without a secure camp for the night, twilight was a gloomy and worrisome time.

Due west, where Seaforth Channel surged into Milbanke Sound, the Inside Passage makes a dog-leg turn north and winds through hundreds of miles of unseen fjords. Staring down Seaforth toward Milbanke Sound, miles before

I'd take that northward turn, I saw only sky and sea. Both appeared the color of skim milk. The horizon was erased. Reflection and reflected melted into one monochromatic canvas from hull to zenith. I had no reference point to aim the bow at. Paddling through this waterscape, hanging weightless as a dream, the winged kayak rode somewhere between two worlds. Such a calm, reflective sea can be dangerous. In a matter of minutes, I nearly dozed off with the paddle loosely gripped.

If it weren't for a southbound prawn boat that suddenly emerged from a hard-to-see passage a quarter-mile ahead, my next landmark for pointing north would have remained hidden. Paddlesore from fourteen continuous hours of progress and lacking sleep after my adventure in Shearwater, it was time to prop the paddle up against a tree. I was so tired that I would have missed the otter family altogether if it hadn't been for a curious sneezing sound—*Stissk! Stissk!*—emerging from an offshore kelp bed.

Five feet away, two almond-shaped heads the color of wet cedar bark corked up. The otters blinked at me. I looked wide-eyed at them. We all three seemed to say, "Where'd YOU come from?"

Their broad foreheads were chiseled down the center with a perfect part. Stiff whiskers punctuated their brows and curved neatly back from their alert noses. Called vibrissae, these extra-sensory preceptors actually vibrate against rocks, fish, crabs, and kelp. They tell the otter what is good pickins—especially in murky water.

Drifting in silhouette, the otters' humped backs and whip tails appeared serpentine. The shape shouted: river otters! Suddenly the larger otter rushed toward me, raising its furred snout skyward to snag a scent of my who-abouts.

Lutra (otter) *canadensis* (since it was first described in Canada) *pacifica* (because this frolicsome individual adores Pacific coastal waterways) is the species' scientific name. River otter is the common name, but "river" is a misnomer in coastal places and a culprit of confusion because it leads to innumerable mistaken identities of *Lutra canadensis* as a sea otter.

It's easy to understand the confusion. In the Pacific Northwest river otters, like sea otters, make their living by the ocean. Dining on crabs, spiny sculpins, gunnel fish, snails, and a favorite delicacy, pinto abalone, river otters, alongside the mink and martin, have evolved to be among the most skilled ocean fishers. A difference between the two otter types is that river otters don't raft up for the night. They galumph ashore. Sea otters (*Hydra lutras*), on the other hand, spend their lives waterborne—including nighttime, when they spool their shoulders, pups, and flippered hind feet in a golden cradle of kelp leaves and float belly to the stars.

Tragically, the sea otter's snuggly, waterproof fur nearly led to its demise. In the early nineteenth century fur traders poured into Bella Bella territory in search of valuable otter pelts, stopping at Milbanke Sound to trade. Quick to capitalize on the profits, the Hudson Bay Company tacked up a trading post on Campbell Island. Within decades, British Columbia and Washington's sea otters were bludgeoned off the face of the coast. Today, new rafts of sea otters have been reintroduced from Alaska. River otters, however, still thrive in their original range along wild stretches of the protected Inside Passage.

People are still an otter's biggest enemy. Around the world, the twelve species of otters see their numbers plummeting through loss of habitat and deliberate killing by humans and other predators. In western Canada alone, trappers kill up to 5500 yearly for their soft pelts. In the wilds, great horned owls, eagles, and large fish snag unwary kits. Bobcats, lynx, wolves, and coyotes stalk otters as they trot between lakes, streams, and their den-like homes.

You can catch whiff of a river otter's home when you are sea kayaking downwind, even by as much as a quarter-mile! The musky smell is unmistakable. Otters are in the family mustelid, as are the notoriously aromatic skunk and the mink, weasel, badger, and marten.

A pair of scent glands hide under a mustelid's tail. To flag territory, river otters drag their tails over driftwood, tree branches, and low-slung ferns. They even gather armfuls of leaves and rub them like handkerchiefs over belly, crotch, and back. They also dribble urine on vegetation. The lingering bouquet serves as an olfactory billboard for sexual receptivity. It clues kin as to how much time has elapsed since the last swabbing. Rabble-rousing otter families can cloak a favorite islet or peninsula with a distinct composite of scents. Long before a kayaker steps ashore to relieve herself, the woods are as odoriferous as a latrine.

In 1983, when I first kayaked through the Inside Passage with Gene Meyers, we stumbled upon otter terrain while searching for a level tent site. I learned to recognize small plots denuded of plants and tamped down to a fine flour as otter rolling patches. Flat and wide enough to erect a two-person tent, they became our last-ditch answer for lodging. Often on the go, otters hunker down at one spot for just a few days at a time. Adults move about within a home range of up to sixty miles, revisiting fishing spots, dens, promontories, and rolling patches. Since it was dusk, and I had no possible camp, I figured it was okay to take temporary shelter in an otter home if no other was available. With a little luck, these sleek swimmers would lead me to such a swatch amid these towering island shores.

With a good frog kick, the largest otter, probably a male, buoyed its square shoulders and chest completely out of the water. He was four-and-a-half feet long, sleek as a comma and one-third tail. His chin bore a silver sheen like reflected moonlight. We locked eyes. What was he thinking? His russet fur glistened with the sea. Uncertain of the danger, he snuffled the air repeatedly. Wavering back and forth cobra-style, he seemed to be triangulating my body size and distance.

Four feet behind me another noise erupted. It sounded like water spewed from a swimmer's snorkel. *Pifff! Pifff! Pifff!* Six more otters popped up. Smaller than the first two, these were undoubtedly the kits. They appeared more nervous, turning heads quickly side to side, eyeing each other, watching their parents, eyeing me. Other than a turn of my head, I floated still as a drift log.

The father, after giving me a thorough once-over, dropped back to the waterline satisfied. He executed a graceful U-turn and flowed back to the clan with tail trailing behind.

Six kits are about the biggest brood a river otter can muster. Two to three is more common. The wonderful thing is that river otters, like their sea otter sisters, have a choice about when to deliver. Due to nature's trick of delayed implantation for in utero eggs, a mother can give birth as much as a year after mating. Yet embryos mature in two months. It's a fascinating option for otter family planning. When fishing is grim, wait 'til spring.

These curious fishers were likely born in late winter. When I packed for this trip, they had been naked, blind, and squirming about in their den, or "holt."

Within a second of the parents' return, the family formed a tight moving cluster. Swimming off, heads pumping in perfect unison, they compassed west. The otters aimed for a jawbone of islands on the light-flooded horizon that I hadn't seen until now. Having nowhere else to go, I followed the eight distinct wakes.

Virtuoso swimmers, the shy otters soon outdistanced me. Four webbed paws and a long, whip-like tail rudder give them great advantage over minks, weasels, and single kayaks. When hurried, otters tuck stubby legs out of harm's way and propel forward by flexing up and down in a continuous wave from head to tail tip. In this fish-like fashion, they can attain speeds of almost 7 mph.

In my heart's prayer, I hoped for an island beach I could camp on for one to three days. Thanks to the otters, an hour before Milbanke Sound, an islet unfolded like a dream. It was ear-shaped with a pocket beach on the leeward side, crowned in spruce and cedar and skirted by a garden of wing kelp. It looked fifty yards wide at most.

The song of a Swainson's thrush rose from an invisible balcony in the greenery. Something splashed. I turned and discovered a seal escorting me shoreward. Without having to lift the paddle, I was carried forward by a tidal current filling the islet's bay. I simply ruddered with the blade to dodge rocks.

After anchoring the kayak leash behind three slippery rocks, I pulled myself up and onto a large drift log for easier walking. Where the bark shucked off, the wood looked lustrous as abalone. Like an elevated walkway, the log stretched seventy feet up the beach onto a peninsula where it had heaved loose. I followed its steeply angled trunk to a tangled root mass and climbed down to the hidden pocket where the roots had grown. Standing beside the eight-foot wide bowl, I was delighted that I could see deep into the wooded island.

I eagerly scouted for a tent site. Yet leather-leaf salal bushes barricaded the island's center as far as I could see. Every few feet a spruce trunk rose up bearded with lichen. I didn't want to crash through and tear up an island. So without attempting to bushwhack any farther, I imagined my tent squeezed into this one lumpy but fortuitously clear spot. Otter signs lay scattered every which way around my sandaled feet. Husks of red rock crab claws had been sucked empty and light as a thimble. Silver ears of abalone were scooped clean. There were shards of mica-thin fish scales, toothpick ribs, vertebrae cemented in a column, and an arrowhead fish tail. Crouching down to lift up the

Swainson's thrush (female)
Catharus ustulatus

The Swainson's enchanting
liquid call is an ascending
tsu-rer-reer-reeer-ree-e-e.

treasures, I accidentally caught sight of a passage into the salal. Was this a portal to somewhere else? What, I wondered, lay on the other side?

Without hesitating, I dropped to my knees and crawled through an arch meant for an otter's shoulders. Branches caught my hair, hooked my sunglasses' cord, thwacked my rib bones. I recalled the tale of Alice tumbling down the rabbit hole. Except I landed in a bed of ginger-speckled chocolate lilies. Pollen the color of cornmeal brushed my shoulders. Where the lilies ended, a fallen tree arrowed off into the thick forest. I stood upright and walked across it like a bridge over a ravine. It led to another passage, this time framed with scarlet huckleberries.

On this one-acre secluded island, I bumped into otter signs without much trying. Scat, piled in neat thumb-thick rolls colored pink by crab shell confetti, crackled under knee. A tamped-down tunnel-trail scampered off under an umbrella of huckleberry, salal, and devil's club. No wider than a car tire, the serpentine path wound up and over fallen branches, through and around a cedar's leviathan roots, leading me to circumnavigate the island's perimeter. It took about twenty minutes.

Long ago, Tlingit girls were terrified to journey into the forest alone for fear they'd be kidnapped by the Land Otter people. One account of a girl who returned home tells how she tore off her clothes and raced wildly around the village naked. She bit anyone who attempted to restrain her. A shaman who tried to heal her got walloped with a rock.

In Tlingit myths, land otters are called "Kuschtas," meaning root people, since they dwell in the roots of trees. Kuschtas can change into otter or human form at will. Their main pastime is kidnapping drowned or near-drowned people to add to their villages. Paddling up to their victims in a canoe—which is really a skate—the Kuschtas offer a kind hand. They are quite persuasive and almost always successful, since they themselves are kidnapped humans who drowned after their own canoes capsized.

The Tlingit feared the Kuschtas precisely because they knew a person's mindscape and could trick the unwary traveler. Sometimes the wily Kuschtas visit the summer camp of an isolated fisher in the guise of a deceased relative such as a long-lost brother or mother. They may seem the perfect dinner guests, offering gifts of halibut, shellfish, and sweet seal meat. But if you eat it, you are toast. Doomed to live among the roots forever.

And the tragic thing is you won't even know you are under a spell. At first, life will seem quite dandy. The roots where you curl up at night will appear to your eyes as a village of fine longhouses. When you sleep, however, you may feel pressed in by something. Something root-like. Eventually, you'll lose human traits in exchange for an otter's. Your lip will grow up toward your nose and become cleft. You'll sprout a fat, furred tail. Your arms will shorten and end in webbed paws. You'll eat only raw fish for the rest of your days, unless, that is, a shaman can find you.

Shamans are the only ones who can break the spell. A Tlingit shaman on her or his youthful vision quest deliberately seeks out Land Otter for the very reason the villagers fear it—the power of transformation. If the apprentice's spirit is strong, the trickster land otter is outwitted. It falls dead at the shaman's

Land Otter Seafood Buffet

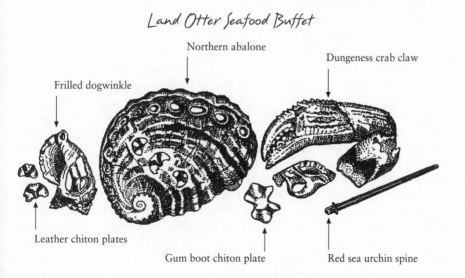

Northern abalone

Dungeness crab claw

Frilled dogwinkle

Leather chiton plates

Gum boot chiton plate

Red sea urchin spine

feet. After which, the shaman slices off otter's tongue, wraps it in medicinal leaves, and tucks it in a charm bundle. Land otters have the most potent spirit power of all the animals. They alone can help retrieve kidnapped souls. They allow the shaman to magically change from human to animal to human again.

With my greenhorn tracking skills, I soon lost the otter trail. The next scat I came to—on a boulder overlooking the sea—was greasy black and littered with shards of fish bone and insect chiton. I realized I was now tracking a weasel or a mink. But as serendipity would have it, I found something else imminently more useful. Towering above that greasy boulder was a great cedar tree. It beckoned me.

I climbed the small cliff to its trunk and found the Holy Grail of that evening's search—a near-level tent spot. I returned to the kayak, shuttled armfuls of gear up and down the cliff, and pitched my tent under an umbrella of fragrant boughs. Lying in the tent that first night, I had the unmistakable sensation of roots pressing up against the tent floor. I unzipped the nylon door, lifted up the tent, and dug out two moon snail shells large as duck eggs and covered in moss—likely deposited by otters years ago.

Henry and Julia Speck, a Kwakiutl family I stayed with on Hope Island in 1983, called the land otter "xomda." They pronounced the word as if they were imitating the sound of a revving motorcycle engine: *HOghh-mm-dah*. The name mimicked the otter's fluttering, throaty call.

Otters are chatterers. They whistle and grunt. They talk amongst themselves in a repertoire of voices. To contact kin, otters emit a terse, one-syllable *chirp!* When threatened or alarmed they growl like a dog. Inquiring, they seem to utter *hah?* Parents talk with each other and the cubs in a sing-song, staccato chuckle. It's a sound I've learned to imitate by vibrating the back of my throat while exhaling. I can raise or lower the tone by pursing my lips.

I awoke in the sun-dappled tent to something wheezing, followed by a choking cough. Otter! I gasped. Maybe with an ill-lodged fish bone? Ducking behind the cedar trunk, I scanned the low-tide beach. Beyond the screen of cedar boughs, below the cliff, a sleek female otter rooted through a mass of kelp. Behind her, two kits sinuous as wrestlers in furry leotards rough-and-tumbled on the beach. Shell bits flew. Growls and excited whoffs were exchanged in the combat. Fat tails swung out and circled back for aided balance. Their copper fur had a mussy look, like they'd just rolled out of the shower. I was thrilled at my good fortune and rifled the tent for binoculars.

I located the father otter fishing in a rocky tide pool. In a matter of seconds he surfaced with a wiggly gunnel fish. Holding the eel-shaped, olive-colored gunnel between his spread forepaws and a rock, he tore off chunks with sharp white canines. His dripping back hunched against the blue sea.

When it comes to food, otters are not cuddly. They are feisty hunters with a carnivorous sweet tooth. Like cormorants and loons, otters float along the water's surface head down, trolling with shifting eyes. Stealthy as submarines, otters can ambush swimming water birds, but they prefer to dine on crabs, fish, chitons, urchins, frogs, and shellfish. If desperate, they have been known to stalk right into the lodge of a muskrat or beaver and knock them dead.

On land, these intelligent hunters ambush rodents and rabbits. Some manage to steal away with a couple of bird's eggs or even a bird. Come winter, otters dive through holes in lake ice and hurl crappies and bluegills up through the opening to crunch on later. Some have punched holes through beaver dams, waited for the water to pour off, and then waded in to munch up marooned fish and frogs.

For a long time, I sat with binoculars held in one hand and a notebook in the other. The father and mother otter were hunting. Working together, they herded spiny sculpin fish into the shallows. The waiting kits gobbled them with gusto. Once the female dug her paws into the mud to excavate a huge moon snail. The youngsters pitched in, digging alongside.

An eagle whistled overhead. Both parents scanned the air and growled to alert the kits. Otters may not be graceful on land, but they are surely swift. Alarmed, they can gallop faster than a human. Not as fast as an eagle, however. The mother raced at the kits in a sprint—springing forward, humping furry spine, grazing forepaws with the back pair. Within seconds she was forty yards up the beach corralling the kits up a bank. They whined and scrabbled, barely reaching a thicket of salal. The eagle passed low over the beach as if there were no commotion at all.

Not wanting to lose sight of this family, I crawled back down the cliff. Like a kid playing cops and robbers, I snuck along the island's edge, ducking behind giant beach logs and boulders. I worked halfway around the island before spying the mother and kits.

They lounged and groomed outside a hidey-hole near a tangle of cedar roots. Out beyond the kelp line in the wind-pleated water, the father continued to fish. His tail snapped spray with each dunk and dive. Fathers rejoin the family after the kits reach six months to help team-teach the youngsters how to become self-sufficient little fishers and hunters. I lay belly down on a beach log watching through a peek-a-boo hole in a log's root mass, utterly enchanted. Seeing these wild creatures—undisturbed, safe—was the antidote to my frightful experience in civilization. I'd come here to find peace. Watching the otters was the ideal activity for just that.

I spent two days playing otter hide and seek. One night, in the pitch dark, something leapt twice on the tent wall as if it were a trampoline; I guessed it was my otter friends, as I discovered a freshly scoured abalone shell outside the tent in the morning. From the screen of the cedar tree I watched the two kits ferry driftwood back and forth on their noses like one yards a ball down a lawn in field hockey. Later they played tug-of-war with what appeared to be a giant gumboot chiton.

I dined on escargot—limpet snails tugged off the beach rocks. These dunce-cap-shaped shellfish skooch against the low-tide rocks, rasping up algae with their sandpaper radulas. Suctioned down like pointy thimbles, they can be buggers to pull loose. But I soon found that a knife blade slid sideways between shell and rock loosened their hold. One flick of a thumb scooped out the white meat. Chewed raw, the snails have the consistency of chewy oysters. Sea salt added the perfect seasoning. "Sea-soning," I laughed, delighted for simple blessings like salt. I gulped them down with fern tea that tasted of sweet licorice.

Later, bathing in the shallows and scrubbing my messy face with a sea-weed leaf, I felt a host of prickly chin hairs sprouting. I didn't care! I liked the evolution. Why bother to tweeze anything? Taking up handfuls of gritty sand, I scrubbed arms, legs, pits, and shoulders. I noticed the fur on my legs was longer and blond from the sun. Lacking aromatic soap, my scent was muskier. Maybe being a hairy, stinky sort of gal would dub me less attractive to any man with harmful intentions. The island was dousing me with its magic. I was growing a new kind of skin.

Drying off, I lay atop a smooth beach log letting the sun-warmed wood release its heat into my back, hips, and legs. The tide was flooding in and waves crashed in stereo from both sides of the log. Who could feel alone out there on the edge of the world? Creation was singing hallelujah for the ocean's return.

I could hear barnacles clicking and hissing all across the beach. Thatched, acorn, and elephant-foot barnacles whispered among themselves of zooplankton and phytoplankton. Long before the water reached their open mouths, they anticipated its return. They twisted about in their calcium tents and nursed the air.

The rising water pooled below the beach log. The seaweeds were shaking out their skirts. In the delicious mud, sea worms wiggled and danced in their tubular burrows. Clams, acres of clams, were thirstily guzzling the millenniums-old ambrosia. Butter clams, western bittersweets, bent-nosed clams, heart cockles—all feasted after a six-hour fast.

The limpet snails I ate for lunch oozed into my arms and legs. I, too, longed for the ocean's soothing touch. Salt spray moistened my lips. I wanted to feel the saltwater's scruffy tongue everywhere! Is there anything more sensuous than an ocean at flood tide? No place on earth is richer in seed and egg. On afternoons like that, I could drink the sea! I was the sea drinking! I was the one being drunk!

6 The Lightkeepers' Quilt

Out on that one-acre coastal island a drumbeat of rain filled a rock pool for otter to lap, swelled a pulsing-red salmonberry for Swainson's thrush, unfurled new skunk-cabbage leaves for Sitka black-tail deer, and inspired a siren of red-legged frogs. But there wasn't much water for me. I couldn't eat enough berries and leaves or find ample pools to quell my thirst.

Water—wild water that is—often requires effort. Sometimes it calls for a pilgrimage. And I've learned that, once found, it often comes hitched with companions: green flecks of moss, hemlock needles, tea-colored tannins, or little red mites.

I was down to one quart of fresh water. It happens all too easily. Camp on an island too small for bears, but also too small for a stream. Stay for days, enchanted by moon snails round as apples, tide pool walls waving pink-tipped anemones, belching otters lounging like Rubens's nudes, and a cloudless blue sky. Meanwhile, eat steamed nettles, raw limpets scooped from the shell, and licorice fern tea under a hot sun. Fail to notice that the rain-filled pools, high in the pockets of beach rock, are beginning to sink, turn yellow and rank with otter urine, and grow thready algae.

I should have filled more water bags at Shearwater Resort three days earlier, but the commotion had spooked me on my way prematurely. Now, with so little left, I decided to ration the remaining tap water for drinking and ferret out a local source for cooking.

But after two hours spent crisscrossing the island, crawling over blowdowns, thwacking salal bushes, untangling my hair from low branches, I was thwarted. Even the wetland mud sprouting its golden torches of skunk cabbage flowers exuded a sulphurous water when pressed underfoot—a liquid thick and dark as coffee grounds. It could be strained in really desperate cases. I told myself I wasn't that desperate. Yet.

Toward late afternoon, however, I was ecstatic to discover a sink-size puddle in the crotch of a drift log. Shaded by cedar boughs, it hadn't evaporated. Sure, it smelled a little of sulfur, spruce needles floated on the surface, and in the deepest part I counted half a dozen squirming mosquito larvae. Their black, worm-like bodies danced to the surface then wriggled back down. I took this as a good sign. I figured if it was fresh enough for them, it was okay for me, as long as I boiled and strained it first.

I scooped five lovely cups into a pink bandana slung over my cookpot as a filter. The cloth was soon stained brown. This water would last me through

Licorice Fern

Polypodium glycyrrhiza

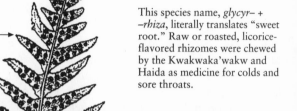

Round, fuzzy, apricot-colored spores dot underside of frond.

This species name, *glycyr–* + *–rhiza*, literally translates "sweet root." Raw or roasted, licorice-flavored rhizomes were chewed by the Kwakwaka'wakw and Haida as medicine for colds and sore throats.

During droughts frond withers brown but promptly turns green after rain, so its other name— Resurrection Fern.

Fern thrives on living and downed red alder and large-leaf maple trunks; also grows in blankets on mossy rocks.

"Footprints"

The genus *Polypodium* means "many footed." Note "footprints" where old leaves broke off.

dinner, but it was a stopgap measure at best. I still needed to find a better water source, and soon. I balanced the full pot over a tripod of stones and lit a fire. After a five-minute, rolling boil, I poured off enough water for tea, then in went cheese tortellini.

Sitting by the fire happily forking up my dinner, I looked out to Watch Island's ink-blot reflection. Swimming quietly past Watch Island, a harbor seal rumpled the still water and sliced the totem pole in two. I clicked my spoon against the cookpot. The seal turned its dark almond-shaped head toward me, stopped drifting, and stared. What does the seal think, I wondered, seeing a two-legger crouched by a smoking fire, gray nylon tent, and two water jugs collapsed on beach gravel?

The next morning, my mouth was dry as thistle down from drinking the ice-tea-colored brine. But as I'd dozed and floundered in my tent that night, I'd heard a foghorn chanting in the distance like a Gregorian monk. *"Commmme Herrrre,"* its monotone voice repeated over and over. *"Commmme Herrrre . . . ."*

The chanting had stopped by the time I woke. I unfolded a marine chart and located a purple teardrop marked "3 sec fl" on Ivory Island. Sure enough, a lighthouse. It lay one nautical mile due west.

I'll tell you now, I am not above begging for water. Without hesitation, I grabbed the two collapsible water sacks, paddled out into the middle of Seaforth Channel and looked around through binoculars. Blinking from the top of a forested headland—Robb Point, my chart said—was a light tower. Just south of the main hump of Ivory Island, Robb Point rises out of the sea like a petrified turtle's head craning to get a better view of the Pacific. The trees on its windward side are sheared of limbs; below the trees are four white buildings with red roofs.

But up close the headland seemed entirely inaccessible—a fortress awash in breaking waves. Seventy-five feet below Ivory Island's three-second flashing light, floating up and down in gray swells, I was stumped to find a landing spot. I reasoned that if I paddled out from under the cliff's shadow right into the strait and waved big arm circles, the lightkeeper would see me. I felt a little silly, but it worked.

Under the light tower, a man appeared on the edge of the cliff. His red plaid shirt sleeves waved big arm circles like a highway flagger signaling a motorist to stop. When he called out, I was surprised to feel a rush of elation. Another human voice!

"Helllllooohh!" He yelled through cupped hands.

"Helllooh!" I yelled back over the surf. "Caaan yooou sparrrre sommme waaterrr?"

The red plaid arms motioned me to paddle around to a small bay east of the light. I'd passed that cove earlier after seeing waves knuckling down then exploding on tire-size rocks. By the time I pulled sideways to a ledge of wave-lashed rock, four faces were smiling down.

"How do you suppose we get you out of that kayak?" Red-Shirt-Sleeves asked. We quickly planned the grand exit. When a wave buoyed me three feet up toward his reach, the keeper would grab hold of the boat. I'd scramble out, latch onto the unmoving rock like a barnacle, and he'd lock onto the kayak. We tried this. Everything went fine until the wave drew away and I was still standing in the kayak. I went down—*zzzzip!*—frantically waving my arms like a cartoon character.

"Whoa there now," the keeper said. I threw myself at the rock and stuck. When I recovered, the introductions began.

"Welcome to Ivory Island. I'm Dennis, and we're the lightkeepers. You need water, eh?" he said, ending his question with the characteristic 'eh?' often heard in Canadian speech.

"Yes," I nodded thankfully, still catching my breath.

A square-shouldered woman with an easy smile reached out her hand next. "Hi. I'm Cynthia, Dennis's wife." I appreciated her strong grip, and I guessed we were about the same age, mid-thirties. "This is our daughter, Heather." Heather looked up at me through dark-rimmed glasses, biting her lip and bobbing with excitement. I could tell I was the most interesting thing she'd seen all week—perhaps all month. Sylvia, who rode sidesaddle on Cynthia's hip, sucked her thumb under a meadow of blonde bangs.

"Are you the famous Audrey Sutherland?" Dennis asked hopefully.

Surprised they would mistake me for the venerated "Grandmother of Kayaking," a spirited solo paddler of sixty-something who's written a book on kayaking Hawaii, I admitted with a bit of embarrassment, "No, I'm the unfamous Jennifer Hahn. Why did you think I might be Audrey?"

"A box arrived by coast guard helicopter two weeks ago, with a note: 'Hold for Audrey Sutherland, kayaker.'"

I wanted to ask more, but just then a wave broke over the ledge. Dennis interrupted, "Let's move her up. Tide's coming in."

With Dennis hoisting the bow and me the stern, we lugged the kayak up a forty-five-degree rock bench, jumping yawning cracks and rounding beached logs, then continued down a walkway to a cement landing pad emblazoned with a white, circled H. We plunked the kayak down far higher than the high-tide line. This confused me because I'd just come to get water. I got the feeling that the lightkeepers hoped I might stay a while.

"Bet you'd like a hot shower?" Cynthia said, confirming my hopes and suspicions.

"I stink that bad, huh?" We all laughed.

"Will you go for a walk with me after you shower?" asked Heather, swinging and tugging my arm as if I were her sister.

Cynthia interrupted, "Heather, Jennifer is probably hungry." She turned to me, "Will you join us for dinner?"

"Oh, I can't intrude!"

"Intrude! People don't drop in here every day, you know."

"Will you?" begged Heather.

A sturdy white bridge joined the helicopter pad on main Ivory Island to the headland where the lightkeepers lived. Below the bridge there was a ravine choked with splintered logs.

"Winter storms bring in those monsters," Dennis explained. "During storms like that, this bridge has ocean boiling under it."

"Really? Then, I bet you've seen some serious storms!"

"Thankfully, not the worst of 'em."

"What's the worst?" I asked, curious about what I might be getting into.

"Well, back in 1904 a tidal wave carried off most of the station. They rebuilt it, of course, but on higher ground. More recently, ten years ago I'd guess, Christmas day, a Force 10 southeaster sent a wave right over the seawall into the house. Tore off stairs and railings. Destroyed the light. Later, the swell took away sections of this bridge."

I was nearly speechless. "Anyone killed?"

"Fortunately, no. The keepers were awake at the time."

We stepped onto the headland. Heather skipped down a red boardwalk ahead of us, oblivious to our stories. She pointed out the garden bed, the compost bin, the senior and junior lightkeepers' houses. We soon reached a green, manicured yard shaded by tall trees on one side with a view of the Pacific as good as an eagle's aerie.

What is it about a lighthouse that strikes a romantic bone? Nothing is so consistent a sentinel, so true a commitment, as that of the "wickie" keeping his light burning. It is the watch-fire that rarely goes out, shining over storm-lashed seas, guiding freighters, fishers, and greenhorns along a wild, convoluted coast— a frequently foggy coast riddled with islands, labyrinthine passages, and invisible reefs. Add winter storm waves that can dwarf a five-story supertanker and it's not hard to understand how lighthouses earn the gratitude of mariners who guide their lives by them.

Most lightstations, I learned, have two keepers, a senior and a junior. Keepers rotate night and day shifts to assure that the light is maintained—winches overhauled, boardwalks rebuilt, weather recorded, foghorn sounded, national flag raised and lowered, rescues performed—365 days a year. It's a profession that is prepared for disaster.

Ivory Island Lightstation was between keepers. The previous keeper had moved to Langara Lightstation and the new keeper had yet to arrive. Dennis and Cynthia were staying temporarily in "the big house" or senior keeper's house. Their real home was Egg Island Light, eighty miles to the south, where Dennis was a junior keeper.

From the outside, the big house looks fully functional. It's a square, two-story, white clapboard with a pyramid roof covered in red shingles. The windows are small to provide protection from the weather, except for a recently added picture window on the leeward side. Built in 1905, it's the oldest dwelling in the Prince Rupert Agency. Even so, because it's on an isolated island smack in the middle of a wilderness, I was surprised to find a normal home inside complete with carpeting, toys scattered about, a favorite threadbare sofa, and the smell of something wonderful cooking.

The sofa was piled with quilt squares, bags of polyester batting, spools of thread, scissors, and a dish of straight pins.

"You're making a quilt!" I exclaimed to Cynthia, leafing through a stack of squares. There was a blue Steller's jay, an animated lighthouse with two arms and a smiley face, a squirrel, a puffin, and a forested island with a lightstation. Each one was in a different style—cross-stitch, applique, embroidery, and paint.

"Cynthia, these are amazing. Did you make them all?"

"Just a few. It's a gift, a surprise for a retiring co-worker. Each of the northern lightstations sent me a square. Even the bachelor keepers. Here, look at this one."

She showed me an orange coast guard helicopter passing a light tower. "The keeper at Langara painted it."

"Nice detail," I said. "So is the lightkeeper quilt your brainchild?"

"Yeah, but I've got helpers. Fil, come in here," Cynthia called into the kitchen. "Fil and her husband Dan are senior keepers at Driad Light. She's been staying here a few days to help with the quilting."

I learned that Fil is short for Filamina. Filamina is Portuguese, five foot two, coal-haired, stout and round as the old country. I guessed she was in her early fifties. She loves to talk, smoke, and laugh. In short, she's good company except for the cigarette smoke.

A timer buzzed in the kitchen. I figured it announced that the wonderful dinner I smelled was ready. But Cynthia said she sets the stove timer to remind her to begin the afternoon weather report.

"Want to come and watch?" she asked.

Because Dennis and Cynthia were covering the eighteen-hour workload together, husband and wife rotated shifts, operating like senior and junior lightkeepers. Cynthia told me that at the turn of the last century it was common practice to have only one married couple watching a station. For the price of one worker, the government got two.

Cynthia and I walked twenty paces down the boardwalk to the foghouse. Named for that Gregorian chanter, the foghorn, it was the size of a one-car garage and contained an eclectic mix of modern and relic technology. Hand drills, planes, and a five-foot bow saw hinted of a time before electricity, when keepers toiled by hand and cut their winter firewood from beach logs. On the east wall, however, a digital display window with red numbers blinked wind speed and direction to one-tenth of a degree.

"Speed 9, direction 17.3," Cynthia noted.

"This is a videograph," she explained, reading the numbers off another display. "It measures the amount of vapor in the air and tells us the distance of visibility."

"How does it do that?" I asked.

"It sends out a beam of high-intensity light and measures what is reflected back. Wave spray will change it, however, and skew the results. Right now it says ten miles."

Back on the boardwalk, we directed our eyes to the sky. "Look out there," Cynthia said, pointing low over Milbanke Sound. "See those layers of flattened white puffs? Those are stratocumulus clouds. They're trapped between two stable layers in the atmosphere that won't allow them to rise, so they spread out horizontally." Cynthia noted in her book, "SC, 2700', 2." Stratocumulus at 2700-feet elevation.

"What's the two for?" I asked.

"The percentage of opaqueness in the cloud. Now look straight up. Those broken up clouds with ragged edges are cumulus fractus."

I strained my memory. "Billowing cumulus, but now they're evaporating?"

"Good. And I'd say they're at eighteen thousand feet, opacity one." Cynthia jotted again, then pointed to the middle of the sky. Her finger stopped at a field of bunched up sheep grazing in blue.

"Those are my favorite clouds," I said. "We call that a mackerel sky."

"We do too," she nodded, "because they look like fish scales. But those same altocumulus seen in early morning can lead to storms by afternoon." Next her finger rose just above the sheep and pointed to a wide gray smudge. It was as if we were looking at the sun through a scuffed soda bottle. "Altostratus. 9000 feet. Opacity three. When you reach an opacity of six plus, which we call a 'ceiling,' you need to have an airplane report." This is important, she explained, because aircraft without certain instruments are only allowed to fly when the ceiling is two hundred feet or higher.

I told her this felt like old wisdom. Wind. Waves. Clouds. What the sky is up to. She replied that it was fun to share it with someone for a change.

To check sea conditions, Cynthia scanned the water in three directions. First she stared south past Cape Swaine and Wurtele Island out to the open Pacific. Next, she squinted west to Susan Rock—a hunch of stone four miles away with a lighted marker. Beyond Susan Rock, McInnes Lighthouse floated seven miles farther out on the horizon. Finally, she checked north up Milbanke Sound. That day the sea looked as if an adz had chipped evenly over its entire surface. Now and then, an odd whitecap blossomed up.

"Two-foot chop, low swell," she wrote. "If it were three-foot, whitecaps would cover it. Four-foot and the whitecaps are rolling."

In the center of the front yard a wood-framed weather box called a Stevenson Screen was affixed to an elevated pole. It looked like a martin house, but with no bird holes. Cynthia opened the box's door. Inside were four thermometers. One dry, one wet, one for minimum, one for maximum, and a clear plastic rain gauge. She noted the temperatures and six millimeters of rain. Then she checked the psychrometric table for the dew point.

"Ten point six for the wet bulb and eleven point seven for the dry. You're supposed to be able to do the entire weather in three minutes. Four if you have a barometric reading, and seven if you have a synopsis."

Cynthia understood the language of weather. While helping with dinner, Dennis confided to me that his wife is his equal at operating the light and deciphering the complex messages written in the sky and on the sea. Seven times each day one or the other relayed these observations via hand-held radio to the coast guard station in Prince Rupert. Such exacting reports build the foundation for the guard's four daily marine forecasts.

Later in the evening, as I dined with the lightkeepers, eating their smoked Canadian bacon and homemade bread—groceries are delivered by supply ship and helicopter—I never imagined that people like the Rose family are going the way of the steamship and totem pole. They're a vanishing breed. Plans were underway, I learned, to automate every lightstation on British Columbia's west coast. High-tech equipment would save taxpayers thousands of dollars.

"They spend sixteen million on a satellite with a five-year life span," mused Dennis. "It gives you a picture of the weather forty-eight hours *after* it happens. Go figure."

"But the real trouble," he continued, "is there's nobody to initiate a quick rescue."

"Do you do a lot of rescues?" I asked, sure he'd mention me in his smart-alecky fashion.

"I did one just three days before you arrived. Remember that foggy period? A fella from your neck of the woods in Washington radioed Ivory from his forty-seven-foot yacht. He was lost. He asked for location information.

"I said, 'Describe where you are.' Then I told him where I thought he was. 'No . . . couldn't be there!' So I asked if he had a GPS—a Global Positioning System. 'Yes.' He had it on, but couldn't read it. I launched the boat in the fog and found him *exactly* where I figured he'd be," he shook his head. "Could have run aground. I tell you, his boat is worth more than the doggone lightstation!"

Dennis paused, then looked at me quizzically. "You always wear a wetsuit, don't you?"

"Of course. Couldn't you tell by the way I smelled?"

"Seriously, with forty-five- to fifty-degree water, I think it's suicide without one. Hate to say it, but every year a few bodies wash up on this coast. With fifteen thousand miles of B.C. shoreline, if something happened, we'd be hard-pressed to find you."

Long after the kids had gone to bed, the four of us continued to sit at the kitchen table drinking tea, talking, and stitching the quilt. As we worked, stories about the family's years on the lights, the other lighthouses up and down the coast, and the animals one comes to know with the passing of seasons, glowed with life. Four sets of hands, Dennis's included, stitched over the white-washed wood table.

"Some of the lights, like Pine, are bird refuges," explained Dennis. "Eleven thousand mated pairs of rhinoceros auklets and storm petrels make their home in the cliffs. There can be four to five thousand birds coming past the lightkeeper's house in one evening.

"One night, the Lucy Island keeper went for a walk and got hit smack in the forehead by a nesting rhinoceros auklet. Came into the house all bleeding. His wife couldn't figure out what had happened. Next day he orders up a pair of hard hats to wear."

Maybe it goes with the isolation of the profession, but Dennis, Fil, and

Cynthia each had the gift of gab. Masters of storytelling, not in the educated sense, but in the down-home, before TVs and VCRs, yarn-spinning sense.

"Auklets," scoffed Dennis, "have the brains of a soda cracker. And not salted either," he shook his head, "I tell ya, only way they know how to land is to run into something. At night—that's when they feed the young—they'll run smack into the house with a beak full of fish. Clip the fish heads clear off. In the morning I find enough fish scattered around the yard—twenty to thirty medium-size herring—to make a good fish stew."

Fil stitched with a cigarette smoldering. Cynthia politely left the nearest window open to draw the smoke out. From somewhere out in the night, two sharp whistles reached our ears.

"What's that calling?" I asked, cupping my hands around my eyes against the dark glass, excited to discover what was out there on that blustery eve.

"Storm petrels," Cynthia said, watching her needled hand drawing white thread up through the blue cloth bordering a lighthouse. She framed each square using an invisible stitch "that takes time to do it right," according to Fil.

She told me calmly, not missing a stitch, "The petrels always come before the storms. They tell us when to put our storm shutters up."

Past the dark window reflection, veering between the outbuildings, the underside of a bird's wings passed in a W formation of white-gray-black. The W looped back and forth as if tethered to an unseen cord that kept it close to the lit window.

"They look like overgrown swallows the way they swoop, dive, bank, return," I said.

We stepped outside, Cynthia in her pink quilted bathrobe and black rubber boots, Fil with cigarette and lighter, and me gallunking along in Dennis's rubber boots.

Fog seeped into our lungs, wet and cool as menthol. Wind needled our skin and flogged our hair. Everywhere, the aroma of sea. Suddenly the air exploded with sound. *BEEEE-OOOOHP!!*

The foghorn! I nearly jumped off the boardwalk. *BEEEE-OOOOHP!!* I wanted to plug my ears, but Cynthia and Fil weren't flinching, so I restrained. Instead, we leaned out from the boardwalk's railing. Surf pounded the cliff below us. No beacon was visible on Susan Rock light four miles out. When the foghorn blasted again, I clenched the railing.

Abruptly, the wind shifted. Our hair flagged seaward. The whistling returned, only louder—a chorus of high, desperate flute notes. We turned, looking up. In the sky above the light were hundreds of yellow birds! Tiny birds, warbler size, crisscrossed the hourglass beam, passing from light into darkness and back into light again. A great yellow wheel of birds spun about the tower like a halo of light, only it was alive, feathered, singing!

"It's spring migration," Fil explained.

Thousands of birds were winging up the coast to their summer nesting grounds. Because of the fog, they could not see the stars they use to navigate. That night, the lighthouse was the brightest of suns. It outshone the heavens.

The warblers were drawn to what ships are warned to avoid.

Fil said, "They're blind from the light." Mesmerized.

"At Driad Point," she continued, "Dan and I collect the exhausted ones and carry them one by one to the dark side of the house."

One mustard-yellow bird fluttered down through the dark sky toward us. We ducked instinctively. I reached out my hand, but Cynthia stopped me. "No, you'll frighten it."

More olive and yellow birds sifted through the column of air between us. Another knocked into the window pane of the foghouse, drawn to the light inside. Its tiny body beat against the glass with fanned-out wings. The gray primary feathers were the size of a child's fingers. It all seemed surreal.

Rain fell on our faces. Silver threads passed through the lit air like static on an old film. The rotating beam spotlighted the storm-battered spruce trees, then the red rooftops, white house boards, and foghouse. It illuminated railings, rose bushes, the fuel tank.

We returned to the house, shaking off the rain. We sat down at the kitchen table again and picked up our quilt squares and sewing needles. But I couldn't stop thinking about the birds.

I wondered how many of the lighthouses on our quilt had beckoned migratory flocks to their electric sun that night? I read the names of thirteen lightstations Cynthia had embroidered on a square: Driad, Egg, Addenbroke, Boat Bluff, McInnes, Pointer, Lawyer, Green, Lucy, Bonilla, Langara, Triple, and Ivory.

As if reading my thoughts, Fil shook her head in disbelief. "By morning we always find five or six dead on the walks." She stitched blue trim on a square that showed a night lighthouse with a beacon streaming out both sides. Behind the light, the sky was filled with a hundred white stars.

"A hundred white stars," I mused to myself, "or are they birds?"

The following day while I waited for Heather to finish her home-school math so we could take a walk, I searched the lawn for warblers and was amazed to find only one. A palm-size Wilson's warbler with an olive saddle, yellow breast feathers, and black brush stroke on its crown, its feet curled like commas.

"Watch for rotting boards," warned Heather, throwing her arms out like a bird, her lanky legs jumping a gap in the slumped boardwalk that led to the far side of Ivory Island. She turned around and smiled proudly. I followed suit, leaping with arms out, Heather-style. Officially, the boardwalk was condemned. A sign said so at the entrance to the woods. But Heather and I passed it with a blind eye, for here was an escape hatch, a portal through which we entered a magical world.

Next to the boardwalk, rising from mossy hummocks, ancient cedars stood sentry. Several of the trunks showed the tell-tale signs of bark gathering: rectangular or V-shaped scars beginning near the ground and tapering to a point twenty feet up or more. Long ago, native women must have come to this forest to peel bark sheets for making cradle bedding, skirts, rain ponchos, and mats— even halibut line, dip nets, and canoe bailers were formed out of bark. Because of its usefulness and sacrifice, the cedar was considered a supernatural being.

A winter wren rattled from the cedar boughs. With 119 notes it has the longest warble of all the songbirds. Its frenetic, hickory-brown body is only as long as my thumb. How do so tiny a pair of lungs create such a symphony? I looked down through the missing planks in the boardwalk. A bird's-eye view unfolded: yellow skunk cabbage flowers brilliant as candle flames, fuchsia salmonberry blossoms, slender combs of deer fern.

Heather knew the same mischievous nature secrets that I did. When the boardwalk passed a beach, we both jumped off and stomped across the mudflats, surprising clams with our foot vibrations. The invisible clams shot thin geysers of saltwater from the sand like hidden squirt guns—exactly as we'd hoped they would. We laughed, though I felt a little mean.

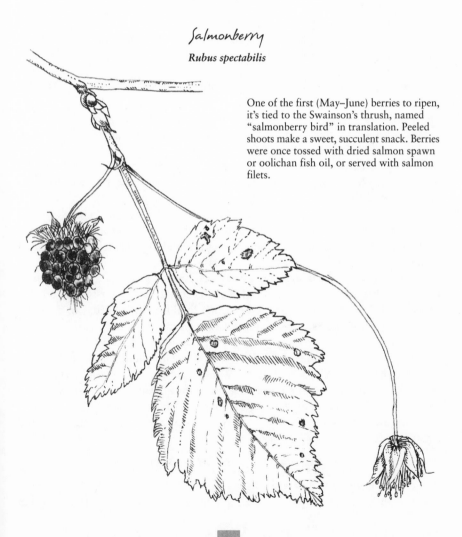

Salmonberry

Rubus spectabilis

One of the first (May–June) berries to ripen, it's tied to the Swainson's thrush, named "salmonberry bird" in translation. Peeled shoots make a sweet, succulent snack. Berries were once tossed with dried salmon spawn or oolichan fish oil, or served with salmon filets.

"Hey Heather," I yelled, swinging a piece of green sea lettuce over my mouth. "This one's delicious! Try it!"

"I know," she said, unimpressed.

We squatted beside pools with barnacles, raking furiously, and poked dried lumps of otter scat thick with pink crab bones. Heather found a raven feather and ran down the beach, waving it up and down as if she were flying. She reminded me of myself as a kid, a tomboy with scabby knees and freckles climbing trees, building forts, and outrunning the neighborhood boys. Only on Ivory Island there were no boys to outrun. The beach, barnacles, clams, and birds were her playmates. I thought about how I would eventually return to Bellingham with its movie theaters, coffeehouses, bike paths, and art galleries. While Heather would return here, time and again, to find her solace and entertainment. There was something altogether disturbing about this. What would I be giving up?

Cynthia was baking bread when we returned. She told me a storm was due late that evening and that now might be a good time to paddle back to my camp and grab all my gear. That is, if I wanted to stay a while longer—being as the weather was declining.

How could I argue? I'd camped and shivered through my share of storms, and would likely continue to do so. So why—when I could eat Cynthia's home-made bread, sip tea, quilt, and be snug and warm with such spirited and jovial companions—leave then? On the other hand, what was the reason I had kayaked to that coast?

Paddling east down Seaforth Channel away from Ivory Island, I was no longer sure. The solitude I once longed for now felt void and purposeless, even dangerous. Jostling through a turbulent tide rip, the newly unfamiliar kayak bucked like a green horse. A wave crashed over the starboard side, swirled around my spray skirt like a spin washer, and poured off. I tried to loosen my hips to the force as I usually do, but I was tight and afraid. I felt uncertain of a wilderness that had been my friend just days before.

Even the magical island where I'd camped for two blissful days now seemed like any other island. Damp. Aloof. Unconcerned by my passing. I quickly rolled up the tent and left a pearled abalone shell filled with cedar in its place.

"Thank you, otters, for keeping me safe," I murmured.

Anxious to return to the lighthouse, I hurried back across the channel. This time, however, I hauled out my kayak at the clam-squirting beach. I stashed it beside the moss-roofed boathouse. Walking up the boardwalk carrying art supplies for sketching and a jar of coveted peanut butter for the Roses, I wondered what was happening to my wild spirit. Had I anesthetized it with domestic amenities? Was I so easily swayed? Two days with running water and electric heat and I was a weenie?

It was high noon, and I was sitting on the island's bluff overlooking the sea and sketching a pinto abalone shell left by an otter when I heard Cynthia running down the red boardwalk with Sylvia jostling in her arms. "Four minutes," she said, "until the coast guard helicopter's here." At the helicopter pad a striped, orange-and-white wind sock wagged northwest. Moments later the *THUB-BUBB* of an approaching chopper beat somewhere overhead. My untrained eye saw nothing but white sky. Then, suddenly, 150 yards above us an orange speck grew into a Sikorski 61 helicopter. It hovered over twisted spruce crowns and log-heaped rocks, then lighted on the cement pad blazed with a circled H.

We all waved. Dennis waited until the blades were just about done spinning before jogging out in his yellow slicker with day-glow armbands.

"GARDE COTIERE," the chopper's side read. "It's a real workhorse," said Cynthia. "Their lifting capacity is somewhere around 4500 pounds. They like to lift around 2500 to 3000 pounds so they don't waste fuel. If it's too heavy it lugs out. If it's too light it doesn't handle well in strong winds."

With the utmost efficiency, Dennis and the chopper crew unloaded and stacked several five-by-eight-foot sheets of plywood and a six-foot aluminum ladder. Before the helicopter crew arrived, Dennis had driven a red Yanmar tractor to the bridge. Now he parked it on top of the plywood so that when the helicopter lifted the wood wouldn't blow away with it.

Cynthia told me, "This flight is a milk run stopping at several lights to deliver supplies and mail. A direct flight from Prince Rupert to Ivory Island is one hour." The helicopter wouldn't arrive at Egg, the Rose's regular home, for three and a half hours. "We never order ice cream there," she laughed.

On a lightstation everything from rubber boots to flannel nightgowns, computers to cross-stitch patterns, is selected through the pages of mail-order catalogs and arrives via Canadian coast guard helicopter or supply ship. Cargo delivered off a ship is shifted by crane onto the east bay where I first landed. A motorized cable winches it up to the station. During emergencies, Dennis launches his rescue boat the same way, but in reverse.

After a round of parting hugs, Fil trotted down the bridge holding her hood against the wind. She waved and stepped aboard. The Sikorski 61 levitated above the spruce. Next stop Fil's house—Driad Lightstation.

Dennis and I loaded the plywood sheet by sheet into a red wagon. Dennis drove tractor and wagon up to the house like a kid's miniature train. Cynthia and I walked to the far side of the yard for the afternoon weather report.

"Cumulofractus. Cumulus. And, over there," she pointed to several massive cauliflower-shaped stacks vaulting above a quilt of white, "stratocumulus with towering cumulus embedded. That's what's bringing the wind."

Later that night, around 10 P.M., the storm shook the house walls and I knew we were in the thick of it. A call came in for me on the Allen radio. It was two New Zealand kayakers staying at Egg Island lighthouse a ways south. They'd heard there was a woman paddling solo up the Inside, staying at Ivory.

"I hope you don't mind that I told them about you," Cynthia said. "They sound very excited that you're just three days north."

I didn't hanker for company, I told Cynthia, but I'd be glad to chat with them.

We lamented about the fog, raged over the storm, and foretold our general routes. They were headed up the Outside Passage. I preferred the fjords and channels. Paddling alone, I wanted to minimize my exposure. I could join them, they said, if I wanted. "Oh, I dunno. That's awfully nice of you, but . . . ."

The unexpected call gave me an itch to get moving again. Over the next two days, as the storm swells subsided, I began to feel a tick of restlessness. Standing on the bluff, watching an Alaska ferry steam by with tourists crowding the deck among colorful tents and lawn chairs, I recalled my excitement at heading out not that long ago. The ferry reminded me of my dream to kayak the entire Inside Passage. The ocean was calling me. I was ready to move on.

The thought of getting back to poking up an island coast soon felt wonderful; the challenge came in the form of convincing my new friends.

"If you stay a few more weeks," Dennis said temptingly, "the coast guard helicopter could carry the kayak and you to Prince Rupert. The chopper would be empty then."

"Women don't come here often," Cynthia lamented later. But the call and the passing ferry had transformed my spirit. I stuck to my vision and Cynthia promised to bake some bon voyage bread.

On my last evening at the light, Cynthia sat in the radio room at her government-issued desk holding a mike. It was 10:40 P.M. and she was waiting to call Prince Rupert with her evening weather report. Voices from other lighthouses up and down the coast warbled from the loudspeaker. Cynthia was familiar with them all.

"That's Point Saint James doing aviations. They make a report every hour." She waited for the channel to clear. I watched her yawn and transcribe her report into the log. The radio opened, and she added her report to the coastal picture.

"Ivory. Good evening. We're overcast 1.2, South .09, two-foot chop with a low southwest swell. In remarks—we have showers all quads." She closed the log. Her report would be typed into a computer at Prince Rupert then read back as part of the 11:45 P.M. marine forecast.

We really jawed it up that night. Cynthia surprised me by sharing a detailed description of her entire first novel, start to finish, plot, characters, and climax. She also told me a few bawdy stories from her past. "That is, before I met Dennis," she said.

I rolled out of bed the next morning at the shining hour of 10:30 A.M. Clouds of baking smells wafted under the bedroom door as I packed my waterproof bags. Downstairs, Heather handed me a scribble of paper with a purple angel. Dennis said, "Boat Bluff lighthouse, four days north, says stop in for coffee."

Cynthia and I lugged my gear down the boardwalk. She handed me a warm loaf of bread. "You come visit now. The Victorian Bed and Breakfast Dennis and I are going to open someday has a free room."

Halfway across Reid Inlet, I turned to wave, but Cynthia was gone. Wind shuffled the still water, but the bread in my lap kept me warm as a lightkeepers' quilt.

7 Reaching

Three days north of Ivory Island, I floated into Jackson Pass at dawn. Ahead, the water's course threaded and narrowed between two forested thumbs. It was one of those mornings when you can count hours between sounds. A trickle of creek water. Silence. Spiraling notes of a Swainson's thrush feathering down the canyon. And again, nothing.

That morning the obsidian water seemed immovably deep. It kept the mysteries of its contents well hidden. Who could guess how many sea stars, spiny rock cod, water-soaked logs, and husks of animal bones lingered in the unseeable darkness. I was reminded of a Bella Bella Native myth that tells of an entire kingdom living under the sea's dark lid. Flippered and finned supernatural creatures sit beside their longhouse fire, abalone eyes sparkling. In their dimly lit lodge, salmon, halibut, and horse clams on drying racks ladder right up to the smoke hole. The house posts, carved like whales and sea lions, swim to life in answer to magical songs. The roof boards drip with anemones. And in the rafters, hollow tubes of bull kelp used to store eulachon fish oil hang easy as ropes.

Golden bulbs of bull kelp specked with pollen drifted past the kayak. A fish surfaced from the darkness, neared the bow, then turned. I watched the sail of its dorsal fin breaking the surface as it swam. A fan of Vs spread out behind in a miniature wake. Did he know I could see him as clearly as a mosquito on the back of my hand? I wondered if this is what an eagle watches, the minute wakes of careless fish too near the surface.

Days before, I'd been sitting in my tent savoring a gnatless cup of cocoa when I heard a tremendous splash. In seconds, I was standing upright outside the tent in my long johns scanning the water for something BIG. Then I saw it. Ten feet offshore—an eagle swimming. Yes, swimming.

Its huge brown wings rowed the still water, stirring the cloud reflections into a dozen pleats. I knew at once that the eagle had likely hooked and was towing a sizable fish. But the catch was too heavy to haul skyward. Like most birds of prey eagles have a locking mechanism in their feet so they can clasp onto fish, snakes, rabbits, and other small mammals when they are airborne. But in this case, the eagle was waterborne. Once the talons lock, the claws can't let loose until their load is removed.

I recalled a story Dennis, the Ivory Island lightkeeper, told of watching an eagle fishing in a storm. *It was a young one. Dove headfirst into a wave and emerged with a huge salmon. Fish must have weighed ten or fifteen pounds. The eagle could hardly lift it above the water. Next thing you know, along comes a big wave. Plunges the eagle under just like that. I never saw it resurface.*

This bird, however, was swimming to an island of seaweed-covered rocks a few feet offshore. With his wings still dripping, he gave a tremendous heave upward and half jumped, half bobbled up the rocks.

Out of the water, the fish looked to be a salmon about the length of my arm. It was almost as long as the eagle was tall. Standing atop the fish, beating its wings dry, the eagle rearranged its cargo so it lay headfirst like a pontoon. Then it lifted into the air with the salmon gripped in its golden hooks, mouth opening and closing, tail thwacking as if swimming in an ocean of blue sky.

The increasingly waverly water beside my drifting kayak told me the current was speeding up. Still, I floated unconcerned on a river of sky reflections. Blue to the south, gray-bottomed cumulus to the north. Just then a sound, unmistakable to my ear, shot into the air. *Paw-hoooofffff!* It rushed like breath blown through a hose, only magnified. The noise sent excitement shivering through my bones, but at the same time a sobering sense of vulnerability as to where the whale would surface next. I turned to see the shining, obsidian back and tall dorsal fin of an orca disappearing into the ripple line of the incoming wind twenty-five yards away.

For the longest time there was silence. Then I heard a second *Paw-hooooffff,* only this time the sound crossed a great distance before reaching my ears. I turned toward Finlayson Channel where I had paddled the day before. Almost imperceptible against the gray backdrop of Pooley Island rose a funnel of whitish air. The last insubstantial cloud burst of whale breath hung like an omen. In seconds it too was gone.

West of Jackson Pass, I crossed two-mile-wide Finlayson Sound in rolling gray seas, narrowly avoiding a southbound freighter. I swung north following the precipitous shoreline of Cone Island (locally called China Cap) to Klemtu, a Native village. It was three days since I'd left the Ivory Island lightkeepers and I was still a half day from the next lighthouse, Boat Bluff, where I'd been invited to stop for coffee.

Klemtu was unmistakable. A huge red-and-white tower reminiscent of a giant soup can flanked a hill at the south end. An impressive public wharf spanned the mountainous shoreline between the south settlement, where pastel tract homes marched up slope, and the business side of the village to the north, where an Imperial Oil Company float loomed. Paddling alongside the wharf, I waved to some laughing, raven-haired, cherub-faced kids leaning from the rail of a moored trawler. Their father looked up, too, waving a paintbrush.

At the store, I passed over the squishy Wonder Bread for sturdier pilot biscuits, then carried a container of ketchup and fries over to the oil company float where I'd tied *Yemaya.* The young man locking up the gas pump for the night said I could camp on the lower gas float as long as I packed up by 7 A.M. Sitting inside the open tent door and eating cold fries I watched a purse seiner charge up Klemtu Passage fifty yards off. White frothed beneath the bow. Soon, huge rollers smashed my tippy float, rocking it like a bathtub toy. Icy water clupped through the planks, soaking the tent floor and me. I jumped up. Three elders eyed the whole scene from the wharf above. One shook his head in disapproval. He whispered something to the others.

"American fishing boat going to Alaska. Always in a hurry. They don't like to follow the no-wake signs," he said frowning. "Did you see a sign posted at the south end of the pass?" he asked. "Sometimes it blows down."

Before I could answer, two of the men dressed in nylon windbreakers with fishing insignias strode down the gangplank to the lower pier and wordlessly began moving a rowboat away from one corner. Next, they nodded at my tent. I caught on and the three of us carried the wet tent to the dry planks where the rowboat had been.

"There, now you'll be safe," said the man who was still atop the wharf. "Where you coming from?"

"Bella Bella," I answered. The silver-haired man smiled.

"Where you headed?"

"Prince Rupert."

"How many miles you paddle today?" asked another.

"Eleven, I guess."

"You must get strong arms, huh?"

"Sore ones," I said. They laughed and wished me a good night's sleep as they shuffled up the gangplank.

Nowhere north of Klemtu was there level ground. At Boat Bluff Lightstation, keepers Bob and Andy used a crane to lift my loaded kayak up the steep shore to a slab of poured concrete. I thought I was just stopping in for coffee, but I spent a lovely night in Bob and Barb's guest bedroom overlooking the cliffs of Sarah Island. On the morning I left, the current ran so swiftly in canyon-like Boat Bluff Pass that Bob had to hold the boat firmly while his wife helped me stow four bottles of their homebrew beer complete with yeast clouding the bottom.

"Camping won't be easy north of here, eh?" Bob forewarned as I shoved off. Over the next three days, the reality of his words settled in with a thud. By dusk I often had zilch prospects.

The first night I ferreted out a lumpy island rank with otter urine in Graham Reach, but the swift tidal stream nearly carried off a seat cushion and a food bag while I was unpacking the hatches. The second night up Graham Reach, utterly desperate, I hoisted the kayak onto a narrow rock ledge and climbed twenty feet up a fissure in the angled cliff. I hoped to peek into the forest above and beat out a tent spot. Where the cliff stopped, the forest shot up at a dizzying angle. Every inch sprouted salal, spruce, and cedar. Immediately to the left, however, an old cedar with a scoop-neck trunk crawled along the earth, then thrust itself out from the scrubby mountain forest and vaulted over the sea into the open. Now that had potential, I thought.

After schlepping armloads of gear up the fissure, I built a lumpy foundation around the table-like portion of the cedar trunk. Dry bags, food duffels, dry box, chart case, water jugs—everything but tent, pad, and sleeping bag—jammed together like bricks in a crude house foundation. I wrapped the lumpy platform with a tarp and tucked in the loose ends. Minus one pole, the misshapen tent fit perfectly on top. Inside, I slept fitfully, as if on a loosely-lashed raft adrift in the Pacific. I was startled once to find a weasel pawing at the tarp trying to unearth the food duffel. I was relieved it wasn't a bear!

I had arrived at the land of "Reaches," three channel-like passages rounding the northwest corner of sixty-mile-long Princess Royal Island. I suspected the cartographer-explorers had a tongue-in-cheek reason for such fitting place names. For forty miles, the Reaches reach and reach.

Where Tolmie Channel ends, Graham Reach tongues eighteen wind-blown miles north. Graham Reach passes into Butedale Passage for three brief miles then hitches up to Fraser Reach, which arrows northwest for an additional twelve miles. After a dog-leg turn west, Fraser becomes McKay Reach. Staring at braided blue mountain silhouettes for hours without any evident visual change over bow or stern, I concluded that "reaches" are so named because you come to think you'll never reach the end.

For three days I paddled these narrow slots hemmed in by stunning three and four thousand-foot mountains rising from forested shores to luminous snowfields. Sunlight ushered in late and left early. Every mile began to look confusingly similar—walls of olive fucus and barnacles at tide level, then steep, scrubby evergreen forests above. But for the presence of three side inlets—the Green, Khutze, and Aaltanhash—carved into the mainland, I'd have had few navigational aids for tracking my slow progress. But every now and then the trees would break open to a quartz-white veil of falling water.

The falls. Ah, the singing, tumbling, roaring, snorting falls. Fusion of voices and applause, they never failed to rejuvenate my weary spirit. I would sprint up to their turbulent, bubbling feet, paddle in place against the race of current, and await the cool, churning mist as it settled on my lashes and the minute hairs of my face and neck, then drifted into the hollows of my jacket.

On the third night, at the end of Graham Reach and near the start of Fraser Reach, I found a mosquito-infested quagmire of black mud and skunk cabbage. I was so delighted for flat ground, I danced across the beach and sang opera to the nearby waterfall. Across the bay, deafening, wedding-cake-tiered Butedale Falls boomed down a scooped evergreen valley. Butedale is the mother of all falls scouring the Reaches. Her bottom tier alone is tall as a cruise ship and wide as a warehouse. Her song is a harsh pandemonium of baritone thunderclap, ear-ringing detonations, and roaring jet engines. The heavy discharge of water from Butedale Falls has been used as an auditory guide for mariners during pea-soup weather.

Decades ago, the Canadian Fishing Company tapped the falls' fulminous power to drive a water turbine known as a Pelton wheel and generate electricity for an enormous salmon cannery on the south shore. A hidden mountain lake provided perpetual water. The turbine received its high-pressure juice through a cedar-plank pipe ringed with barrel hoops that directed the lake water down the staggeringly steep slope to the cannery. The water pipe narrowed as it arched seaward, building pressure as it dropped to feed the turbine. In its heyday, Butedale would light up like an emerald city. Now it molders on pilings as the forest and sea seep back.

Butedale Falls roared all night, mosquitoes whined, and Sitka black-tailed deer, bless their hungry stomachs, munched skunk cabbage inches from the nylon tent walls. I had mistakenly camped in the midst of the local salad bar. Deer actively seek calcium-rich skunk cabbage leaves and its cheery yellow spathe—a hood-like bract cloaking the flowery spike. The odiferous cabbage is one of the first plants to emerge from the primal goo each spring when there's not much else around. Deer just hammer it. But the heavy pruning job doesn't seem to bother the cabbages, which can live up to seventy years. (That's ten deer lives by comparison.) How deer—and bears and geese for that matter—can handle the plant's needle-like calcium oxalate crystals is a mystery. Humans and other animals who sample the tempting greenery are quickly dissuaded from ever doing it again by a fiery irritation caused by the crystals embedding themselves in tongue, cheeks, and gums. First Nations ate skunk cabbage leaves only after repeated boiling and pouring off the water after each boiling, which destroys the calcium oxalate.

At one point, I couldn't sleep for the din of molars grinding and leaves tearing. I unzipped the door, picked up the heavy plastic chart bag and the *Sailing Directions* book and slammed them together: WHAM-WHAM-WHAM! The loud smacks shook the forest, delivered me from insomnia frustration, and closed down the bar. Just to be sure they knew I meant business, I drew out my harmonica and played two raucous rounds of "Oh Susanna," whaling on the long low notes and twittering on the highs.

"Like that? Now I'd like to get some sleep! Thank you!" I paused, listening. I imagined the deer standing still as tree trunks in the blackness, waded up to their knobby knees in mud, molars paused in mid-chew. But I never heard another rasping bite.

***

At 4:30 A.M. the watch alarm *zee-ba-deeped*. After being pummeled and slammed around by Graham Reach's afternoon winds, I had vowed to launch before sunrise. The electronic call jarred me from a terrifying dream. *Over Butedale Bay, a lurid orange mushroom cloud roiled and smoked and was about to scorch me alive! My last thought was "I'll never see loved ones and family again!"*

From inside the tent, I could hear Butedale Falls resonating like Dante's flaming inferno.

By 6 A.M. I was sitting half asleep in my loaded kayak munching a bowl of granola while a swarm of gnats had breakfast too—me. Over the din of Butedale Falls, the VHF radio gargled out the daily weather synopsis. A low-pressure system was slogging north. South winds would shift west as the front passed. I looked out at the tranquil mirror of Fraser Reach. Troops of

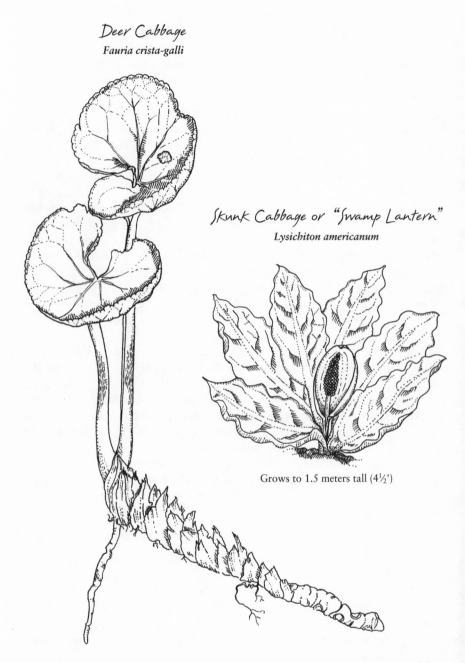

Deer Cabbage
Fauria crista-galli

Skunk Cabbage or "Swamp Lantern"
Lysichiton americanum

Grows to 1.5 meters tall (4½')

evergreen mountains bandaged with snowfields marched upside-down to the horizon. I sloshed my empty bowl in the sunlit water and pushed off, unable to restrain from singing an oldie, "Feeling Groovy." To make it more timely, I made up new lines: "Paddling down ol' Fraser Reach, looking for smooo-ooth seas, and feeling grooo-ooveeee."

Sunlight poured in spears over the Klekane Crest down into Fraser Reach. In local legends, the rays are called Sun's eyelashes. I dipped my fingers in the soothing water and imagined every worry flowing away. I hadn't a clue if the day's weather forecast would translate into wind on face, rudder, or beam. Turned out it would be all three.

The high wavy bathtub ring of sea tar lichen smudging the western cliffs should have been my first warning. Sea tar lichen love salt spray. Spray is generated from waves—BIG ones. In protected bays, sea tar lies in a horizontal bar across the rocky intertidal shore. Its line mirrors the water's personality. Flat for calm water. Zigzagged for tumultuous seas. In Fraser Reach the line looked like someone had motored along the cliff in a storm while a passenger held out a brush dipped in black tar. Not a good sign.

An hour later, the rear horizon darkened to indigo blue. For some goofy reason I dismissed the ominous, distant wind as a localized disturbance. I figured, wrongly, that Klekane Inlet, having been sun baked for an hour, was gushing cool air from the snowfields down into Fraser Reach while the warmer, less dense air was rising and dissipating. The "localized disturbance" slammed into me like a sack of ice. In no time, whitecaps hissed and leapt across the reach. The largest waves rolled over the stern with a smash. I couldn't believe their sudden size. It became paramount to judge the "thrashers" ahead of time so I could speed up or brace and ride them out. With dizzying frequency, I glanced backward every few seconds mentally bracing for the grand slams.

If that weren't enough, fifty yards out from *Yemaya*'s bow, acres of leaping white waves signaled a burly tide rip. I cupped one ear to identify the sound. Sure enough, the static of a white water river confirmed my suspicions. Out of caution, I steered the kayak toward the cliff. Even though I knew vertical rock offers no emergency haul-out, I craved the psychological safety of land in case I flipped. Within seconds I suffered from my poor judgment. Near the cliff, reflection waves slammed off the wall and reared up under the hull. The cliff edge was the sloshiest, roughest place to ride through a converging tide rip! I bounced along sucked violently toward the froth of the narrowing Reach. Water pushed and shoved to get past the bottleneck. Waves piled up like grunting football linemen to block the kayak's course.

Breathing hard, paddling harder, I sprinted for all I was worth into the middle of the pack. Fifty yards of chaos and I'd be through it. My shoulders and torso worked with a force that pained my sternum. Waves shook the kayak as if it were scudding over a giant washboard. I braced and gasped and held my hips as loose as a gate hinge. Spray slapped the deck and swatted my arms and face.

Staying upright was expending so much energy, I needed to be assured I was getting somewhere for the effort. I shot a glance at the cliff. I expected to see it zinging by. On the contrary, my movement was nearly undetectable! What the hell?

Paddling full throttle yet no progress? I knew I couldn't maintain the manic pace without something giving. But what was I to do? I just kept digging in the paddle blades and hoping. I knew from experience that current is *supposed* to flow through rips. Eventually I would come out the far side. Within a few minutes, I noticed the bow passing a bright cluster of purple sea stars hanging on the cliff. Perhaps I had pushed through the worst of it. I was moving ahead. Yes, I was. The chop was decreasing.

Moments later, a creature splashed up beside the bow. I jumped. Slick flippers disappeared into a green wave as the seal zoomed between me and the cliff.

"*You're* surprised? Well, ME, TOO!" I yelled, heart thumping. I turned to watch the seal zip past and caught a foaming wave up to my armpits. My body fizzled like shook soda pop. I needed a break SOON! The seal threaded toward the bow, then charged the cliff again. I couldn't believe my eyes. A kayak-size pullout was cleaved into the wall. It formed a visible eddy inside a bulge in the cliff. I yowled for joy. A resting place at last!

Steering a ferry angle, I torqued the kayak forty degrees to the current and back-paddled. Wind pushed from behind. Waves jostled the hull. But the ferry angle held. *Yemaya* skittered sideways across the waves. Without the angle's remarkable effect, I could have blown by the indent in an instant. Now I thanked my lucky stars for having practiced ferry angles the previous spring. Three hard, fast strokes urged the kayak to park neatly inside the bight. The cliff jumped straight up but the uneven surface provided a handhold. Current roared at a frantic speed beyond the eddyline. I yanked a snack bag from behind the seat. With gloved hands, I couldn't open the double ziplock fast enough. I inhaled a glove full of dried apricots. Then another. *Not enough!* I stuffed down two home-dried bananas. They immediately vacuum-sealed to the roof of my mouth.

"*Holy crow!*" I couldn't for the life of me get them unstuck. I shoveled and clucked my tongue. I was dancing on my edge. Short of sleep, pushed to my physical limit, and now unable to swallow . . . I tore off my neoprene glove and plucked them loose.

"Please . . . just a place . . . to step . . . from the kayak . . . and rest," I prayed through labored breath.

Since Butedale I'd counted two emergency bivouacs. One, a rock ledge flat enough to drag a kayak up (for a brief while). Two, a tumbling boulder creek spilling out from a steep forest. Emergency rest spots. Not big enough to roll out a sleeping bag much less a tent. My *Marine Atlas* didn't show one, but I *believed* that somewhere down the long neck of Fraser Reach I'd find a take-out. I looked north at the green fields of catapulting waves. I imagined fighting this for thirteen more gruesome miles. The thought made me weak. I wanted someone to take my hand and lead me home.

I wanted to quit!

But my body knew it was dangerous to dwell in the bight much longer. I was getting soft—better to keep moving. I eased the bow forward. Something flashed under the overhang ten feet ahead. A soaking-wet animal with a long tail, flattened forehead, sideward ears—a-a-an otter, for gosh sake! It peered nervously from the shadows.

"Otter," I said softly, "I didn't mean to frighten you."

The slick otter paced back and forth. Its heavy brown tail sulked behind. Hickory fur spiked up along it's mussy humped back.

"I'm so relieved and happy for your company!" I said. It felt tremendously comforting to be in the presence of a soul who thrived in rough waters.

I pinched some cedar from *Yemaya*'s deck boughs and dropped it in the sea. "Blessings of urchins and fishes, Otter!" I pushed free of the bight and jostled into the Reach again, elated and more at ease.

A half hour passed. Winds gusted fifteen knots. I bobbled over another convergence in the pipe of Fraser Reach. One skookum roller surfed *Yemaya* sideways. I slammed a paddle brace and swung her bow forward again. I stayed upright in the forty-five-degree water, but it felt like a near capsize. I guessed that in two and a half hours I'd plodded only five miles. My frazzled nerves craved a break. I alternately opened and closed my hands to relieve the stiffness. My body felt dangerously fatigued. If I flipped I wasn't sure I would have the quickness of mind to roll upright or the energy to self-rescue with the paddle float. As far as I could squint, the Reach kept reaching. Kingcome Point, where Fraser turned into McKay Reach, looked like a distant blue crease in a long crumpled cloth.

Nonetheless, I prayed again for a place to rest. A hundred yards ahead, a mudslide had toppled several spruce trees over the cliff. Their upturned root masses still clung to the mountain, but their trunks angled down into the sea like a thirty-degree ladder. As I floated nearer I realized they obscured an indent in the cliffy shore. The tree closest to the indent was in the lee.

I pulled up to its barnacled trunk. A crazy idea dawned as I held to its branches. If I could just get myself up the trunk, I could hoist the kayak up after me. The kayak would roll up the branches like a log dragged up a skid road.

Sane kayakers don't jump from moving kayaks into trees. I wasn't sane, I was desperate. A two-foot wave whooshed the kayak treeward, I leapt upright and hugged the slimy trunk. Down plunged the boat. I squeezed and held on, dangling my toes in the cockpit so the kayak wouldn't sail off. Up soared the next wave. I bent my knees with the kayak's rise, then pushed off the boat's floor and sprang onto the trunk, pushing my feet against the tree's lowest branches. Limbs crumbled underfoot. Punky white splinters tumbled into the water below. I began slipping downward on the seaweed-slick trunk, raked by leagues of barnacles and mussel shells.

Thrashing about in an underwater forest of branches blazoned an image so terrifying that it blessed my hands and feet with amazing strength and dexterity. I dug my gloved fingers into the mussels and squeezed my legs against the trunk for all I was worth. I began wriggling up through the slippery branches like a spider stringing a web. Only my gossamer was a nylon bowline clipped to my flotation vest with a carabiner.

Ten feet up the spruce, inside a nest of needled branches, I twisted around, hitched the bowline to a sturdy limb, then turned back toward the boat. I dug my boots against the tree limbs, wrapped a bight of rope around my glove, and heaved with both hands. Up jerked the bow! I was frankly surprised. After pulling up the rope's slack, I jerked hard again. The kayak kept jolting up the trunk. I was amazed it didn't fall off, but the higher, thickly needled branches cradled it in a V-shaped trough of limbs. I yanked and pulled, inching backward up through the trunk's branches until the stern rested six feet above the water. I wanted the kayak well above the smashing wake of cruise ships, ferries, and freighters. I tied it off with a fist of locking hitches.

The rope had gnawed a groove in my gloves, but I had no time to marvel. I dug the food bag from the front hatch, and scurried up the trunk to terra firma. At least I hoped it was terra firma. Wishful thinking.

When I stepped down from the root mass, the earth moved under foot. Nothing was firmly anchored here. Toppled trunks, branches, and cleaved earth littered the next sixty feet up slope. But then the forest plateaued and the trees grew upright. Something told me to get myself up there. I picked my way through the scaffolding of branches, climbed toppled trunks like walkways, and balanced on pillars of soil so unstable I worried that I might upset the entire freighter of mud and tree trunks and slide down the mountainside into Fraser Reach. As I climbed, I found myself grimly composing an obituary:

"Kayaker found smothered to death in Fraser Reach mudslide. Authorities say the woman summoned help on her VHF radio, but then lost contact. Search parties recovered (that may be too optimistic, I thought) the woman's crushed body in a muddy crevasse only after dogs were boated to the scene. Her kayak was discovered mysteriously tied to a tree, which is what alerted a passing pleasure boater."

I reached the plateau. Back away from the cliff, hidden by a wall of rock, a mossy swatch lay out of the wind. A cup of nodding violets sprouted in a fissure. Beyond thankfulness, edging on worship, I threw myself on the moss, kissed the violets, and sobbed.

"What a goofy idea, *SOLO* paddling!" I scoffed to no one in particular.

Three pilot biscuits slathered with peanut butter eased the tension and tears. Exhausted, I pulled the hood over my head and fell asleep still wearing the flotation vest and kayak skirt.

"*AUK! AUK! AUK!*" a pesky raven nattered.

"Go away, I'm trying to sleep."

Raven gargled a second alarm call. "*AUK! AWWWK!*"

"What IS IT! Are you hungry TOO?" I squinted up at the bristly triangular silhouette perched in the branches of a Sitka spruce. The branches weren't moving! The wind had died down! I could hardly believe my eyes. I scrambled to the cliff's edge. For miles in both directions whitecaps had vanished. How quickly that sea rearranged herself. She shifted her myriad moods in hours or moments. The Reach lay as calm as the languorous, silken sea I had launched in earlier that morning.

I glanced at my watch. "Holy smokes!" I gasped. Two plus hours had passed since I lay down. The irony hit me like a cold fish—if I'd slept in that morning, I would have been just fine.

I picked my way down to the kayak tree then stopped short. The tree's crown was lifted completely out of the water. The diving-board tip trailed streamers of kelp. Still tied in the branches, but now seven feet above the water, the kayak was poised like a bobsled waiting to take off. The tide had dropped a whopping five feet while I slept!

Crawling back down the thicket of branches I wondered how I'd ever managed to heave the kayak up as I far as I did. Adrenaline knew no limits.

As I started to untie the bowline, the boat lurched down the incline. The sheer weight of a 250-pound kayak was enough to pull me off balance. I had to devise something to slow the descent. I wrapped the rope around a branch stub for a brake lever. Feeding it out inch by inch, the kayak rappelled beautifully down the trunk, cradled by the uncanny V of branches that steered its course. The stern plunged into the sea with such force it disappeared under a blossom of white before rebounding. I was amazed that the cockpit didn't fill with water or the rope snap. When all was dunked and done, the kayak bobbed to the surface and waited patiently to be hauled back for mounting.

Reentering a kayak while hanging from a tree is tricky business. It calls for as much luck as buffoonery. On the first attempt, the kayak shot away when my toes knocked the fore deck. Still hanging from the trunk, I tip-toed the cockpit back into place. On the second attempt I dropped to a squat then to my butt so fast I surprised myself I had legs.

Along the far shore, a green sailboat with a white mast motored serenely north. It was *Dancer*, a vessel I'd seen moored at the Butedale cannery. The crew hadn't a clue about the weather I'd been through. I admired their good fortune of a late start as I turned *Yemaya*'s bow toward distant Kingcome Point.

The wind came up again two hours later. My fingers stung from crab-clawing the paddle shaft. My wrists burned with tendonitis from the repetitive twist of a paddle blade feathered for the wind.

A cheery British Columbia ferry chugged up mid-channel, smoke stacks billowing back. From the side decks, dozens of arms shot up in waves. I burst into tears and waved the paddle in sweeping arcs. It was my friend, Captain James, whose ferry shuttled me to Bella Bella. Before debarking, the captain had called me up into the wheelhouse to discuss kayak unloading logistics. When I told him about my solo trip he had instructed me in a kind, fatherly tone to be sure and radio him when *The Queen of the North* passed. Miraculously, he had spotted my little kayak. I imagined his public announcement: "Folks, may I have your attention. This very moment my friend Jennifer is soloing the Inside Passage in a kayak. If you can believe that, look out the port side and give her a wave. I dropped her in Bella Bella about three weeks ago." I melted with gratitude for his kind gesture.

The Queen of the North's wake hit *Yemaya* as she rounded a mild rip off a bulging point. Again, I couldn't have situated myself worse. Great sloshers thumped together and rose up to my shoulders as the swell from the ferry's wake was trapped in the rip. I remembered a story Dennis had told me about a fisher who flipped his skiff in a similar wake and drowned. Waves crane upward when they meet opposing current and are forced to slow down. The oomph they forgo in speed must be transferred into height. I steered a fishtail course through the big green rollers. They broke against the cliff just after I passed.

Beyond the outcrop, a tiny cove eked out of the shoreline. At last, a rest spot! I was delighted by the prospect of crawling from the boat until I realized the walls were steep as a quarry. House-size sea stacks clotted the open water. Each one was crusted with blue mussels and slick fronds of wing kelp. Waves rushed between the stacks and flushed out white.

Flat tent sites were definitely available. They lay twenty feet up atop the fractured pillars. I would need climbing gear to haul myself up. I'd climbed enough for one day. Disheartened, I chomped on pilot biscuits and moldy cheddar cheese and pondered what to do. I'd already peed once in my wetsuit for lack of a pullout, so I chugged water and steeped in a "puddle of warmth."

Using the *Marine Atlas,* I measured the remaining miles to Kingcome Point (or "Come, King Point," as I had renamed the coy sucker). All I really wanted was to get the day over with. My sleep-deprived mind lumbered toward drunken looniness. My arms and shoulders moved only because they didn't know what else to do. Frazzled to the core, I pondered firing three Olin emergency flares at the windshield of the next passing boat. But after the ferry no other vessels came along.

What drives the spirit when the body is a tired, life-weary husk? Poet Dylan Thomas lauded the "green fuse," and the metaphor struck a decent chord. Somewhere inside the husk of my body burned a tenacious wick. I didn't understand the why or how of it. But I distinctly felt its presence. After I rested in the swill of the sea stacks, that wick or fuse or whatever you call it took up the paddle and led me out the cove. I followed it north.

Two miles later I came to a waterfall. I hadn't an ounce of energy to charge the outflow and paddle into the lovely spray. I laid my paddle across the combing and dropped my hands to the sides of the kayak. A sound emerged from the partly hollow fiberglass drum—a likable, satisfying sound. *Blap!*

Blap! that's all. But I enjoyed the surprise so much, I dropped my hands again. This time heels first, fingers second. *Thunk. Tap.*

I strung the sounds together. *Thunk-tap-blap!*

I drummed the kayak hard like a conga. *THUNK-TAP. THUNK-TAP-BLAP!*

The cliff returned the sound in an echo. *THUNK-TAP. THUNK-TAP-BLAP!*

It bounced the spunky rhythm back like it had a life all its own—a heartbeat made audible by two hands, a kayak, and a mountain.

That was MY voice I was hearing. My SPIRIT talking. My LIFE supercharged by a MOUNTAIN. I rocked my hands, tapped my tired fingers, and there amid the *thunk-thunk-thunk tap-tap-blap* my childlike sense of wonder returned. I'd jumpstarted my green fuse.

I looked around and wherever I looked I saw beauty. It dawned like a slow brightening that comes only after a long darkness. I dipped my hands in the sea again and wiggled my fingers. For the first time, I saw the chartreuse whips of cedar rising like hopeful flames beside the falls. I paddled closer. The churning mist generated enough inner energy for me to round the last point and find camp. Beside a creek I stumbled across a lovely, eight-foot square of tamped earth. The blunt white saw cuts indicated it had been hacked out of the woods recently. It was as level as a dance floor, and I made the best use of it—dancing a happy jig—before shaking out the tent.

The very next day, fog rolled in at Point Cumming. I was plodding out of McKay Reach planning to cross Douglas Channel to Hartley Bay, a Native village voted dry by its residents. Rumor had it that the local store carried Häagen-Dazs ice cream. Here was my reward for three days of fiendish winds. But as I neared Douglas Channel, the cool dense fog pushed like a steamroller out of the mountains. It rolled down the valleys and spilled out into the sea. It rolled right over Point Cumming, *Yemaya*, and my ice-cream dream. I could taste the dream melting on my tongue as fog enveloped the kayak in a blanket of mist. It was a mist so fine I imagined a cloud of uncorked champagne. It made my skin feel effervescent.

The clear, calm night before and high humidity at sundown had laid down the perfect conditions for radiation fog. The absence of cloud cover allowed the land to shiver away its heat overnight. Moist air near the ground quickly chilled and condensed. Come morning, the lightest zephyr, maybe three knots, puffed the fog down Douglas Channel like a flying carpet. This fog was as opaque as shower glass and taller than the trees. Before I could take a compass fix, it obscured the three-mile-wide crossing over Douglas Channel to Hartley Bay.

I held out hope. Radiation fog usually burns off by late morning, unlike sea fog which can dawdle around a coast for days, socking in hundreds of miles and leaving boaters stranded. I poked north up Douglas Channel hugging the low-tide cliffs, awed by breadcrumb sponges, strawberry anemones, and scarlet blood stars looming brilliantly in the mist. Just in case it didn't burn off soon, I wanted a place to haul out. For miles, the land, what I could see of it, was a depressing battlefield of ragged stumps and mud oozing right into the intertidal pools. Fog bandaged the worst of the logging company's ransacking. Damn them! I wanted to scream and did, two lungs full of fog.

Then I saw it quite by accident—the island nearest Hartley Bay. Promise Island it's called. I smiled at the name as if it were my own private joke. I quickly took a compass reading and outfitted the deck with safety gear: flare gun, extra rounds, hand-held flare, and foghorn. I blew the paddle float up half-way and listened to the VHF weather report: *Douglas Channel, moderate afternoon winds.*

It was high noon. Wind-blown ripples striated Douglas Channel's surface. A two-knot ebb flushed south. Through curtains of fog I saw the same green-hulled sailboat I'd seen at Butedale Falls and Fraser Reach skimming silently into Douglas Channel toward Hartley Bay. It looked like a distant ghost ship, but it gave me courage. Someone else was either stupid or brave enough to navigate in fog. I sent out a cedar prayer and pushed off.

To account for drift, I aimed northwest up Douglas Channel. The rocking of the boat caused the needle of my hiker's compass to stick frequently, as it was not well damped like the pricier, domed deck compasses typically used for navigation. To keep the needle level, I tried to paddle as if I had a plate balanced on my head.

Over my shoulder, three or four miles away I guessed, the drone of a large ship vibrated over the socked-in sea from the direction of Wright Sound. The ship's horn sounded one long blast five seconds in duration every two minutes. I imagined the great hulk of steel, long as a football field, cleaving the fog beyond Point Cumming. The ship sounded eerily close.

Point Cumming lies smack on the south rim of Wright Sound. In the *Marine Atlas,* Wright Sound resembled the head of an octopus with eight channels twisting away from its core. Counterclockwise they are named McKay Reach, Verney Passage, Douglas Channel, Stewart Narrows, Grenville Channel, Cridge and Lewis Passes, and Whale Channel. Even without the fog, Wright Sound looked like an easy place to get turned around.

Groping through a shipping channel in fog was the last thing I needed. I had reduced those risks by paddling three miles up Douglas to Verney Pass. It wasn't long, an hour maybe, and Promise Island dropped its foggy shawl long enough to show its tree crowns. I looked across the last remaining stretch of channel toward Hartley Bay and saw a little sun bobbing along the water's surface.

My Goddess, it was an orange. A perfectly round offering of fruit. Fresh fruit! I stretched my arm toward it, still half suspecting it to be an aberration, until I clutched the firm roundness in my palm. I turned it over and over. No punctures. Perfect. I held it to the sky with a thank you. I sank my nails into the peel, tore open the sweet pulpy flesh with my teeth, and sucked its juice as it drooled down my chin. I had reached and gone to heaven.

The gift orange that rolled into my outstretched palm was the beginning of a horn of plenty. At Hartley Bay I tied up to the public wharf alongside *Dancer,* the sailboat I'd been tracking for two days. Dick, a Stanford University physics professor and his shipmate, Juan, a mechanic, invited me inside their galley to escape the sudden downpour and share a mug of instant chicken noodle soup. We hit it off so well that when we realized we were traveling north at the same speed, they invited me to rendezvous each evening over the next few days for dinner and a dry berth. In the morning I'd fly off up a portion of gorgeous, mountain-hemmed, forty-five-mile Grenville Channel, and at 5 P.M. I'd radio *Dancer* to find out where they'd dropped anchor.

"Dancer, do you read me? This is Jennifer, over."

"Jennifer, it's as if you're standing here now. Hope you like fresh salmon! Juan just hooked one and is cleaning it on the back deck. We're at the waterfall in Lowe Inlet."

I'd turn off Grenville Channel into Lowe Inlet after nineteen miles of bone-weary paddling with visions of grilled salmon and cheerful company. We'd eat, tell stories, and laugh into the night, then I'd exit off *Dancer*'s stern the next morning and go on my way.

The third night up Grenville, after fighting a three-knot current through the narrowest part of the channel (which is one-fifth of a mile wide and runs like a whitewater river), I radioed *Dancer* and confessed I was just too tuckered to paddle two more miles. I had to bow out.

In the middle of the night a north wind shook the still woods. My creekside tent rocked and swayed. For two days the north wind pushed against *Yemaya*'s progress. As I inched closer to Prince Rupert, the boat traffic increased and so did the glacial outflow of the Skeena River. Twelve miles from Prince Rupert, a barrel-chested Native man en route to the dentist in a fiberglass skiff "wooed" me into his boat (kayak and all) by cheerfully saying he "won't take no for an answer." I was beat from current, waves, and endless winds. He was well-meaning and friendly, so I finally obliged, in part because he promised "I'll tell you about the candlefish—oo-lah-kin—harvest, and the history of this place." I am a sucker for that kind of talk.

Turns out I was delighted for his unexpected company the last twelve miles of the journey across the Skeena River Delta. This knowledgeable fisher explained all the intricacies of catching candlefish—a kind of smelt—in the traditional method. He told how the finger-length fish were netted from canoes, buried in pits in the beach "until they got good and stinky," tossed into bentwood cedar boxes, and boiled with hot rocks and water. When the fish oil floated to the top, women skimmed off the rich residue with horn spoons and poured it into kelp tubes. Japanese scientists, he told me, call it "miracle oil" for it helps fight colds and fevers and helps the heart beat stronger. I recalled my first gulp of this odorous miracle. I burped up dead fish gas for three days afterward.

But to my chagrin, I arrived at Prince Rupert the same way I came in before—hitching.

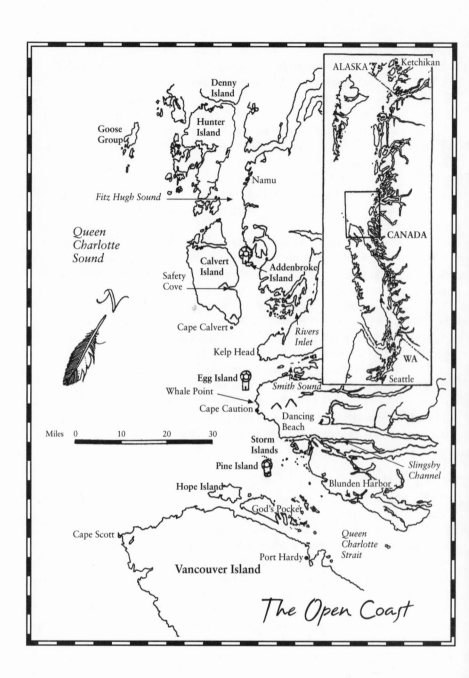

The Open Coast

Part 3

The Open Coast: Queen Charlotte Sound and Cape Caution

Summer Solstice, 100 miles, 9 days

l haada seagai gu un shanzudie gum langung.
People should not rest on the ocean.

—Haida saying

8 Eating Urchin

Tides and seasons had flooded and ebbed since my last solo paddle. It was almost summer solstice again. I was on a ferry bound for Namu, British Columbia. Rumbling away from the Port Hardy docks, headed east toward Queen Charlotte Strait, I leapt at the deck railing waving to my boyfriend—a khaki speck standing in front of a Volvo station wagon parked at a bend in the road. Excitement pummeled my heart. Tears streamed down my face. We hurled wild trills over the lengthening comet-tail wake of the *Taku*. Back and forth, farther and farther, until I could hear only water.

"The *Taku* will arrive in Namu at 5 A.M.," a cheery voice announced over the ferry's loudspeakers. On his coffee break, the friendly captain told me, "You'll have the honor of being the first paddler to use the ferry's hydraulic kayak lift."

At 4:30 A.M. hot tea and two lumps of sugar arrived at my sleeping bag, compliments of the crew. Soon, I was watching my loaded kayak sink gently down to the sea.

"How's it feel to be our first kayaker?" asked a crewman steadying the boat as I slipped into the cockpit and took up the paddle.

"Gosh, I feel like a queen."

"Well, Kayak Queen, the captain says to send his very best wishes for a safe voyage. He's watching you right now."

I looked across a small sea of early rising passengers and crew, but saw no captain. "Where is he?"

"Up there!" laughed the crewman, pointing to a little remote camera lens on the top of the ferry's door. "He's watching you through that camera!"

I waved and flashed a big grin. I appreciated the captain's concern. I could use a kayak hatch full of good wishes.

But before I made nineteen miles, I'd punctured a seeping hole in the kayak's floor after nailing the hull on the rocks below Addenbroke Lighthouse in a sloppy landing. After bushwhacking up a deer trail to the top of the island, I was befriended by two lonely lightkeepers—both bachelors. As I timidly sipped their stash of Wisers whiskey, they shared their stories of loss. A wife "gone crazy from isolation" and a long-ago lightkeeper murdered for a can of expensive paint. When I prepared to leave the next morning, the loneliest keeper, the one who'd been left by his wife, exaggerated the severity of the weather conditions in an attempt to forestall my leaving. Departing the island, Coast Guard-strength duct tape mending the kayak's damaged hull, I felt like *he* was the shipwrecked sailor in need of rescue, not me.

Edging along Fitz Hugh Sound, which was a raven's whisker from low tide, I was hungry as a sun star. Unable to restrain ravenous fingers, I fumbled for a leaf of nori draped like a spent balloon on the shoreline cliff. But I zipped past. Ungloved fingers grazed toothed barnacles and bled red. The ocean's blood and my own tasted of salt.

On deck beneath the chart cover, the tide tables read:

Low: -1.4', 8:30 A.M.

High: 16.1', 3:25 P.M.

Tide tables chalk off the fullness or emptiness of the moon's drinking vessel—the earth's continental shores. Knowing when the tide is lowest is useful information for gauging an appetite. Potential seafood buffets lie exposed. It tells the weasel when best to run away with the sea star. That day in Fitz Hugh Sound the moon's gravitational thirst would guzzle seventeen feet of ocean in seven hours. That's an exceptionally large dining hall.

The moon is always thirsty for the ocean, whether turned darkly away or full-facing, and that night the moon would float dark as December over Hunter Island. Already I could feel her nearness drinking the sea from beneath my hull. The ebb current pouring out of the Sound was so swift I could measure it dropping from the cliff.

Beside my elbow, growing taller by the minute, rose a vast, living sea wall quilted with ocean creatures and dripping seaweeds. Its jeweled surface glistened and crackled in the sunshine. Beaded here with rose anemones, there with oval buttons of black Katy chitons, over there with a hollow-toothed barnacle, and behind that droopy popweed with the open skull of an oyster. This rich intertidal necklace is one of the treasure troves of sea kayaking. I could explore a marine world without even getting my boots wet.

Below the hull, scarlet feather duster worms swayed easy as flowers from calcified stalks. Bread sponges, cratered and pocked as moonscapes, glowed chartreuse green from fissures. Wedged in the lips of a crevasse, bunches of Pacific mussels smiled fat orange grins under blue hard hats. A clownish decorator crab groped about in sea lettuce. Tiny hooks on the crab's head and back allow it to camouflage its shell with bits of algae clutter. It trundled by like a high school parade float under a profusion of sea lettuce roses. Some scientists believe this mobile garden is a convenient grazing source as well as a disguise. A breeze chipped the sea's surface and the decorator crab disappeared into stained glass oblivion.

The world viewed through the sea's shifting surface evoked an Impressionist's canvas. Colors shivered and coiled, sea stars and mussels slid into ochre-violet ribbons, sea lettuce blurred, everywhere a wind seemed present. Squinting down past the kayak's shadow into deep water, creatures were transformed into luminous patches of carnelian, rose, and fuchsia.

Intertidal places, where water conceals the shore twice each day then draws its protective sleeve away, make for rugged living quarters. Animals and plants that evolved in this narrow belt thrive in extremes. Soaked in saltwater at high tide, then splayed out to the sun, galloping surf, rain storms, and gale-force winds during low tide, they are survivors of a lunar-crazed, shape-shifting country—a country that is desert as often as it is ocean. Consequently, more living and dying occurs in this narrow pulse than anywhere else on earth.

I soon discovered that if I made a V with boat and cliff, a breakwater formed. Wavelets ironed smooth. Swatches of red focused into pie-size sea urchins. Not a meager handful, nor a baker's dozen, but hundreds of giant red urchins blazed like wildfire on a fur of swaying sea lettuce. From the depth on my chart, I guessed this tribe might be chewing on sea algae another forty feet down, but they disappeared into a frost of white plumed anemones.

The giant red urchin, which tips the scale at one pound, is the heftiest urchin on the Pacific Coast. Its oval exoskeleton blossoms seven inches across and can reach ten inches. Add a 360-degree armor of spines and you're looking at a basketball-size porcupine with a voracious appetite for kelp. Five equidistant rows of tubular feet rise up the side of an urchin's body. The urchin's mouth hides underneath.

Red urchins are in the family "spiny skin" or echinoderm. Other spiny skins include the sea cucumber, a worm-like animal resembling a rubber war club with a mop of tentacles at one end for swabbing up plankton. Once the tentacles are saturated, the cuke merely hauls the mop inside its tubular body and, lickety-split, cleans it off as you might a hand dipped in chocolate syrup.

Sea stars, whose rays can number as many as twenty-three, are also echinoderms. "Starfish," the most common name for sea stars, is a misnomer, since they haven't a bone in common with fish. If you lifted a sea star's legs so that the tips all touched on top, you would have the skeletal mimic of a sea urchin. Like the urchin, the sea star's mouth is underneath.

One primary difference between the two is their dining style. Sea stars would be embarrassing dinner guests. Extruding gelatinous bellies on top of their platters of food is a regular affair. Urchins, like you and me, digest their food in secret.

Perhaps the kin most similar to urchins are the sand dollars. If you look carefully, a sand dollar is merely a sea urchin in flattened form. Hold a living creature in your hand and you'll feel a cat's tongue roughness. That's because, above and below, the coin-shaped disk is shingled with thousands of minute spines. Underwater, the dark purple-brown spines seem almost velvety in appearance. Spent sand dollars bleach white and lose their spines, revealing a delicate flower stamped beneath. The stippled petals are for the protrusion of tube feet. Like sea urchins, sand dollars travel by wave-like movements of spines and tube feet.

Millions of years ago when the first Lawrence-of-Arabia urchins left the rocky coast and struck out across the sand to search for new territory, the most successful evolved ever shorter spines and flattened out from a dome to a shovel. Given an evolutionary journey that spanned millennia, they eventually developed the skill of plowing through the sand and straining out minute food particles. Some varieties even feed collectively, tipping on end like a wagon-wheel fence line. Sea urchins thrive on shores with firm bottoms. Tidal channels harbor the densest cities of red urchin—sometimes more than thirty per square yard. Sand dollars by their very name tell you where they live and feed.

Besides the color red, sea urchins also come in purple and green. The purple ones are the smallest. Unlike other urchins, their blunt, inch-long spines lie flat like a blowdown of trees. Green urchins are bristly and about the size and shape of a horse chestnut burr.

Green, purple, and red sea urchins are edible. I discovered that in 1983 back in British Columbia's Octopus Islands when my dream of a solo kayak adventure whispered its awakening. Stuffing beach rocks into unzipped wetsuits, five of us sank like ship anchors to the foot of Octopus Island. With only one mammalian breath per dive, as we dropped we viewed the quickly passing cliff animated with swaying sea anemones, sunflower sea stars large as our torsos, and gumboot chitons scarlet and elongated as cow's tongues. We almost missed the giant red urchins. Four of them were teetering across the cliff as if on magic stilts.

Alan, the ethnologist among us, pointed them out. Earlier, he'd described how the natives caught and ate urchin—or sea eggs, as they were fondly called. The Old Ones of Haida Gwai (Queen Charlotte Islands) called a stretch of coastline *"Eating sea urchins while you are floating."* Using kelp to anchor their cedar canoes, hunters leaned out still as herons and speared urchins off underwater boulders. A sharpened huckleberry or ironwood spike lashed to the spear's tip pinned the urchin in place. Once caught, the sea eggs were lifted into the canoe and often cracked open on the spot. The Haida simply inserted a finger into the broken shell, scraping out the gonads, and devoured the tasty morsel raw. From the grin of Alan's blue-tinted lips, I could see he hoped to catch one by the stilts for dinner.

Emptying our wetsuits of rock ballast, we popped up to the surface with two urchins in tow. Opening the urchin we found five neat packets of roe clinging to the walls like gelatinous orange slices. Often referred to as roe or eggs, it's really the gonads you eat. Both male and female urchins are harvested for eating, though even a biologist would be hard pressed to tell you the sex.

Passing the urchin half like a bowl, we spooned out the raw roe. There wasn't much else inside. Spit balls of green seaweed. A strange veil of mucus.

Eaten raw, the taste is a wild one. A kayaking pal folds the golden roe into melted butter, garlic, and warm cream cheese for a cracker spread. Urchin is delicious when added to omelets or soups, too.

Traditionally, people all around the Pacific Rim from Japan to Mexico ate urchin. Today, most Westerners flinch at the thought. The Japanese, however, fork out top yen—up to twenty-five dollars a pound—for choice, bright yellow or orange roe. Aesthetic tastes, not taste buds, sense the difference. A professional urchin diver once told me, "The Japanese eat with their eyes." Apparently so. Prices sag below a dollar per pound for less desirable, brown-tinted roe.

Having plucked most of Hokaido and Honshu clean of urchin, "the land of the rising sun" now relies on imports from as far away as Chile, Australia, Denmark, the United States, and Canada. In 1994, Japan gobbled up thirteen million pounds of urchin valued at more than $250 million. One tenth of that was hand-picked by British Columbia's commercially licensed urchin divers. These strictly regulated scuba-clad souls swim along the Inside Passage's kelp beds hour after hour selecting the best urchins.

On the international market, fresh urchin is prized. Within seventy-two hours after live sea eggs are plunked on the docks of Vancouver's processing plants, the golden nuggets are gently removed, rinsed in saline, soaked in a potassium-aluminum solution, dabbed with paper towels, painstakingly arranged in 80- to 300-gram trays, and flown to the far side of the Pacific Rim. From the friendly skies into Tokyo's Tsukiji wholesale fish market and the trucks of sundry sushi companies with names like "Jet Fresh" and "Jet Marine," the urchin—*uni* in Japanese—eventually arrives on a happy tongue.

Staring down into the water of Fitz Hugh Sound, my hungry tongue remembered the briny decadence of the first roe I lapped up in the Octopus Islands decades ago. If I can coax an urchin into my kayak, I will gratefully savor its mousse-like insides spread over pilot biscuits.

Only I had no spear, just bare hands made more determined, perhaps more ingenious, by the hunger of an eleven-mile morning. The closest urchin looks to be at least an arm's length down. But I couldn't be sure. Every fisher worth her salt knows water is a magnifying lens. What lies below looks twenty-five percent bigger than life. How many fish magically shrink as they come hurling by hook and line into the choking air? Besides water's elusive way of making creatures look larger, things, urchin-like things, may appear closer than they are. My mind chewed on this. My stomach rolled up my sleeves.

The clarity of water in Fitz Hugh Sound that afternoon wrapped me in its spell. It held a kind of intoxicating transparency that made me want to jump right out of the kayak cockpit, sprout fins, tail, and hoary whiskers, and swear to live as simply as a sea mammal forever. But as soon as I leaned to the side the water piled underneath the hull's up-current side and nearly flung me over. When I sat upright again it carried the kayak down coast as if by an invisible leash. Unlike the Haida who speared urchins from dugouts, I had no kelp for anchoring.

And where was the kelp anyhow? This cliff provided ideal growing conditions—forty feet of water. At low tide I'd expect to bump over drifts of copper leaves and stipes. The stipes, or stems, of giant kelp and bullwhip kelp are held aloft by gas floats. Consequently, low tide sends languid bullwhip kelp sprawling across the water's surface like a disarray of organ pipes. A handful can anchor a kayak from wind or current. Jacques Cousteau called these dancing ninety-foot long skeins of copper leaves and stems "the sequoias of the sea." Something major was missing.

A story I heard from a marine biologist I'd met earlier on Vancouver Island slowly circled up. Jane Watson called giant red urchins the unequivocal "lawn mowers of the sea." Jane ought to know. For years she's gone on daily scuba dives off Vancouver Island's outermost coast to monitor the balance, or rather imbalance, between urchins and kelp. Watching these hungry blade runners cruise along the sea floor, rhythmic jaws opening and closing on the underside, cutting a winding swath clean as a John Deere mower, is part of Jane's work. John Deeres, like urchins, make no distinction between a prize tea rose and a dandelion. Chomping up tree kelp, giant kelp, wing kelp, and bull whip kelp, as well as sea squirts and tunicates—a soft-skinned ancestor to the urchin cemented to the ocean floor—is all part of a day's cutting, Jane told me.

In spring and summer when the kelp is high and the living easy, urchins mow along the edges of the great undersea kelp forests. Come fall and winter when storms tear up the remaining kelp beds, they hunker down and wait for kelp to drift their way. The urchin's three-inch spines act like strainers to hook shreds of algae. Catching whatever comes hither is called "drift feeding." As my friend Rick Harbo, another marine biologist, likes to say, "The currents are delivering the groceries."

And it's true. Following a slam-bang Pacific storm, rafts of uprooted kelp drift shoreward dragging their golden leaves like the tendrils of a jellyfish. En route, leaves tear loose. Some drop right on top of the urchins' heads. Specialized "feet" grab hold. Working together, the feet and spines pass kelp shreds to the mouth on the underside of the shell the way a line of fire fighters works a hose hand-to-hand toward a hungry fire.

To suction onto kelp or to magically ascend cliffs as swiftly as a high-tech climber, red urchins need only a hydraulic vacuum and mucus. Between the thick ranks of spines, two thousand suction-tipped "feet" act like ropes to yard the urchin vertically up a rock or to snag a passing shred of delicious kelp.

Like starlings, crows, and park pigeons, urchins are amazingly adaptable. During lean times, purple urchins can reabsorb their skeleton and actually shrink their body size. An undersea famine can occur during an El Niño climate cycle when warm, nutrient-poor waters kill cold-water-loving kelps. Red urchins survive the loss by supping on a thin broth of diatoms, tiny microscopic plants pulsing through the ocean current. No one knows how long urchins live. Using computer models, one urchin specialist theorized it could be fifty or more years.

An undersea city of geriatric urchins is devastating. Scientists call the clear-cuts they create "urchin barrens." They nibbled their once luxuriant kelp forest down to a handful of lucky plants hidden in rock crevasses.

Sea otters. Urchins. Kelp. These three protagonists are wedded together by an ever-changing drama of appetites dating back to the first Alaskans. The seafaring Aleuts speared otter from skin kayaks called baidarkas. Aleut hunters were so successful they decimated sea otters from parts of their northernmost range. Consequently, without a predator to keep them in check, the local urchins swelled in number and size. Archaeological digs in Aleut kitchen middens on Amchitka Island—the farthest in the Aleutian chain—revealed shards of enormous urchins cake-layering the beaches. A clan of hungry otters would have feasted on the big fellas—roe, spine, and barrel.

When kelp beds are diminished it's like taking an evolutionary back step. Coastal ecology is oversimplified. Diversity is bereft of algae, plants, abalone, and sea stars. Fish that once hid from predators in the undulating curtains of kelp join the ranks of the homeless.

Below my kayak, the giant red urchin seemed to call to me. As soon as I dipped my naked arm to touch it, fifty-degree water sparkled numbness to my elbow. The boat rocked wildly. I needed something solid to hold on to or I'd spill right over. Looking around, I thought, why not trust my weight to a hefty horse barnacle? They secrete some of the strongest marine cement on this watery planet. It should hold.

Pinching the thumb-size barnacle between my fingers, I leaned the kayak up on its edge. My free arm shuttled back and forth along the cliff. I touched nothing. The urchin was deeper. But how much?

Without sensible pause, I leaned farther . . . a little bit more . . . then nearly upside down. What happened next I might once have pegged as serendipity, but now I believed it was the sea talking to me. With my head half underwater and still no urchin at my fingertips, my hat became waterborne and floated off. I sloshed upright and snatched it up. Shaking it off, I heard a desperate little voice whispering, "*Use the hat to net the urchin.*"

Of course. Holding the hat by its brim, my arm transformed into a makeshift urchin scoop. I felt as wily as an otter.

With hat in hand, the hunt for my seafood dinner transformed into a slow underwater ballet. As my arm swept slowly downward, trails of shivering bubbles roiled from the tilted cap. The white hat settled sweetly around the sea egg like a horseshoe on a stake. At the same moment as I began lifting I imagined the urchin, surprised by this sudden intrusion, beginning to stipple the hat's fabric with leagues of sure-stick'em tube feet. Though, truthfully, I wasn't sure if my scoop had scored until I felt a substantial weight as the prize broke the water's surface. Out of the water, holding the capped urchin on my spray

skirt, I realized the creature fit my hat so utterly well that it proved I have a head the size of an urchin. With the hatted sea porcupine clipped under the deck bungee cord, I paddled us to shore.

Floating through the Inside Passage, taking on the work of a fisher or a gatherer, I felt like a sea otter or weasel searching out, capturing, and killing for my life. Cunning and patience evolved. The five senses bristled awake, growing eyeteeth, sprouting whiskers.

I know this much: There is nothing quite like hunkering over a beach fire tending a freshly caught lingcod resting in a fry pan atop a quilt of coals, then afterward leaving shore to paddle over some icy strait. I feel the vigorous sinew of the fish swelling inside my own strong arms, the eyes seeing again through my own cod-black pupils. The fish resurfaces.

Every wild creature has to fuel itself. Glaucous-winged gulls tweeze crabs from kelp beds then drop them like hand grenades—*ker-splat*—on headlands before devouring their demolished victims. At low tide, black bears paw over beach rocks and nuzzle up shore crabs. A weasel runs away with yet another sea star.

Wendell Berry said it well enough. "The shortest distance from the earth to your mouth is the best." The interstate miles stretching from my mouth to a vacuum-sealed soup packet is a lot greater than the distance spanned by a clam to my cookpot. Biting into an apple plucked and airlifted from a tree growing seven thousand miles away in New Zealand requires some innate imagination to be thankful of its roots. And so, traveling along this fecund coastline, I started to follow my external cues.

I took my seat at the intertidal table. Plucking mussels from white-whiskered headlands where waves soaked my sleeves I felt a kind of belonging—belonging not just to my appetite, but to the tide, moon, and booming waves. The boundaries separating us fell away like scales.

At its most basic, eating urchin is refueling. At its most profound, eating urchin is shape-changing, carrying the wisdom and muscle-twitch and perspective of another being inside of you. Eating with thankfulness that which grows close at hand became a prayer of sorts.

It was a good sixty feet from the water's edge to the kitchen beach log I straddled. I set the animal in front of me. Surprisingly, the sea urchin tiptoed on its red stilts across the log's curve headed straight for the sea. How amazing that it teetered toward the ocean side of the log, not the forest. I watched it tumble off, uninjured.

Solomon Wilson, a Haida elder born in 1887 and hereditary chief of Haina Village or "Sunshine-house Village," said that urchins, abalone, and cockles found alive in the woods were revered as good omens by the Haida. If a person ate the animal raw on the spot, carried the shell home, hid it in some secret place, and never mentioned it again, good fortune would follow.

I scooped the urchin off the beach. Dozens of scarlet, blunt-tipped spines danced against my soft palms. Fine grooves like those on a knife-sharpening file were etched in the spine's surface. A sheath of magenta skin shone with life. Where each spine spoked out from the skin an ochre sleeve rose up to hold it, just as the flight muscle of a bird gathers around each individual feather.

"You are beautiful, urchin," I said. "More like a blood-red sun than a sea creature."

At age five, with tiny hands pressed together like butterfly wings and eyes squinted tight in concentration, I prayed these words at every Lutheran dinner:

Come Lord Jesus be our guest and to these gifts may we be blessed. Amen.

I was reciting exactly the words every Lutheran kid on our block recited as a quick route to our pork chops and Pillsbury Crescent Rolls, Birdseye unfrozen vegetables, and glass of whole milk. It was a generic dinner prayer for a generic dinner. I spoke the grace quickly and in a near whisper— *ComeLordJesusbeourguest*—not to thank Jesus, but to be given permission to eat. I spoke it by rote night after night because I didn't know the reason for the prayer.

Thirty years later on this wave-washed beach holding an urchin in my rough hands, my heart was not afraid to speak out loud, to talk with everything. Harlequin duck. Cedar tree. Blue-handed hermit crab. Frilled dogwinkle. Eel grass. Drift log. Sea. These were my companions, teachers, elders, and some were my nourishment. Salmonberry. Pickleweed. Sitka rose.

Sea Urchin, you are my sister, I said returning her to the earth. Kneeling down beside her, I could hear my friend Whitebear saying, "You must try to do some things from your knees."

I unsheathed my knife. The stainless blade bears this stamp:

AR

MADRONA

Adrienne Richards, a gifted knife maker on Lopez Island, forged the blade and shaped the wood handle. It fits my grip as if a part of me. I like that. Long ago I nicked some hide from the leather sheath and cemented a cowry shell in the hollow. It's a symbol as close to labia as I can imagine. Adrienne might appreciate that. Crafting tools with hammer and flame, she inspired an image of

Brigitte, the Irish goddess of fire. On the knife cord, I've strung a glass "eye bead" to remind me that I must use the knife with mercy. Three ovoid blue irises watched me as I began my work.

I turned the urchin upside-down on the gravel. It teetered, but I held it still by gripping it between the spines with one hand. Pacific Northwest species do not have venomous spines as some tropical urchins do.

On the urchin's underside, a wreath of glossy red flesh hid the mouth. Its uncanny resemblance to a vulva unnerved me slightly. Behind the O-ed lips hid five spade-shaped teeth joined like flower petals. This peculiar chewing apparatus led me to wonder if this wet-toothed cave wasn't the origin of the Northwest Coast's snapping vagina myths, in which dentations sometimes line the vagina like snake teeth.

I closed my eyes for a moment. The urchin spines rotated on their sockets inside my palms. Waves hushed their white breath up the broadening beach. A raven chortled. Killing does not come easy.

When I finally speared the center through the five white teeth and began rocking the blade to break the shell, the spines reacted forcefully, collapsing inward like felled trees. They blocked the knife's work. I tried to break through them. The grating sound of knife on porcelain sideswiped my focus. Do sea otters feel the pangs of killing urchins for their dinner?

"Knife be swift to free this spirit," I heard myself say.

One more rasping cut and the urchin cracked in two equal halves. I tipped them over. Sea water, minced sea lettuce, and intestines spilled out. Clinging to the inside walls were five segments of pumpkin-orange urchin meat. Each crescent moon of slippery seeds was as wide as my thumb.

I scooped a fleck of roe onto my knife, smeared the seeds on my tongue. They felt cool like the sea and tasted of oysters and salt. I ate slowly, feeling the coolness melt on my tongue, slide cool down my throat. I ate until the urchin bowls were empty.

Thirty feet above my head, huge brown wings row over, hushing softly as they pass. A bald eagle. It felt like a sign. I reached for the empty urchin. Though the innards were gone, the spines still rotated about on their own will. For a long while I held the restless urchin halves on my lap and looked out.

The sky over Calvert Island is lapis lazuli and ash, the color of a Stellar's jay. It was time. I'd waited, but I didn't know why. Now it came to me. I broke one spine from the urchin's body and put it in the pouch around my neck. I broke a sprig of cedar from the boughs on my kayak's stern, crumbling the fragrant leaves into the empty urchin halves. Crouching at the edge of the sea, I nudged the bowls adrift. They bobbed on the still water like tea cups.

Ebb tide carried them south away from the beach. Where the urchin floated free of the inlet, wind splintered the ocean's surface into a thousand mirrors. The sea turned to fire. Now the urchin cups drifted as if carried by a lighted voyager, a funeral pyre burning silently toward Queen Charlotte Sound. My ancestors, Danish Vikings, honored their dead this way. This was my offering.

9 Whale Watching Me

Looking south across four-mile-wide Rivers Inlet, the kayak rode up and down in buttery swells while I considered the options. I was two days south of Addenbroke Island and feeling the personality of the wide Pacific beginning to dominate the quieter channels that flagged her side. Should I leapfrog island to island in a zigzag southeast-to-south route? Or, because it was a relatively calm morning, perhaps I could be courageous and take the straightest line across no matter the exposure? I chose to parallel a necklace of islets up the inlet, then reevaluate partway across.

What I loved most about long kayak crossings is how the sea overtook all my senses. Eventually, halfway across, I'd be completely deprived of the aroma of soil, ferns, forest, rock. Following a multi-mile crossing, the returning aroma of the land never failed to stir my heart with gratitude.

The water rimming the once distant island on the far side of Rivers Inlet was spunky, alive. With each incoming swell, *Yemaya* danced toward the bouldered perimeter then soared backward with the rebound wave. The rhythm was mesmerizing. And while I was watching to be sure the bow didn't puncture again, I was also playing with the energy of the sea—back paddling at just the right moment, forward stroking to get back into the dance step.

At last, tired, I paddled out of the swells to the leeward side of the forested island, removed my glasses, laid down the paddle, and drifted. A winter wren trilled its territorial symphony. Below me, a school of herring jumped at the sight of my predator-size boat. A curious seal zoomed out of sight in the dark water. Next time I looked down, it lay perfectly still in *Yemaya*'s shadow staring up at me from three feet under the surface, its flippers folded as if in prayer.

The Rivers Inlet-Smith Inlet Basin is exactly what its name implies—a heartland of rivers and creeks, twenty of them to be precise. All five species of Pacific salmon—sockeye, chum, pink, chinook, and coho—once thrived here in salmon heaven. Long ago, when the world's greatest sockeye runs swarmed the plushly forested river valleys, this was a place of mythic proportions. One enormous salmon is reported to have towed a fisher in his boat five miles down the inlet.

So what happened? It's a story that repeats itself up and down the coast. In the name of progress and profit, nineteenth-century investors sealed the fame of these legendary salmon runs by clapping them into the tin coffins of twenty clickity-clackity canneries. More recently, reckless logging companies shaved away enough old-growth fir, hemlock, and cedar to suffocate much of the river's remaining sockeye salmon eggs with silt. Rivers Inlet's sockeye numbers plunged from over three million in the late 1960s to sixty-five thousand now. One-of-a-kind subspecies were driven to extinction.

As I paddled along the inlet's south shore I noted derelict canneries moldered on rotting pilings. Deep inside the inlet's nooks, sport fishing lodges of modest and immodest proportions catered to an international clientele.

South of Sharbau Island, on the south shore of River's Inlet, I passed an aluminum skiff with two friendly fishers who told me they were lodging at Goose Bay. One steered the motor prop while the other grappled with a pole bent to sea just like a fish hook. Record-breaking salmon haven't surfaced in Rivers Inlet since the 1950s when the heftiest chinook reeled in by sport fishing tackle tipped the scales to eighty-two pounds. After a few minutes of tugging and reeling, a sixteen-inch orange rock fish surfaced.

"Oh well," the man said, shrugging. "Nice eagle food. Watch this. They love to come down and get a handout."

He whistled like one might call a family dog. Two bald eagles floated down from the crown of spruce and circled the boat's bow. Their wings and white tail fans tilted with each wind gust. One whistled back plaintively. The fisher whistled again and tossed the fish. The larger bird dropped to the water with yellow talons outspread. It swung powerful legs backward and snagged the fish. Eagle and wriggling prey rose from the sea. With the fish as ballast, the eagle was no longer tossed by the gusting wind. Like one animal now, they banked toward a spruce tree.

"That fish just grew wings," I shouted.

"Great big ones," the man yelled back, opening arms wide.

Grant and Barry at Addenbroke Lighthouse had told me that the resident eagles recognized the distinctive buzz a fishing reel makes as a fish runs with the hook. The whirring brings them out of the trees toward the fishing skiff.

For the next three miles, I beat down Rivers Inlet against a ripping headwind. Every so often I tucked the kayak behind a leeward point to catch my breath, then bucked west again. It was exhausting. I was hoping to find a camp soon. A half-mile ahead was land's end—Kelp Head—the last protected anchorage before encountering the Pacific's full-bore exposure.

An aluminum skiff with two more fishers came busting around the headland as I approached. I waved, hoping to get a report on sea conditions. Fifty feet distant the pilot was yelling something, but I couldn't make out a word. Then a gust snapped my hat off. In the last two minutes the wind seemed to have gotten noticeably worse.

I sprinted for the floating hat and the skiff motored alongside. A father and son huddled in fluorescent orange float vests. Behind them a plastic tub with two halibut as big as pizza pans flopped about.

"How are the seas beyond Kelp Head?"

"Until a half hour ago, we were having a great time out here." He pointed to the fish. "Two halibut, small ones, five pounds, but what the hey? Came in 'cause we were taking waves over the side. Where you headed?"

"Cape Caution."

"Really? You don't want to go out there now. Sea's building—fast. Wait 'til tomorrow. Weather's supposed to improve. Wind's gonna die down to nothing."

Nothing?! I felt a geyser of joy gushing inside me at those words. "GREAT! Well, thanks for saving me a look."

"Good luck. Be safe."

I headed in to make camp on a sandy beach just inside Kelp Head.

Paddling toward Kelp Head the next day, my heart held still while I measured the danger. I was leaving a cove of vertical trees and entering the wind's house—though no one was home right then, as the fisher had promised. Even on a calm day I could see that outer Kelp Head was a wind-pressed country. Bushes crawled across the rocks like prostrating monks to avoid the blast of Pacific storms. Full-grown trees twisted into bonsai with mere brush strokes for needles. Grasses grew in alert wedges like someone's blown-back hair. Every plant left me with a mistaken impression of a wind still present. I felt terror filling my heart just looking at them.

I'd dreaded this leg of the journey through Queen Charlotte Sound and around Cape Caution ever since I'd talked on the phone a year before with kayak guru Randel Washburne. He'd warned, "Wait for a weather break."

That break had come. I was ready for my second "threshold."

Place names can tell you a lot about the personality of local waters. The names along this stretch of open coast would give the most daring pause: Safety Cove, Storm Islands, God's Pocket, Cape Caution, Shelter Bay, Sorrow Island. Looking at a *Marine Atlas*, it's easy to see how the ocean can grow so nasty here. There is nothing but open ocean for forty grueling miles.

But exposure is only part of the challenge. Chaotic water conditions haunt the region, especially during ebb tides. Imagine Queen Charlotte Sound as a huge drainage ditch transporting the water from hundreds of miles of fjords out to the open Pacific, from Fitz Hugh Sound in the north to Queen Charlotte Strait in the southeast. That means the ebb flows west. Ocean swells pushed by sea winds galumph east. Everything is trying to pass in opposite directions through the same portal between Cape Scott on Vancouver Island to the south and Cape Calvert on Calvert Island to the north. The result: sumo wrestling matches under your hull.

Even with a zephyr westerly and moderate swells, the Queen's Pond, as Queen Charlotte Sound is fondly known, can deal a dirty deck. Diesel tugs towing log booms have idled for half a month waiting for better weather in which to cross. In severe cases, hurricane-force winds have whipped the waves to almost unbelievable heights of ninety to a hundred feet! Seaworthy purse seiners have been battered to shreds near Pine Island. Cape Caution, with its fast-shoaling bottom, has wreaked havoc on many a boat and life.

All this darkened my mind as I paddled out through the placid bay and around land's end. To distract myself as I worked into the first swells, I reviewed the day's ambitious route in my head. Fourteen miles to Cape Caution, two miles around it, then seven more to Slingsby Channel. Slingsby offered the first escape route where I could turn east and travel up a fjord if I needed to.

Rounding Kelp Head, the bow vaulted up an astonishingly large wall of green water and sank softly into the wave's trough. I felt swallowed. I couldn't see the horizon inside that opaque scoop. That first big swell skittered the kayak sideways at an alarming speed. I was rushing back toward the headland. Surf pounded fifteen yards away. My heart drummed like a lovelorn grouse inside the hull of my yellow jacket.

My mind reeled. I expected to smash into the headland any second. DO SOMETHING! Adrenaline bolted into my arms and hands. I lunged the paddle blade into the glassy wall to speed up. The kayak rose. The view returned. I emerged forty yards from the pounding surf line. Shaken, I was surprised to be so far out.

Things under water appear twenty-five percent larger than they are. Under the lens of fear, things seem even more magnified. I was rife with fear. Where did reality end and imagination begin? My worst frailty was not physical, but in my mind—shunting my fantastical imaginings of spilling over, sinking helplessly, choking in a cold frightening sea. I could drown a thousand deaths today and never leave the boat.

True, the swells were bigger than I'd expected. But were they only amplified by the headland or the ebb tide? It was too early to tell. I had to keep going to know. If I only knew then that by the end of the day I'd be eye to eye with a whale, the tumultuous seas would have been easier to handle. But at the time, only the next fifteen feet mattered—the distance between me and the next cresting wave.

I lost sight of the horizon again and again. I felt a tinge of relief every time the kayak rose from a trough. My eyes quickly remembered to sharpen on those upswings, to take in vital details and hold them in a gestalt before I fell back into the valley. There was only the measure of rise and fall. How many rises and falls were there between here and Cape Caution?

Receding headlands appeared in layers of mussel-shell blue trimmed in oyster gray toward the misty horizon as far as I could see south down the rugged coast. A handful of island outposts lay scattered between.

My mind flicked like a Rolodex full of snapshots of solo kayakers I'd known. I recalled the names of adventurous men and women who, through luck and solid judgment, had logged years of experience under their hulls, and died doing what they loved. One day, the sea embraced them and didn't let go.

Did I really need to do this section after all? Why risk my life to paddle this treacherous piece of coast? Once I committed, I might be unable to land for untold miles. What if the wind picked up? Ambling along at 3 or 4 mph, I might not have the speed to escape to safety. I'd just have to deal. God, was I loony?

I looked west to Queen Charlotte Sound and the milky Pacific warbling on the horizon. It felt as if the sea were a huge reverberating drum skin stretched across the Pacific Rim. And somewhere far beyond, where human eyes couldn't see, a huge mallet hit the surface. It shook the drum skin sending swells out toward the edge where I paddled. What if the wind's mallet struck harder?

I glanced east to the mainland where I'd come from. Waves exploded in a spray of white manes along rock cliffs. I shuddered at the sound of their KAHH-BOOM! I felt nauseated, taut-stomached.

I looked north over my stern. Blue-shouldered Calvert Island watched from the horizon like a big brother. There wasn't a boat in sight from Calvert Island south. Not a human anywhere. I was alone. Rising, falling. Atop the next swell, I glanced toward the land again. Two bald eagles hunched on a skeleton shore pine looked out to sea.

Other life besides me! I spoke to them.

"Eagles, I am so scared," I yelled.

I sank into another trough.

When I came up, the eagles' heads had turned. Their golden bills were arrowed right on the kayak. I felt pierced by their gaze.

I dropped into the next trough praying aloud. *I need strength to make this long and difficult journey. Pleeeease, help me be strong.* And as I rose over the crest I felt something powerful pass between bird and human like an invisible zap of electrical current. Immediately I felt calmer. I palpably released all of my frenetic tension and dread. Bold confidence leapt into my heart like a torch ignited by an unseen spark. I turned to the eagles and raised my paddle.

"Thank you for watching over me," I shouted. "I wish you many fish and children!"

The Bella Bella people say eagles open the door to the spirit world. After praying to them, I relaxed and sank the paddle blade in deeper. I committed my everything to the journey.

Two marbled murrelets corked up beside the cockpit inches from my paddle blade. Each bird looked no bigger than my fist. Just a brown and white swirl of feathers and a conic head. As we passed in opposite directions, their tiny feet stroked so fast—one-two-one-two—that their heads bobbed.

Ah, maybe, it wasn't size after all, I mused. Maybe it was adaptability and persistence.

Marbled murrelets are the epitome of both. Sleeping all night in old-growth forests miles inland. Winging to the coast before sunrise. Feeding all day on ocean herring. Returning to nesting sites in the mossy branches after sundown. They looked like they belonged out there. I decided, admiring their ease, that I belonged there, too.

After seeing the eagles and murrelets and realizing I was not really entirely alone, I passed over a threshold. I slipped into a state of mind as simple as this: surrender. Whatever awaited me was okay. I was exactly where I needed to be. This life. This open coast. This body. I had been plopped into my rightful place: upright in the waves in that little grin of a kayak. The moment felt utterly full and intoxicating.

Though just minutes before everything seemed perfectly wrong, it now seemed perfectly right—even the danger. And danger was everywhere—the forty-five-degree water below my tush, the rock-buttressed shore, the no-nonsense overture of the swells hammering the rocky coast fifty yards away. Yet, I swear on forty sacred texts, I loved that tilt toward danger. It felt beautiful, because it amped my six senses. I was ALIVE!

Looking around, I thought I'd never felt such a powerful place. The crashing surf now looked astoundingly beautiful. It was no longer frightening. I felt drawn to it. Tempting fate, I drifted to within a few feet of an exploding reef and watched. Glassy waves curled over the rocks and rumbled white. As the waves withdrew, I was rewarded by the song of a dozen waterfalls pouring over tiered stone and hula-dancing sea palms.

Three miles down the open coast, all was well. False Egg Island towered off-shore marking north Smith Sound. The "real" Egg Island, complete with light-house, was visible four miles farther down coast at the southern flank of Smith Sound. The hair-raising ocean swells had ironed out to a kiddy pool. Wind was a whisper on my cheek. Ebb tide was flushing me south at a thrilling speed. I

Rare Sea Palms
Postelsia palmaeformis

Thrive on surf-pummeled, wild coasts.

made progress faster than expected. Only one thing seemed rotten in paradise that morning—the air. It stank of sulfur and putrid eggs—like a pulp mill!

I couldn't believe I was paddling through the heart of a wilderness Eden, yet the stench of the paper mills on Vancouver Island reached my nose. I'd know that nauseating odor anywhere, even seventeen miles north of Vancouver Island, for crow's sake!

Then I saw the real culprit: a cloud as tall as a sail mast, but misty and funnel-shaped. It was unmistakable against the spruce trees of False Egg Island. Only then did I register the true source of the smell. I'd inhaled the same sulfurous odor at Ivory Island lighthouse. Never one to miss a gag, Dennis, the lightkeeper, had accused me of farting at the dinner table—though he knew full well that a couple of gray whales had just belched under his kitchen window. Now I laughed at myself as I watched the "toxic pulp mill cloud" drift off and a new cloud appear.

Before paddling closer, I asked the whale to let me be an observer, not a threat. Floating twenty yards away, watching with binoculars, I could see a bulging cap of water where the gray whale shuttled back and forth like a forty-foot school bus. Every so often, its back burst above the sea and an enormous spray of shrimpy gas shot up from twin blow holes. I was pleasantly drenched, or maybe I should say stenched, for I felt like a floating houseplant just misted with some fertilizer made of fish entrails.

Sixteenth-century mariners believed a whale's spout could upend their boats. In 1554, Pierre Belm wrote erroneously of the right whale (so called because it did not sink when killed) that it exhales a jet of water "sometimes with such violence that ships have been capsized by it." Ancient navigational charts writhed with sea monsters half whale, half serpent, spewing geysers as powerful as Old Faithful. Of course it was all nonsense and fish-tales.

The gentle gray whale puffing off False Egg Island exhaled a misty plume then folded into a graceful dive. As the whale disappeared, the bumps of its spine turned over link by link like a chain. The water boiled and sudsed. I imagined the great whale feeding in the sun-lit curtains down below. Scientists used to think grays plowed through the bottom mud like giant bulldozers. But that's not the case. Their skin is far too sensitive and easily abraded. Besides, the benthic critters that the grays eat live in the top two centimeters of sludge.

With the advent of the Aqua-Lung, scuba divers were the first to ogle a gray whale chowing down. Gray whales forage leaned over on their right sides with their jaw parallel to, but not scraping, the sea floor. They cruise along the bottom whoofing up tiny crustaceans, shrimps, and sea butterflies. Hovering above a yummy colony of tube-dwelling amphipods, the whale depresses its muscular tongue, creating a pulsing suction. The morsels are vacuumed up like fleas from a carpet.

Each "pulse" leaves an imprint in the ocean sediment. Divers have measured imprints spanning three feet by five feet—the size of your refrigerator or a whale's head. During one feeding dive, a gray whale might leave six impressions all lined up like stitches on a quilt. Some whorl out from a central point, like the petals of a daisy. These are the hieroglyphics of appetite.

As appetites go, gray whales are generalists. Besides bottom-feeding, they can skim along the surface swallowing up crab larvae. Sometimes they hunt together. They corral schools of bait fish and take turns diving through the shimmering cloud, mouth open. They've even been known to suck up clams and kelp.

Gray whales gulp up sediment, too, but only by coincidence. To separate the morsels from the ooze, a gray whale has its own in-house colander called baleen. I like to imagine the whale's mouth like a giant storm grate straining the muddy water through a comb of vertical bones that hang from the upper jaw. Tiny creatures are imprisoned inside the 360 or so bars of baleen. The tongue rises to the rooftop, forcing the water out. Sludge gushes out, too, leaving a sediment trail. These mud plumes are large enough to see from a passing airplane.

Scientists estimate an average gray whale disturbs fifty-seven acres of the Bering Sea floor in its summer feeding orgy. It's no wonder they forage so much. Gray whales are the marathoners of the cetacean world. Each year they log up to fourteen thousand miles round-trip, swimming from the ice-clogged arctic to the womb-warm lagoons of Mexico and back. In the five months a gray spends between migrations it gains more than eleven thousand pounds in rendered oil, or up to thirty percent of its body weight. Come fall, when the gray turns tail and heads south, it will begin a fast lasting up to eight months. Imagine sitting down over one summer to eat all the food you would need for a fourteen-thousand-mile marathon swim. With all that weight, how would you get up from the table?

The answer is you'd roll down to the sea and float. Millions of years ago the gray whale's ancestors abandoned terra firma and returned to the ocean. Their bodies became pisciform, like fish. Their hind legs vanished or, as in the right whale, phantom leg bones still float in the flesh where the pelvis would be.

Other land clues remain hidden in the gray's anatomy. A whale fetus is blanketed in downy hair and has nostrils on the end of its nose like a deer. Later, the nostrils migrate to the top of the skull. Like human mammals, grays breathe with lungs. Only they must elevate their blow holes above the sea for every breath. Imagine sprinting to your housetop every time you needed to inhale a gulp of air. Baby whales are nursed by their streamlined mothers through two mammary slits where hidden nipples erupt with Godiva-rich milk that's forty percent fat!

All that fat helps the newborns thicken up with a layer of blubber. Born with scant insulation—the equivalent of a summer sweater—in the tepid Baja lagoons, they build up a polar explorer's jacket to travel north to the arctic. Millennia ago, when whale hair became obsolete, blubber became all the rage. Adult gray whales sport a half-foot-thick coat of it.

Whale blubber is the ultimate "energy bar." The Ironman grays burn blubber for fuel to enable them to cruise halfway around the world. The Aleuts,

Makahs, and Nootkas knew this. They burned whale blubber for fuel too. Aleuts ignited it in their lamps. Makahs and Nootkas tossed rendered whale oil into their fires to impress visitors with the light show. As food, whale oil was the caviar of the Northwest Coast, jealously guarded by the chief.

Along the trade routes, whale oil was as good as gold. In 1856, one whaling captain noted that the Makahs of Washington sold eight thousand dollars worth of whale oil. Aleuts exchanged one fifteen-gallon skin of whale oil for one caribou. Consider that an average-size gray whale thirty-five to forty-five feet long yielded twenty-five to thirty-five barrels of oil, and that's a lot of caribou. Never mind the whale steaks the Aleuts froze in their permafrost cellars, or the whalebone they used as house beams. A nineteenth-century whale oil barrel, give or take a cooper's hand measurements, stored thirty-one and a half gallons. By that kind of math, a group of Aleut hunter-traders might gain seventy-three caribou from one large whale.

From the arctic to Cape Alava, Washington, since as early as 1 A.D., whaling cults evolved. Eight waxing moons before a hunt, a Nootka whaler bathed in snow-fed lakes, rivers, or the ocean. He scrubbed his body with nettles. He swam slowly in the sea, breathing like a whale. He prayed. An Aleut whaler sought out secret caves to paint pictographs of sea animals he wished to hunt. Sacred acts made the hunter's spirit strong. Whaling, after all, was dangerous spirituality. A crew might spend days at sea, vulnerable to storms and angry harpooned whales.

On Vancouver Island, a Nootka chief floated his dugout canoe within an arm's length of a whale before throwing the first honorary harpoon. Apparently his marksmanship wasn't the keenest, (according to James Jewitt, who was held captive at Nootka Sound by Chief Maquinna, the royal highness hunted for fifty-three days, struck eight whales, but got only one). Making the first strike was nonetheless one of the highest Nootka honors. When a whale spouted, a hunter struck the animal behind the flipper with an arrow on a removable shaft. A string of seal-skin buoys was fastened to the harpoon. The rigged line, woven of sinew and cedar bark, might stretch more than seven hundred feet as it bobbled and dragged behind the fleeing whale. This system made it possible to get in a second and third harpoon and finally a sharp lance.

The Makah whalers of Washington added an ingenious twist: diving from the canoe and sewing up the whale's lips. This was because three to four days might elapse before a group of weary canoeists, towing a dead forty-ton whale, reached the excited village. No one dared risk sinking the beloved creature by allowing seawater to pour into its open craw.

Aleuts, on the other hand, counted on their prize sinking. Their baidarkas, or skin kayaks, made for lousy tugboats. Instead, they attempted to poison the whale. After rubbing a slate-tip spear with aconite—a deadly alkaloid poison derived from the monkshood plant—an Aleut whale hunter fired the toxic projectile from atop a wood board fixed to his kayak deck. If the spear struck the whale, he let the wounded creature flee.

Aconite, once used worldwide as a hunting poison, causes lung and heart failure. A whale laboring under aconite poisoning slowed enough to allow more lances to strike. Eventually, it drowned and sank. That of course was part of the plan. The Aleut whaler kayaked home empty-handed and left the rest to chance. Several days later, decomposition gases bobbed the whale to the ocean's surface. If a hunter had extremely good juju, the whale washed up near his village's shore.

Often as not, unfortunately, the manic Aleutian currents carried the bloated prize out to sea. In some cases, the dead whale drifted to an island with opportunistic neighbors. A hunter had one last trick up his salmon-skin sleeve (Aleut kayakers often donned stylish and waterproof "salmon leather" jackets and boots). Each whaler's spear shaft showed signature designs. If a hunter's markings were recognized by relatives, he could lay claim to his catch. Nonetheless, many a fine catch simply floated away.

Not all the whale was used, as people often think. Even if a dead whale did bump up against land's end, the carcass's flesh had often turned rancid. Whale meat was consumed only if fresh. Blubber doesn't spoil as easily. It was flensed and, in the case of the Nootka, tossed in wood troughs, then melted with fire-scorched rocks. Prize whalebones were selected for clubs and tools. The Makahs jammed whale ribs, skulls, and mandibles into embankments to control erosion. But the bulk of the skeleton sank into the beach unused.

By 1790, unbeknownst to America's first whalers, the "American Whale Fishery," as it was called, started hauling sail around Cape Horn and up the Pacific coast. Lucrative markets in whalebone, ambergris, spermaceti, ivory, and whale oil fueled the multi-year voyages out of ports such as Nantucket and New Bedford.

Soon the world's oceans became a free-for-all slaughterhouse. Sperm whales were lanced off Chile and Peru. Northern right whales and bowheads were hauled up in fluke chains in the Bering Sea and Arctic Ocean. California grays were bomb-lanced in their birthing lagoons in Baja, Mexico.

By 1846, the American whaling fleet had grown to a phenomenal 678 ships and barks, thirty-five brigs, and twenty schooners. The investments connected with the whaling business totaled $70,000,000. Almost seventy thousand Americans made their living from the spoils of whaling. They outfitted rigs with multiple long boats, prepared stores for two dozen crewmen, and manufactured "bomb-guns" that could be fired from the shoulder like a musket. These state-of-the-art whale bazookas lobbed a twenty-one-inch lance through the whale's fibrous blubber and flesh, after which it exploded. Whales, for the first time in whaling history, had a trifling chance.

Whale products ranged from the commonplace to vogue fashion. Baleen was cut into flexible frames for umbrellas, corsets, and hoopskirts. Ambergris, a waxy musk scraped from the whale's bowels, was mixed into perfumes. Spermaceti, from the head cavity of the sperm whale, was melted into sperm candles and stirred into pomades. Teeth were carved into pendants and paperweights.

The most famous hunter of gray whales was likely Captain Charles Melville

Scammon (1825–1911). Credited with discovering his namesake, Scammon's Lagoon, a whale nursery folded discreetly into Baja's Pacific coast, Scammon actually learned about it from a Mexican. Both whaler and scientist, Captain Scammon published a remarkably accurate natural history opus in 1874, *The Marine Mammals of the North-western Coast of North America, Together with an Account of the American Whale-Fishery*. Although the book was doomed to be a financial failure (Scammon purchased unsold copies from his San Francisco publisher for the price of paper), the book is now a classic, unmatched for its graphic descriptions of the 1800s whaling era. Captain Scammon describes the harpooning of a gray whale:

"When the spout of the long-sought prey is discovered in the distance, and the welcome cry of the men on the outlook is heard, the ship, fore and aft, becomes the scene of hopeful excitement. All hands are called . . . orders are vehemently given and responded to. The boats . . . are hoisted and swung; and when the time comes for lowering, they are dropped into the water with every man in his place . . . in approaching the whale, the officer . . . orders the 'harpooniersman' by word or motion to stand ready, with his weapon poised, as a rattling, rippling sound is heard, and a huge black form breaks the water, with the harsh, ringing noise of its first respiration. Instantly the deadly spear flies from ready hands, and plunges into the mammoth creature. The water is lashed into a pyramid of bloody foam, the boat is 'fast,' and the whale in vain endeavors to escape by running over the surface of the sea, then diving to the depths below; but its human pursuers still cling to the line attached to the fatal harpoon. The whale rises again to the surface, in some degree exhausted. Another boat approaches, and darts its murderous weapons, and the pursuit is continued with renewed vigor. When, at last, a vital part is pierced, the animal deeply crimsons its pathway with its remaining life-blood, and lashes the sea into clouds of spray in its dying contortions . . . the ship bears down under reduced sail, and the whale is secured by the ponderous fluke-chain. The boats are again hoisted, and all hands are on board. Everyone is cheerful, and works with a will; up goes the cutting gear and the implements are in readiness for cutting-in the whale . . . and the animal is soon stripped of its rich covering . . . ."

Within three years, Scammon's Lagoon was deserted for lack of whales. Whalers continued to line the coast of California, hunting off of points where the great migration passed close to shore and setting up oil rendering stations in the bays. Other ships sailed down on top of the southbound migrating whales and killed them en route to Mexico. Others still swarmed the arctic summer grounds to lance the grays while they fed on fat-rich krill. In less than thirty years, the gray whale population dropped from somewhere around fifteen or twenty thousand to perhaps fewer than two thousand. It's no wonder. "The outside coast," writes Scammon, "was lined with ships, from San Diego southward to Cape St. Lucas."

The lone survivors that swam into the twentieth century gave birth to the generation I celebrated off my kayak bow. Today, because of legal protection, approximately twenty-five thousand grays migrate along the coast. Some scientists speculate they have outstripped their food supply.

At one point, I was afraid I'd floated too close to the feeding whale off False Egg Island. It spooked and disappeared.

"I'm sorry to scare you from your lunch," I apologized to the whale.

Alone again and feeling sad for disturbing my friend's mealtime, I paddled on. A quarter-mile later on the south side of False Egg Island, the paper mill stench returned. My whole body shook with delight.

Where would the whale surface next?

I drifted. I waited. I twisted around to look in all directions. I waited some more, then decided to munch on a granola bar. Forty yards away, vapor spewed up. A gray mottled dome, crusty with barnacles, rose then submerged. I tapped my deck to let the whale know where I was.

I couldn't believe my luck. *Pa-hooff!* Two more grays spouted and flashed near Smith Sound to the south. Their white tail flukes rimmed with black scallops fanned above the silky sea like gigantic butterflies before vanishing. I wanted to meld with those giant wings, ten feet across from "wing tip to wing tip," to fly away with the whales into the infinite blue sea.

A paddle's reach away, spray exploded up. A barnacled island appeared. I nearly leapt out of my cockpit. I exhaled so fast I thought I'd blown my lungs out my mouth. When I recovered, I was puzzled at the bits of white floating across the water.

Was it shrimp bits? No, it was my half-chewed granola bar! "Hah! Got me back for interrupting *your* feeding!" I laughed out loud.

This rough-elbowed, fertile coast was not for light hearts or light stomachs. I sang to keep my mind, spirit, and body working calmly together while crossing Smith Sound's four-mile-wide mouth.

At Protection Cove on the Sound's south tip, I crawled stiffly up a rock outcrop and radioed Egg Island Lighthouse. I felt like a rusty-jointed action figure after four hours in the cockpit. I hoped to make contact with the lightkeepers and ask them to call the coast guard and update my float plan. For peace of mind, I needed someone to know I was heading around Cape Caution today—in case something troublesome happened. Besides, I felt a strong affinity with Egg Island. The Rose family, my dear lightkeeper friends from Ivory Island, had lived and worked as junior keepers there with Stan, the senior keeper. Though I'd never met Stan and his wife, I'd heard about their family from the Roses, who had transferred to Pine Island Lightstation.

The wedge-shaped island, which the Kwakiutl named "Pinched," lay two miles offshore. Trees fenced the crown. In a small clearing the light storked up.

"Egg Island, do you read me? Over."

"I read you. Switch to 09. Over."

"This is Jennifer Hahn. I'm a solo kayaker. Could you please pass a message to Comox Coast Guard to update my float plan? I'm at Protection Cove headed south to Cape Caution."

"Jennifer Hahn? That name sounds familiar. Have you been up this way before?"

A woman's voice came through the radio speaker. She sounded so kind and friendly, I immediately felt like I had a friend up there at the blinking light atop the rock massif.

"Yes. I'm friends with Dennis and Cynthia Rose, your former lightkeeper neighbors."

"That's right. Didn't you meet them on Ivory Island?"

"Good memory."

"Yes . . . well Stan is passing that message on to Comox right now."

I remembered how the Rose family lightkeepers worked as a tag team. The Egg Island keepers did the same. I also recalled the tight interweaving of the community of lights that thread the British Columbia coast. Over handheld radios and telephones, they share more than news of the weather. They chat about station repairs, health, gardens, kids, and visitors—including me.

"Your float plan is updated for Cape Caution, Stan says."

"Oh, thank you so much! Your little blinking light is kind of a beacon for my heart. Over and out."

She laughed as if she were on the beach beside me. "Take care now. We'll be thinking of you. Over and out."

I couldn't help but wear my heart on my lips. I felt so raw, so vulnerable. The lighthouse winked from 275 vertical feet atop Egg Island's fortress. I turned the radio off. A new lifeline linked the Egg Island keepers and me. I thought about the other friendships I'd formed in just three days. The B.C. ferry captain's wishes as I splashed down at Namu. Then Grant and Barry's company at Addenbroke Lighthouse. Next, the friendly voice of a Comox Coast Guardsman jotting down my first float plan. And only yesterday the fisher at Kelp Head. A safety net of newfound friends was being woven where once I'd only myself to count on. It helped me feel as though someone was watching over me.

The amazing thing was someone *was* watching. Every two miles, as if on cue, an aloof bald eagle knitted a shore pine with its golden feet. I prayed to each one.

Protection Cove was still as an aquarium. I looked down through reflections of shore pine, white sky, and hemlock. A dusky blue sun star with fifteen legs drifted half an inch off the bottom. I wondered if it was dreaming. A flurry of shore crabs tussled and tumbled over one another to get at what looked like a bag of white fish skin. Another dozen stood by waiting. A Dungeness crab jogged sideways beside my cockpit. Sculpins the color of granite lay motionless on the sea floor, disclosed only by their distinctive kite outline. Eel grasses with red algae drifted in scarves. A mallard duck flew over, raspy voiced and excited.

Everything—current, waves, wind—was tranquil. It was the ocean's siesta time. Slack tide. The moment before the river turned around. Silence before the deluge. I couldn't believe how calm and lovely the sea conditions had become after the intense interlude at Kelp Head. I felt endlessly thankful that I hadn't turned back then.

Five miles from Cape Caution, the coast guard weather report still advised "winds light and variable." It was tempting to take a siesta myself—to sketch, swim, or poke around paradise a while. But open coasts have a way of keeping you moving.

I rounded Ness Neck, a hatchet-shaped headland striking back at the waves. In my atlas I'd penned "whale" here because it is the Kwakiutl name for the area. And wouldn't you know it, right there off the blade end I heard the hollow inhale of a whale. I could hardly believe the synchronicity. Even after hundreds of years this ancient place name held true. There was hope in this.

I stopped. Floated. Surf pounded the granite headland. A gull circled and mewed plaintively. The sea broke open again. A dark curve rose up. *Pah-wuff!*

Out to sea, a tourist cruise ship with Tahitian-turquoise logos and three hundred windows clipped by. Did anyone see this marvelous brother of ours breathing our same waters? Another *pah-wuff!* I grabbed binoculars, focusing them on the whale. It's gone. Beyond the sudsing water where it dove, a sparkle caught my eye. On the ship's upper deck a revolving ballroom mirror sparkled through the plate glass picture windows. Gowned ladies and tuxedoed gentlemen circled to unheard music.

In our own way, we are all dancing.

Cape Caution's white navigation light blinked in the distance. I aimed the bow just right of it. I wanted to stay slightly offshore. "Forehead" is the Kwakiutl name for the cape. From a distance, the boulder-strewn, granite headland protrudes much like a nose from a forehead of cliffs and trees. It is a cape that stirs humility and begs patience.

"Timing is everything," Randel Washburne had warned. It took my friend Kim Kirby eight days before she and a friend found a window they could use to kayak around the frightening Cape. Fog and sixteen-foot breakers nixed their safe progress. Paddling north from Seattle, they took false refuge in Slingsby Channel. They got stuck there. Waves as tall as the kayak was long blocked the channel's mouth.

I couldn't believe I was now approaching the dreaded moment. The western swell lifted and rolled the kayak like a behemoth hand rocking a cradle. I kept squinting ahead for the tidal stream running directly agrain of Cape Caution's tip. Where was the typical scour-line of whitecaps that signals a tidal rip? I didn't like it that I hadn't found it. I didn't want those kind of surprises sneaking up on me.

Everywhere the sea was a not-too-threatening tumultuous gray chop. Nonetheless, hobgoblins niggled my mind. Was I too low in the water to catch approaching danger in time? Should I swing farther out to sea to avoid colliding with potential rips? Although Queen Charlotte Sound was calm by most standards, the Cape itself was white toothed, bursting with explosions of spray.

But nothing happened. Nothing! After days . . . weeks . . . months of self-aggravated, doomsday scenes played over and over I could hardly believe my eyes. No eat-you-up and spit-you-out tide rips! No sixteen-foot breakers! Just low swell. Meager winds. Choppy surface waves. And now, after six hours, I still had tidal current running in my favor! Cape Caution is one of those rare places on the coast where the current splits because of a T-shaped oceanography. After the incoming tide enters Queen Charlotte Sound between Vancouver Island and Calvert Island it hits the British Columbia mainland and flows two directions along the shore. Half the flood tide bounds north up Fitz Hugh Sound. Half muddles south into Queen Charlotte Strait, sluicing behind Vancouver Island. On that morning I hitched the ebb current exiting Fitz Hugh Sound south down the open coast. At Cape Caution, the tide was changing guards. So I would again "go with the flow" and ride the flood south for six more hours—an almost unheard of timing—into the throat between Vancouver Island and the mainland. Hallelujah!

The kayak bucked up and over the waves ricocheting off Cape Caution. It rolled under the heave of the ocean swells. I didn't mind any of it. I knew that capes tend to concentrate swell and wave energy because of reflection and refraction. Without thinking, when the chop intensified, I loosened hips, leaned forward, and stroked faster. I danced with the kayak, following its lead. How many times had I instructed my kayak students: "Loose hips don't sink ships." The kayak swayed gracefully beneath me. Yet my head and spine kept vertical as if connected by a string to the sky. This technique helps maintain a crucial center of gravity. I exhaled long soothing breaths.

On the starboard side, a blast shot up. I lurched in the seat. Immediately, the boat became less stable. Beside the cockpit, the water boiled white. A dark form sank from sight. I wanted to cry. I wanted to laugh. A gray whale was accompanying me in the choppy tidal current around Cape Caution!

"Hi ho, whale friend. Keep your eye on me," I yelled. "And please don't knock me over!"

The waves were erratic now, and I could hardly turn to watch the whale, who was surfacing now on the other side of me. He dove right under! I could hardly believe it.

A voluminous cloud of mist rocketed off the bow. A barnacled forehead rose out of the sea ahead of me—big as an upturned wheelbarrow. Water poured off the whale's immense throat, and a beautiful, knobby snout appeared. The whale was spy-hopping to get a look at me. Nose pointed skyward, it gyrated slowly with its head above water while its flukes beat back and forth to keep it upright.

The whale's mottled skin reminded me of one of those curious images of the night sky taken through an astronomer's telescope. Bursts of white nebulas, sprays of starry barnacles, and shooting asteroids—the marks of scrapes—

patterned the hide. But the eye—oh that gentle eye! Just above its down-curved grin, set inside a cowry shell of folds, I met the whale's dark orb staring out from a universe of stars. Though only visible for seconds, the eye looked out wide as all curiosity. When it sank into the waves and disappeared I felt like I'd been looked at by the eye of God.

Now the whale surfaced behind. I heard the blow, and wondered, half nervous, half ecstatic, where it would come up next.

But I never saw the gray whale again.

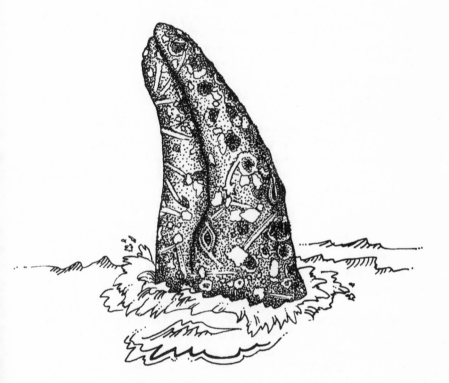

10   The Blue Trade Bead

Long ago in the time before time, when animals could speak and bears walked upright leaving human footprints, the people were canoeing home in Queen Charlotte Strait when they were overtaken by a storm. In those days, the canoes were as huge as the biggest cedar trees. Some could carry dozens of people— young men and women, as well as grandparents, children, and everyone's dearest possessions were packed in waterproof bags of halibut skin and bentwood boxes with tight lids.

Terrified that the storm would swamp the boats or batter them to splinters on the rocks, the people prayed for help. A devilfish surfaced in the waves. The sea monster guided their canoes safely to the entrance at Blunden Harbor.

George Hunt Jr., a Kwakiutl carver, told me a less embellished form of that story from the railing of the Alaska ferry. I was delighted to learn that George's famous grandfather, George Hunt, had known one of my heroes, Northwest Coast Native ethnographer Franz Boas. Apparently, great-grandfather Hunt ran the Hudson Bay Store at Fort Rupert in the early nineteenth century. Fluent in both English and Kwakiutl, Hunt was hired as a translator by Boas. I'd seen Hunt's name dozens of times in Boas texts. He served as an invaluable aide recording and interpreting Kwakiutl myths, prayers, and ceremonies.

Surfing through Queen Charlotte Strait—barreling tail wind, snapping hair, soaked sleeves, low sun—once again I found myself desperate for a spot to haul out and camp. The coastline offered nothing remotely appealing: boulders, cliffs, seaweed-slick rocks. So I prayed. *Please, just a tiny beach out of the chilly air.*

Soon after, the waves cuffed me by a keyhole in the rocks. In the split second as I passed it, my eyes locked on a shimmering blue bay in the distance. It flashed, then disappeared like a blown match.

What was that?

Already downwind, I quickly swiped a sleeve across the salt spray on the chart cover and leaned forward in the cockpit to check. Months before on a whim I'd scrawled a Kwakiutl place name on the chart beside this blink-and-you-miss-it passage. It was called O-stowa-lis—"small opening beach." A mile farther was a larger passage. This was a godsend. It took me out of the tiresome wind. The old names had worked their magic again.

The narrow cut turned into a river of stones at low tide. At high tide it was just wide and deep enough to float a kayak. The tide was dropping. Barnacled rocks scraped the hull. I had just enough time to jump out of the boat and line it through the quarter-mile passage before it dried up.

As I left behind the white noise of surf and floated the boat down this transitory stream flanked with fern and spruce, time seemed to warp, then fold backward. It was as if I were stepping back into an ephemeral, if not enchanted, world. The air smelled of vanilla leaf and mushrooms. A Swainson's thrush netted me in its waterfall of notes. The watery corridor was disappearing beneath me as I moved forward, closing access for another six hours. I couldn't have turned back if I tried.

Looking down the spyglass passage toward Blunden Harbor, I could make out a curious white scratch on the far shore. At the stream's end, I slipped into the kayak and paddled across the harbor toward the brightness.

The scratch turned into an extraordinary midden of white shells. Fantastic, I thought, landing on the white crunch of broken cockle, horse clam, and butter clam shells. It must be an old village site. Middens are kitchen refuse heaps. Long ago, women cracked clams, scooped out the meat, and tossed the shells in front of the longhouse door, much like my great-grandfather shelled peas.

A friend who works with the Lummi Nation in northwest Washington told me a fascinating detail about middens. On Sucia Island in Puget Sound one inch of midden height equals three hundred years of habitation. After landing on the beach, I propped the nine-foot paddle against the eroding shell bank. The drift of shells and dirt measured seven feet tall! How long since George Hunt Jr.'s people hushed cedar canoes up to these white shells?

Fireweed and cedar had long since taken over. But glancing around a bit, I discovered the old village lived on in pockets everywhere. Carved figures peered from a burial island across the harbor. Toppled house posts leaned from the hedge above the beach. I scrambled up the bank and rested my palm on a gargantuan post. Wave-like grooves rippled the surface—the signature of a master carver's adz. When I reached my arms around the base of the post, my fingers didn't meet.

Rummaging under a carpet of thimbleberry, I found several longhouse planks measuring up to fifteen feet long, half an arm wide, and one palm deep. Native wood harvesters were so skilled they could split planks from a cedar trunk without killing the tree! But more often, trees were felled by burning or hacking away at the trunk with adzes. This laborious process took slave laborers two to three days. After being felled, the logs were skidded atop poles to the water. It took an average of two hundred men—pushing, prying, heaving, hauling, and grunting—twenty-four hours to transport one log from the forest to the sea. Even then, the job was far from over. The prize had to be towed behind a canoe to the winter village site, then split.

Northwest coast longhouses were magnificent communal dwellings sheltering sixty or more people from an extended family. To understand their astounding size, imagine entering a basketball court framed by massive, hand-hewn cedar planks and posts. Now, fancy two courts side by side for a wealthy chief's house. One of the largest longhouses I've heard of loomed in the San Juans. The monstrosity grew from a chief's ingenious idea of butting two longhouses together into an L-shape to deal with scrawny beach space.

Always, the people faced the sea. Their enormous houses stood eave to eave in rows rimming the beach edge, one of the few level places on the mountain-flanked Inside Passage. For added room, people fashioned wood decks on pilings over the sea much as we build them today for our barbecues, hot tubs, and potted gardens. They had angled walls for back rests and were popular gathering places for yarning, gossiping, and gambling.

Captain Meares, during his first voyage to the coast in 1788, left a wonderfully detailed account of his visit to the Wickaninnish longhouse on northwest Vancouver Island.

"On entering the house we were absolutely astonished at the vast area it enclosed. . . . Three enormous trees, rudely carved and painted, formed the rafters, which were supported at the ends and in the middle by gigantic images carved out of huge blocks of timber. . . . The trees that supported the roof were of a size which would render the mast of a first-rate man-of-war diminutive on a comparison with them; indeed our curiosity as well as our astonishment was on its utmost stretch, when we considered the strength which must be necessary to raise these enormous beams to their present elevation; how could such strength be found by a people wholly unacquainted with mechanic powers? The door by which we entered this extraordinary fabric was the mouth of one of these huge images . . . ."

Seaward of the houses, totem poles often towered like vertical columns of acrobats balancing shoulder upon shoulder to heights of four stories or more. Exquisitely carved eagles, wolves, salmon, bears, frogs, whales, humans, and mythic beings such as Thunderbird, Sisiutl, and Moon proclaimed and documented family lineages, rights, and privileges.

I rapped my knuckles on a long-house plank to check its soundness. Sadly, it was punky with rot and made only a dull *hap-hap-hap*. A pileated woodpecker echoed back—*tuk-tuk-tuk-TUK!*—from a cedar snag behind the old village. Carvers often honored the woodpecker as their guardian spirit. My mind drifted. The seasons ebbed backward, as if out to sea. Time was warping, turning inside out.

Tuk-tuk-tuk-tuk-TUK! It is winter. The Blunden people have invited neighboring clans to crowd into the chief's longhouse for a potlatch. The celebration is to honor a marriage. *Tuk-tuk-tuk-TUK!* Drummers in abalone-button blankets beat time on a log plank. Raven-of-the-North-End-of-the-World dances into the room backward, clapping his mask's enormous three-foot beak. *Tuk-tuk-TUK!* His shredded cedar bark robe shivers with mischief. It conceals hands tugging cords that snap the bill open and shut. *Tuk-TUK!* Raven circles the blazing fire four times then vanishes behind a painted screen.

The crowd buzzes. The children ahhh and poke. They know what will happen next. Firelight trembles on their excited faces. Wood smoke wafts out the roof where two massive planks are shoved aside. Behind the dance screen, a trickster is screaming into a hollow tube of kelp buried under the floor.

Bear-Mother Totem Pole
Village Island, B.C.

Onlookers jump as blood-curdling cannibal cries rise mysteriously from the fire pit where the tube trumpets.

A Tlingit elder from Ketchikan explained it this way, "Winter was a time for singing, dancing, potlatching, and storytelling. We worked six months and we played six months."

The word potlatch is from Chinook jargon, a trade pidgin once used along the coast. It means "to give." Blankets, eulachon fish oil in bentwood boxes, and other gifts were given to guests witnessing the event. It was a time of great pride, a time for showing off the masks and dances owned by the host family and for transferring rights and privileges.

One of the most magical places I've ever slept is an ancient longhouse in Gwayasdums on Gilford Island just southeast of Queen Charlotte Strait. In 1983, at the invitation of a village carver and teacher, a group of friends and I unrolled our bags on the wood-chip floor. The air inside the longhouse carried the enchanting tang of yellow and red cedar. Two magnificent house posts carved like preying wolves, or perhaps bears, flanked the door. Lying under the sharp-toothed silhouettes, I imagined that these fierce guardians would either devour my bad dreams or inspire some. I woke after a deep and restful sleep to a raindrop conga on the roof.

Tuk-tuk-TUK! The red-crowned pileated woodpecker dove through the cool evening air above the sinking house posts. I needed to find a place to sleep before dark. Out of respect for the people whose ancestors once lived here and the spirits of the dead, I climbed down to the water's edge and asked if the beach might allow me one night's rest. The answer felt affirmative. I would have looked elsewhere if I'd gotten weird vibes.

I grabbed the tent and headed around the curve of the beach. Along the way, I passed a surprising, if not disturbing, museum of artifacts. A rusty iron winch cloaked in barnacles and resembling a human torso, had been propped upright on a stump. Some humorous soul had added to this unlikely Venus a stone head with a scrap-metal cap. Driftwood logs glittered with a kaleidoscope of scavenged objects: shards of colorful glass, broken china plates, tea-cup handles, ice-blue bottles.

When I returned to the kayak for another armful of gear, a dinghy and a skiff had landed beside the kayak. Two couples were already milling down the beach, raking the shells looking for God knows what. Beach-combing seemed to be a regular activity out there. I decided to watch and see what they might find.

Each hunter possessed a unique style. One woman squatted in front of a large square she'd drawn in the slope. Carefully, she raked shell bits through her parted fingers. Another artful woman dug shallow holes with a rusty screwdriver. Farther away, a man paced up and down the slope in a systematic grid search.

The people were so intent on looking, I figured they might have lost something dear. Perhaps a wedding ring? Puzzled, I walked down to greet them and ask if I might be of help. As I approached, two wet dogs charged down the beach, chasing scents of their own. They nuzzled my crotch.

"Oh we haven't lost anything," the man said, "Ask my wife to show you what she found."

The woman with the screwdriver laughed and reached into her shorts pocket.

"If you look hard enough, you can find Indian trade beads in the beach sand." She held her palm out for me to see. One glass bead the size of a half-inch bolt glowed Noxema-jar blue.

"Amazing. Real trade beads?"

Later, I'd see it printed in a travel guide to the Inside Passage: You can find trade beads at Blunden Harbor. It read like an open invitation.

Though I felt uncomfortable with what they were doing, the bead diggers were friendly folks. They'd sailed up from Seattle. Gus, their gangly, black and yellow dog-child had an ingenious streak. He could dive for clams and rocks and blow bubbles out his nostrils like a swimmer. The nice couple even offered to store my food bags aboard their sailboat for the night, so the wolves and bears wouldn't come looking.

"Wolves and bears?" I repeated, trying not to sound too alarmed.

"Oh yes!" said Lu. "A wolf was stalking a deer right here where we're standing earlier this afternoon."

"Here?" I said, pointing to the ground to be sure I was hearing it right.

"Yes, we saw the wolf hiding in those bushes," she motioned toward the thimbleberry thicket a hand's reach away. "The deer was grazing on seaweed. We watched them from our sailboat."

It struck me then how convenient it would be to have a sailboat from which to watch the wilds while I lounged or slept.

"Did it kill the deer?"

"No, the deer ran off."

"That's good." What else could I say, even if it sounded inane. Sleeping by myself out here, I felt more affinity with the deer.

Lu must have read my thoughts.

"Are you alone?" she asked concerned.

We launched into all the usual questions and answers. How long I'd been out, where I was headed, why I would want to do this kind of thing by myself.

Finally, the friendly couple told me if I got scared, I could unroll my bag on their galley floor.

"Gosh, thanks," I said, "but I think I'll be fine."

Franz Boas's Kwakiutl informants told him "ole'gade" means "having wolves." Later in the evening, I was sitting in my tent flossing my teeth when a deep, chiseled bawl rose above the forest and echoed from island to island across the inlet. The fur on my arms and neck rose.

It was the most powerful and mournful sound I had ever heard. When it repeated, the cry was so full of resonance I felt as if I were sitting inside the throat of the wolf.

Across the dark bay where I'd eked through the canoe passage, more wolves echoed the first. For breathless minutes, the pack sirened back and forth. I strained to listen for individual voices. How many wolves were out there— four? six? Packs usually embrace a half dozen or so family members, but some run as large as thirty or more wolves.

Something *klunked* and splashed in the bay. I stared out the tent screen into the darkness. A pensive silence followed.

Hello?

No answer. It was dark as a wolf's den. My pupils widened. Nature has a dandy way of growing extra ears and orbs in anticipation of close encounters.

More wolves yawled from a new direction in the harbor. Under the cloak of darkness, the pack was trotting invisibly through the familiar woods and along the shore. Only the imprint of their voices gave me any idea where they lurked. Were they coming closer? Maybe it was the ventriloquy of echoes that made my camp feel surrounded.

I remembered the wolf stalking the deer. Lordy, they wouldn't be stalking me now, would they? Childhood myths came back to haunt me: "Peter and the Wolf," "Little Red Riding Hood," and "The Three Little Pigs." *I'll huff and I'll puff and I'll BLOWWWWWWwww your house down!*

Of course not, silly. Get a grip. Those are fairy tales. A wolf wouldn't hurt you. My mind repeated known facts: THERE ARE NO RECORDED HUMAN DEATHS FROM WOLF ATTACKS. WOLVES PREY ON RABBITS, DEER, OTTERS, BEAVERS, AND RACCOONS. But my animal-body wouldn't respond to logic. It heeded some visceral nerve of its own.

My sense of isolation deepened with each sonorous cry. The wails seemed to dissolve the very curtain of time. I was tumbling back ten thousand years to the Ice Age. I was falling, falling into prey. I was rabbit hunkered in tall grass. I was deer munching seaweed on Blunden Beach. I was First Woman shivering in a hide lean-to.

Something splashed in the bay a second time. Wide-eyed, I scanned the blackness. Perhaps the spirits were returning to count their missing trade beads— returning disguised as wolves. Had anyone asked permission at all? But who would they ask? Where had the villagers gone?

It was lonely and frightening lying there all alone. To soothe myself, I tried to remember how Hunt and Boas described the Kwakiutl people's relationship with wolves. I tried to think back to when my European ancestors crossed paths with the First Nations on the coast. When the Grimm Brothers met the supernatural Myth People. When things turned inside out.

The First People must have been astonished when Europeans appeared along their shores. The first to look in was my Danish brother of sorts, navigator Vitus Bering. In 1741, the Czar financed an expedition to claim land out yonder of Kamchatka (a.k.a., the Aleutians) for Russia. From the south horizon came Mexico's Juan Perez in 1774. Perez sailed into the area of Haida Gwai, then Nootka Sound on Vancouver Island. In the following decades, more empire-financed explorers arrived—Francisco Bodega y Quadra, who claimed the land for Spain, James Cook, and, finally, George Vancouver, who counterclaimed the land for his majesty, the King of England.

Soon, profiteering trade ships packed with "King George men" from England, "Boston men," French, and Spaniards squeezed into village harbors bearing beautiful and magical things—copper kettles, iron chisels, calico, blankets, buttons, needles, and beads. They dropped anchor in villages such as Blunden Bay and exchanged trinkets for furs.

Europeans brought malaise too. Rum. Muskets. Gun powder. They seeded epidemics—smallpox and tuberculosis from which the people had no immunity. In fact, the single most tragic calamity to befall the First Nations was a smallpox epidemic started in 1863. Within two years, it had killed twenty thousand, almost one-third of the coast's vibrant population.

The epidemic started in Fort Victoria on south Vancouver Island. Northern coastal tribes often visited the Hudson Bay Company settlement established there in 1843. They arrived in huge canoe fleets and camped on the outskirts to trade. In April, a white man with smallpox arrived by ship from San Francisco. Regardless of dire warnings in the Victoria newspaper, the disease reached the encampments with alarming speed. People died in frightful numbers.

Smallpox's incubation period was usually a week to seventeen days. One tenacious form, hemoragic smallpox, knocked you dead in five to seven days. People bled to death internally. Panicked, civic officials darkened the camps and chased the people north. The sick canoed toward home. Every village they visited ignited with the dread disease. Raiding parties preyed on the weak travelers and unknowingly carried smallpox home with their booty. The epidemic engulfed the coast like a prairie fire, then swept into the interior.

Powerful shamans failed to chase away the sickness. In desperation, some of those inflicted tried drinking a mixture concocted from bumpy crab shells in a belief that like cured like. The crab's carapace mimicked the look of smallpox with its pustular eruptions. Others tried bathing their swollen, feverish bodies in cooling seawater. Hence, Smallpox Bay on San Juan Island. But the lesions continued to spread across torso, back, arms, legs, and even to soles and palms. They worked into the spleen, liver, and other viscera. The fatality rate was staggering. Entire villages perished. Miraculously, one Kwakiutl man infected with smallpox was cured by wolves. I'd read the haunting story in Boas's works.

During the decades of smallpox, a man named Fool had helped a wounded wolf by removing a deer bone jammed sideways in the animal's mouth. Two years later, Fool was traveling with his wife and family. He encountered the wolf again.

"It was in the summer of 1871," he told Boas. "We were headed home, traveling in a large canoe. We came to Rock Bay at the north side of Seymour Narrows." There his family found abandoned "four nice boxes full of very good clothing on the beach; and also two flour bags and all kinds of food." No one was around. They loaded up the supplies. Ten days later the family fell sick with smallpox.

"We all lay in bed in our tent. I was lying among them. Now I saw that all our bodies swelled and were dark red. Our skins burst open and I did not know that they were all dead." Fool had been asleep, but startled to "many wolves who came whining and others howling." Two of the wolves began meticulously licking his body. They vomited white foam all over his body.

"They did not treat me well when they turned me over . . . ."

Again they licked him off, and he saw that they had licked the scabs from his sores. "Now I saw that I was lying among my dead past nephews." Afraid, Fool crawled to the shelter of a thick spruce tree and shivered with no bedding. Two wolves came and lay beside him.

At daybreak, Fool felt strong enough to stand up. He recognized one wolf as "the one who had been in trouble with the bone. He sat down seaward from me and nudged me with his nose that I should lie on my back, and he vomited and pushed his nose against the lower end of my sternum. He vomited the magic power into me. Then I dreamed of the wolf who was still sitting there. In my dream he became a man, laughed and spoke and said, 'Now take care, friend, now this shaman-maker has gone into you. Now you will cure the sick and you will catch the souls of the sick and you will throw sickness into anyone whom you wish to die among your tribe. Now they will be afraid of you.' Then I woke up and my body was trembling and my mind was different after this, for all the wolves had left me. Now I was a shaman."

"You'll live through this too," I told myself, shivering in the tent. "When you fall asleep you won't hear the wolves howling and whining."

I had other pressing matters. I had to pee badly.

Squatting at the shore, headlamp glowing, I was horrified to see scarlet stains on the beach shells. *Sweet Jesus!* Was it the deer's blood?

I dashed the headlamp beam all around.

Lordy! Again.

It was coming from me!

Women explorers have myriad challenges to deal with, such as smelling like wounded animals each month. I rinsed to get rid of the scent. A Hesquiat myth has it that wherever a woman's menstrual blood falls, clusters of red bunchberries grow. Likewise, the Strait's Salish name for the Indian pipe plant is wolf's urine. Wherever a wolf urinates, the ghostly white Indian pipe sprouts up. What would my odorous pee propagate?

It didn't take long. I had just ducked into the tent again when a set of oars clunked and splashed offshore. I stood up and scanned the darkness. Soon after, a chatty stranger rowed up in his dinghy. He must have seen the light. Eager to engage in a conversation, he explained he was out for a midnight stroll. Great, I thought, and what have you seen? He invited me out to his sailboat to enjoy tea with him and a buddy.

Yeah, right, at 11:30 P.M. I told him no thanks, have to get up early.

He oared away, yelling cheerfully, "Come on out if you change your mind. I'm a night owl."

Back in my tent, I turned off the headlamp when I remembered how revealing a tent silhouette can be. But I still felt naked as I peeled off wet shorts and shirt, leaving breasts and bum exposed. Wolves I could handle, but lonesome, possibly horny, humans I wasn't ready for. I slipped on dry clothes, lay down, and zipped up the sleeping bag.

I tried to erase the image of a dinghy rowing up while I slept. I tried to visualize white light around the tent fly. I tried to forget the unexpected visitor. But I couldn't. Yet, darn it all, I needed to rest. Tomorrow I had to face Queen Charlotte Strait for twenty more miles. I couldn't imagine paddling rag-tag seas on zero sleep.

To comfort myself, I thought about Lu and Al, the kind couple who convinced me to stow the food bags aboard their sailboat. Lu and Al . . . just out in the bay . . . fast asleep in dreamland . . . rocking on their cozy brig *Louise*. I'd spotted the mast light shining like a star above the bay.

"If you get in trouble, just scream. We'll hear you and come to help," Al said earlier to soothe any worries.

"Or unroll your bag in the galley. Gus would love the company," Lu added laughing. It was a comforting thought having that big domesticated "wolf" lying at my side. In fact, the more I thought about goofy, bubble-blowing Gus, Al, Lu, and *Louise* in the bay, the more I wanted to be there.

So I went.

I paddled across the dark water at midnight, my headlamp illuminating the blue nylon sleeping bag wadded under the deck bungee. I was glad for the option of a sailboat, yet I felt like a wimp leaving my tent because of a pack of wolves and a stranger in a dinghy. But then, I hadn't slept a wink since the wolf howls began. More than anything, I wanted to fall safely asleep.

The boat was farther than I thought. At night, it's hard to check my center of gravity. Balance goes helter-skelter in the dark. Like trying to do yoga with your eyes closed. Was I leaning too far right, or was the kayak packed too hastily with poor weight distribution? The last thing I wanted was to spill over out there in the black bay.

I knocked on *Louise*'s hull.

"Lu? Al?"

I knocked again. "LUU-U . . . AAA-L!"

Nothing. I couldn't wake them. So much for Al's advice to "scream from shore."

In the morning, Gus—who came to my rescue by barking and getting everyone up—woke me in the galley with a fat slobbery kiss. As Lu cooked us all oatmeal, I leaned over *Louise*'s side and stuffed my food bags into the kayak's open hatches. Al spilled the beans and told me that Lu had hidden a trade bead in the yellow duffel.

"It's folded in a piece of paper. I didn't want you to throw it out by accident," he whispered.

It was a sweet gift and I'm sure a bit of a sacrifice for Lu. Yesterday, she'd told me, disheartened, that she'd only found one. When I opened the note on shore it read:

Yes, it's a Blunden Indian midden bead.

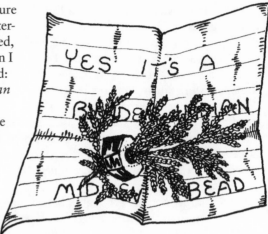

I held the trade bead to the sky. Octagonal with diamond facets, it glowed the most amazing cobalt blue.

Blue glass trade beads were the most popular color in demand from European traders. The Hudson's Bay Company doled them out like expensive coins: six green or yellow beads the size of a pea or three slightly larger blue beads for one beaver pelt.

Holding the bead between my thumb and index finger, I think of the places it might have been—a fringed dance tunic? A necklace? A rattle? Was it traded for beaver, otter? Given as a wedding gift? I'd once read that the Tlingits threw strings of seed beads into the ocean before beginning a coastal journey to hunt or trade. Such offerings carried prayers for a safe and prosperous journey.

Something told me the bead wasn't mine to keep. It belonged here at Blunden Harbor near this ancient site of rotting house posts, broken glass dreams, and midden shells, near the wolves and the honored spirits of the dead buried on the island.

Wolf tracks disappeared into the sea where I loaded my kayak. It was as if they were looking for the bead.

But if I buried the bead on the beach, someone would just dig it up again. I made a plan.

As I pushed off into the foggy morning, a belted kingfisher looped the mist. The blue-gray fisher pumped its wings like a bellows and disappeared south. I followed. Fog and silence pervaded everything. Even a paddle stroke seemed loud. Misty islets dotted Blunden Harbor's wide southern entrance. Near a kneecap of rock, a loon trailed a ripple reflecting white sky. I turned the bow toward it. The animals were telling me what to do.

I stopped beside the rock. I opened my dry box and lifted out the deerskin pouch full of talismans. I unfolded the note paper with the blue trade bead. How beautiful the bead would look hanging on the soft deerskin fringe—a gift evoking friends met on the journey, a touchstone back to the ancient mariners of this coast.

But no, that was not my plan. I remembered the voice inside me. Two stories crossed my mind that soft morning:

Late in the nineteenth century, Seattle's *Post-Intelligencer* newspaper and the Seattle Chamber of Commerce sponsored an Alaska tour aboard the

City of Seattle. After anchoring at Tongass Island just north of the British Columbia–Alaska border, the passengers and crew explored a "deserted" Tlingit village. It was summer, so the inhabitants were gone, temporarily, to their summer camps. The ignorant visitors, knowing no better, sawed the most striking totem pole in two and carried it to the ship. Back in Seattle, the Tongass pole was resurrected as the Pioneer Square totem. The Tlingits eventually filed theft charges, so the pole was paid for by the city.

Another theft story, this one more tragic. At Village Island just southeast of Queen Charlotte Strait in December 1921 one of the last great potlatches was busted up by William Halliday, the Indian agent in Alert Bay, under Section 149 of the Indian Act. Following a mass arrest, forty-five people were charged for potlatching, making speeches, dancing, arranging items to be gifted, and carrying gifts to the guests.

The potlatch artifacts—let me clarify artifacts: they were an entire village's gorgeously carved masks, headdresses, dance capes, and coppers (shield-like symbols of wealth)—were inventoried, crated, and conveniently shipped to Victoria Memorial Museum (now the National Museum of Man in Ottawa) and the Royal Ontario Museum in Toronto.

Even before the goods left Alert Bay, however, George Heye, a New York collector, purchased thirty objects. The Superintendent General of Indian Affairs, Duncan Campbell Scott, whisked a few more items aside for his personal collection.

The potlatch goods (most of them anyway) were finally repatriated more than a half century later. Two Native-run museums funded and built for the purpose now care for the pieces—the U'mista Center in Alert Bay and the Kwagiulth Museum and Cultural Center at Cape Mudge on Quadra Island. Years ago, I stood in the longhouse-styled room in Alert Bay. Surrounded by masks of mythic birds, bear, eagle, wolf, and the wild woman Dzunukwa with her O of a red mouth, I too stood astonished, my mouth also in a round O. My spirit had never seen such power in art.

Long ago, people who had been captured by raiding parties, then returned to their homes, either by a retaliatory raid or ransom payment, were said to have "u'mista." Confiscated masks and coppers that are repatriated also have u'mista. I knew in my heart that this blue trade bead carried u'mista.

I opened the pouch and lifted out a sprig of cedar. The bead's hole slid nicely over the stem. I said a prayer and tossed the blue trade bead overboard at the harbor's entrance. It disappeared. My small repatriation.

Later that same day, a traveler told me, a pod of hungry transient orcas had blocked the entrance to Blunden Harbor with a hundred corralled dolphins inside. People anchored inside the harbor leaned from their boat decks horrified as a systematic killing frenzy reddened the water. The orca calves were being taught to hunt, he said.

In the old myths, Wolf and Orca are two forms of the same animal—the mythic Seawolf. When wolf tracks enter the ocean, it is said, an orca comes alive. Wolf spirits gone to the sea.

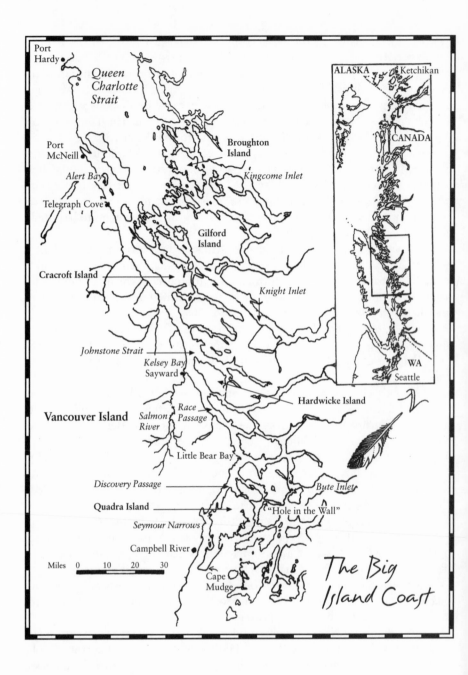

Port
Hardy

Queen
Charlotte
Strait

Port
McNeill

Alert Bay

Telegraph Cove

Broughton
Island

Kingcome Inlet

Gilford
Island

Cracroft Island

Knight Inlet

Johnstone Strait

Kelsey Bay
Sayward

Race
Passage

Hardwicke Island

Vancouver Island

Salmon
River

Little Bear Bay

Discovery Passage

Bute Inlet

Quadra Island

"Hole in the Wall"

Seymour Narrows

Campbell River

Miles   0   10   20   30

Cape
Mudge

The Big
Island Coast

ALASKA   Ketchikan

CANADA

WA
Seattle

Part 4

The Big Island Coast: South Along Vancouver Island, British Columbia

Mid-summer, 119 miles, 7 days

Those black fish are human all right! All Indians up and down the coast say that. If you talk to whales, they seem to understand. I have whistled to them and had them stand right up in the water. They rose three times straight up in answer to three whistles . . . If you lie down in a boat they will come round whistling—calling—to you.

—Chief Harry Assu

11 Rock, Scissors, Paper

"Leading-Spouter-of-the-World" was the first killer whale. A great hunter, who like Wolf hunted in packs, he was a supernatural being who shined good luck on hunters who crossed his watery path. Long ago, when a person saw killer whales near him as he paddled, he threw goat tallow and diorite into the water. It is said the souls of sea hunters go to the killer whales.

Johnstone Strait, three days' paddle from Blunden Harbor, is orca whale heaven. Rivers of salmon and cod flagged the cool, deep fjords and inlets. A "rubbing beach" at Robson Bight Ecological Reserve—an orca sanctuary established in 1982 to protect their habitat—is a favorite haunt. Here, one day's paddle south of Queen Charlotte Strait, the orcas love to push their thirty-foot bodies along the river gravel much like a baseball player sliding into home plate.

These were familiar waters. I'd come here three times before to see the beautiful creatures breathing and rolling in the mist. But it still nearly stopped my breath when, rounding a point south of Robson Bight Ecological Reserve, a pod of orcas surrounded the kayak. The six-foot-tall dorsal fin of a male sailed by only twenty feet away. Black and white forms warbled through the translucent sea on all sides. Vaporous breath saturated the sunlit air and hung

like spirits. I hardly had time to breathe myself and they were gone in a dive, just after the great male—perhaps "Leading-Spouter-of-the-World"—lobbed his tail on the surface with a WHACK!

Johnstone Strait after sundown has a way of swallowing you whole. It was summer and I'd come here to complete the southern half of the Inside Passage. But the light had shifted from the long daylight of solstice I enjoyed along the "Open Coast." The land had hemmed in and with it came the tidal current and funneled winds. All too soon, the last copper light burnished the tree tops, then slipped off the jagged crest. Dwarfed by the giant shadows of mountains, I had no choice but to float down a narrowing waterway squeezed between the shoulder of Vancouver Island and the alpen upheaval of the mainland. A mile or two ahead of the kayak's bow, the water forked to thread around Hardwicke Island. I paddled hurriedly, veering right toward Kelsey Bay, racing the narrowing light on the throat of Johnstone Strait. Before darkness pooled, I hoped to unfurl my sleeping bag triumphantly atop Kelsey Bay's thirty-foot-tall government wharf.

Fortunately, Johnstone Strait's obligatory afternoon winds had blown themselves out. But an opposing tidal stream was increasing rapidly. It pushed stubbornly against the hull like a moving sidewalk. After paddling twenty-three miles from Cracroft Island, I felt sloppy, slow-witted, and hazily worried. How long would dusk linger? How much farther was it, for heaven's sake? Inhaling shadows of basalt, cedar, hemlock, and fir triggered a primal instinct fueled by darkness. Night smells different. I'd recognize it blindfolded.

Not far ahead, the bay offered its own specters of tail-twister currents and trickster waves. The *Marine Atlas* warns mariners of its treachery. Earlier I had cracked the book's spine to page thirty-six for an aerial view of Johnstone Strait. I found Kelsey Bay—a logging settlement hugging the west shore of the much grander Salmon Bay. It was a meager notch under the forested brow of Newcastle Ridge. Then, for a sneak preview, I bypassed Kelsey Bay and browsed down the strait's south fork. My finger stopped on a flagged arrow in mid-channel indicating that the current flies up to six knots. "*Race Passage*," read the italic script. Do tell.

Wise small crafters and greenhorns probably wouldn't attempt to navigate Kelsey Bay at dark. Especially given that a capsize might entitle them to a tour of Race Passage. But Kelsey Bay evoked the sweet ring of home for this seat-of-the-pants navigator. I'd moored there once before. Twelve years earlier, six of us tied up at the government wharf in the sailboat *Leucothea*. Now I tried to recall every detail to help me recognize it in the dark.

I remembered how rusted ship hulks were used to block the bay's south end. They made a cheap breakwater for a log-booming ground. Over the years they'd transformed into whimsical giant planters sprouting wildflowers, bushes, and alder trees. The public wharf towered north of the boom. The beefy pilings, tall as a tree house, were nonetheless susceptible to crashing waves if a feisty northeasterly scudded past.

When at last my kayak floated into Kelsey Bay, a pizza-size whirlpool sucked past the kayak's stern and twirled away. Without warning, lickety-split, my 250-pound craft was sucked into the bay like a fir needle. In an instant, it zoomed toward an odious, churning ridge of black water. Perhaps it was two or four feet tall, twenty or forty yards long—size is difficult to grasp from such a low vantage. All I knew for sure was I suddenly felt like a dog hair sucked toward the rollers of a Kenmore vacuum.

The dog hair climbed, then stalled on the wave's rising shoulder. Getting tilted backward, then sideways, triggered my muscles to begin slamming the paddle down and forward like a manic windmill. Ineffective, quixotic, against the force at first, then ever so slowwwly the boat pulled up over the top. On the wave's back face the dog hair wasted no time on views. It shot forward—more like a surfboard than anything—on a plume of white water. Instantaneously, two more waves rose up. *Up and over, fishtail. Up and over into calmness.* I had arrived.

Before long, water-soaked, dripping, I reached the stilts of a creosote-black pier. I didn't know it wasn't the government wharf. Twelve years and darkness prevented a positive ID. Hazy floodlights illuminated a quaint cottage with a boat launch and a rind of beach. Nice camp spot, I thought, less gear hauling than the wharf. But a sign with peeled paint looked like it read:

PRIVATE PROPERTY

It was too dark to tell, but I figured in logger country it's always wiser to ask permission before flying a flag to the wind.

Stopping with paddle across lap, I tried to get a read on the white cottage wreathed by a picket fence. The place had a friendly feel to it. Quaint, of 1950s vintage, with a host of grandparently lawn accoutrements—geranium planters shaped like white chickens, a string of miniature lanterns bobbling above the sundeck, and a road runner whose yellow feet went round and round in the wind atop the gate.

I figured I'd meet an elderly retired couple with sturdy Old World stances, a matron drying her hands on a paisley apron after washing the dinner dishes. So I landed on the gravel beach, rubbed the salt stains from my hands and face, and trudged up the newly mowed lawn. "A lawn!" I sighed, bending to swipe my palm over the dewy blades. How amazingly soft it felt. It was 8:30 P.M. when I stood on the cottage's unlit wood porch. No dog barked. No one yet suspected a stranger was loitering at the side door. Through the sheer-curtained window I saw two men talking at a kitchen table.

I paused, hesitant. Perhaps I should tiptoe back to the beach, make an inconspicuous camp, and sneak off at sunrise? Yet curiosity held my feet in place. *New things often begin with a shred of apprehension.* This credo passed into mind and settled the gut instinct to take flight.

So instead of bolting, I watched through the curtain. The leaner of the two men looked as though he'd lived a lot of life outdoors. A graying Marlboro kind of man—weathered, square-jawed as a deck of cards. His blue-and-white flannel shirt was unbuttoned to the chest pockets, which held a pair of reading glasses and cigarettes. Momentarily, he bent to light a cigarette, waved the match out, and reached for a newspaper.

The other fellow, also flannel-shirted but softer-shouldered, sat with his back to the door. His neck was sun browned, thick and deeply creased, his hair wolf-silver. Every now and then he'd lean forward as if to sip from a mug of coffee. His left ear cupped a hearing aid.

When I knocked, it was the soft-shouldered man who turned in his chair and pushed aside the curtain. Upon seeing me, a grin plumped his ruddy cheeks. He threw back his head in joy, as if to say, "Why hello, what a nice surprise!" He was just about to open the door when a female voice came from out of view. It put me at ease immediately.

A raven-haired Italian beauty with geisha-smooth skin and eyebrows perfect as a sumi artist's brush strokes swung out the door. She was nothing close to a matron. Her knee-length red kimono, bare legs, and mischievous smile seemed out of place in a logging community. Yet her bright blue eyes spoke of surviving hard times.

Before I could speak, a stew of home-cooking aromas whirled out the open door and mixed with the damp bite of iodine and grass. Suddenly, I longed to be invited inside. But I was only asking about the beach.

"Hello! Oh . . . my . . . you look all wet. Are you okay?" the woman says, leading me gently inside by the arm.

Suddenly, I was standing in the center of a warm kitchen feeling like a dripping spectacle washed up by the Kelsey Bay tide. "Ss-sorry to bother you," I stammered.

"No, it's no bother." The gentle man's voice felt warm as honeyed tea.

"My name's Jennifer. I'm kayaking, uh, from uh-laska. And I wondered, where, uh, I might pitch my tent—"

There was a pause, as if the room and the people were still taking in my words, then an explosion of warmth and familial openness.

"Right here!" the woman jumped in, throwing her arms out in wide gesture.

"Yes, right here!" echoed the older gentleman like it was a delightful idea.

"Alaska, you say?" His eyes searched mine in disbelief at what his hearing aid had just picked up.

Before I knew it, the door had closed behind me.

Introductions went round. Doug smoked. Lars owned the cottage. And Margarite, well, she was my best girlfriend now.

"Here, take this chair," Doug offered, sliding into a different one.

"Hang your wet coat behind the door. You must be cold," Lars said, concerned as my own father.

"How long have you been out?"

All attention had shifted to me, seeing to it that I was warm, comfortable, and made welcome.

"You're probably hungry." It was a statement more than a question from

Margarite. I would soon discover that in her overzealous, gracious-hostess role, she would make me her sister, confidante, and heroine, too. Within minutes she had dashed together a plate of pork chops, sautéed onions, potatoes, salsa, and beer in a frosted mug heavy enough for a kayaker to heave ho and grunt.

"How about some coffee? Tea?" Doug offered.

"Tea sounds great."

"Want some whiskey in it?" Margarite suggested. It was as natural as if she was asking if I wanted some milk or sugar.

"Oh . . . no thanks." I figured it was best to keep my wits about me in a house with two men and a woman in a red kimono. But I could see mild disappointment, as though I'd answered the question wrong and crossed some invisible line of ingratitude or, worse, prudishness. So I waved toward the bottle in Margarite's hands.

"What the heck, a bump of whiskey'd be great."

She smiled approvingly and the whiskey poured like water.

"Just a little though, don't want to fall asleep in my pork chops." My acceptance restored ease.

Doug nodded toward the cup of laced tea I raised to my lips. "Yeah, that'll warm ya up!"

Around this gray Formica table, I recognized kind, hard-working, good-timing folks like my own welder father. Plaid flannel shirts elbow-worn and frayed at the collar, work-faded blue jeans with a wallet ghost on the back pocket, callused hands, and thick, dirt-ringed fingernails. I knew their straight-forward, trusting ways from growing up in blue-collar Milwaukee, Wisconsin. I sawed off a mouthful of chop, drank the ninety-proof tea, answered a trainload of curious questions, and asked a few myself.

Conversation began immediately to clear up who was who and related to whom, and what I'd seen on the journey. I talked about a whale I'd almost hit head on that afternoon, the twisting current and strange waves in Kelsey Bay, and the spring storms I'd encountered in Alaska in June.

Before I'd finished Margarite's home-cooked dinner, we were all laughing easily. I'd transformed from a stranger hiding in the wet cocoon of my jacket into a headlong family friend.

Mozart played softly in the background from a tape player. Lars, it turned out, is a classical music buff. Lars also told me he's a contractor and was logging the mountain behind us for future home sites. Doug ran the skidder. He and Lars had been buds for fifteen years.

"We've run a lot a jobs together," said Doug. "Lars is one of the best in the business."

As if to dismiss the compliment, Lars gestured with his coffee cup to an invisible peak rising behind the kitchen wall. Newcastle Ridge pulls itself out of the sea like a petrified tidal wave ready to crash at any moment on the settlement of Kelsey Bay. "We'll go up the mountain in the morning," he said, "and you can see what our loggin's about."

"Up the mountain in the morning." It sounded like a folk song refrain. I figured that as a literate human who'd spent a great deal of her life inking, stapling, highlighting, glue-sticking, filing, and wadding reams of paper, I ought to visit the source. Especially considering that one ton of paper chews up almost thirteen tons of wood.

British Columbia shelters the earth's last vestige of large coastal temperate rainforest—eight million acres. But the government long ago deafened its ears to concerns about the hack-and-destroy practices of corporate logging in ancient forests. Why whimper when you can fill the coffers with easy cash from old-growth liquidation? I'd seen the rusted spoils of big-time corporate clear-cutting all up and down the evergreen coast. The Canadian Council of Forest Industries estimates that one acre of forest is cut in Canada every thirteen seconds. Vancouver Island has been shaved of almost sixty-five percent of its original old-growth forests. Even the British Columbia government agrees that the province's ancient forests are being felled at a rate forty percent faster than is deemed sustainable. The global tragedy is that we are losing the last magnificent rainforest in North America.

Lars was felling second-growth fir, hemlock, and cedar. His operation was a "small, family kind of business . . . cutting a swath for home sites with standing trees skirtin' the edges." I knew that leaving trees standing carries on the genetic diversity for the next generation. Lars seemed to recognize this without saying so.

"Jennifer, do you like bubble baths?" Margarite asked as she whisked away the empty dinner plate. She was smiling coyly, as if this is a girl-to-girl secret.

I already knew from the variety of bubble scents on her bathroom shelf that hot baths were Margarite's elixir for feeling good. So I said the magic words. "Yes, I'd love one." Of the bath scents, I chose "Tranquility"; of the face masks, it was "Passion Fruit." At which point, I had to laugh out loud.

"What's so funny?"

"I never imagined, hours ago, paddling through dicey waves, slapping high-fives off the north point, that tonight I'd be taking a bubble bath in a claw-foot tub, wearing a tropical fruit face mask. It's so surprising . . . so funny!"

Margarite giggled, scrunched her shoulders to her ears in a gesture that suggested she, perhaps, was happier than I was for my change of plans tonight.

"What I really mean, Margarite, is this is a *great* treat."

Margarite waved me through another door one down from the bath. Inside was a guest room with a quilt-covered bed, a fireplace with hangers to dry clothes on, and a television. A simple, corn husk cross hung in the corner and a curtained window was positioned right above the bed.

"Is this okay?" she asked.

"Okay?" I was a bit bewildered. "You mean this is my room for the night?" Apparently the tent was a moot point.

"Of course you're sleeping inside, silly," scolded Margarite like an over-protective mother. "I'm not going to let you sleep outside in the cold!"

After stretching fresh sheets over the mattress, we returned to the kitchen and waited for the tub to fill. But soon we were all so caught up in conversation that the bath overflowed with bubbles.

As the evening seemed to wax, not wane, it was vividly apparent that I was as much entertainment for them as they were curiosity to me. In this sleepy little town tucked in a mountainous valley, a female stranger paddling in from Alaska was a breath of fresh air, although Margarite was a whirlwind unto herself and kept the evening full with surprises.

She goaded me, "Come on, Jennifer, look inside. You'll like these. I bought them for Lars a couple of weeks ago." Margarite had placed a small red, silk-covered box with a miniature brass clasp on the kitchen table in front of me.

I lifted the box's lid. Inside were two sterling ball bearings streaked with rainbow colors. Each bearing the size of a plum.

Margarite picked up the balls. "These are Lars's balls," she laughed.

I looked around, a tad embarrassed. But then Lars laughed. And Doug laughed. So I laughed.

"Go ahead, roll 'em 'round in your hands." She put the balls on her cupped palm. They clanged and chimed as they rolled over and over, round and round.

"Chinese healing balls. See, here's this little book that tells all the pressure points in your hand."

"A kayaker like you should have a pair," said Lars. "They work wonders on my arthritis."

I picked up the booklet. Margarite went and sat on Lars's lap, wrapping an arm around his neck. Lars smiled and patted her thigh. I guessed he was sixty and she, mid-forties.

"Jennifer, just so you know who's with who, I'm Lars's mistress."

"Great," I said for lack of something more inventive. But mostly I was hoping Doug wasn't too lonely.

As the night grew later, my suspicions were overridden. Everyone carried chairs into the guest room turned video theater. Margarite paraded in with foot-tall floats made of bubbly wine and ice cream. One for Lars and one for me. Doug lit up another cigarette.

Margarite punched in a video—*Fawlty Towers* with John Cleese. Soon the punch lines had us guffawing and slapping our knees.

Margarite's high-pitched giggling made high notes in our river of talk. "Isn't this funny? Oh-ohh, now watch what's going to happen next. Isn't this just hilarious, Jennifer?"

More scenes, more cigarettes. The blue smoke clouds settled in a layer overhead like a temperature inversion. I wanted to dive inside the parfait dish and bury my nose in its smoke-free coolness. Soon the empty ice cream drinks were whisked away and a cold beer set on a napkin.

"You're gonna make me a hippo, Margarite."

"Oh, you're buff, Jennifer. Real buff."

I got embarrassed for a split second, then retorted, "Well, you aren't so bad, either . . . Sissssster!"

She smiled and playfully whapped Lars's knee as if to say, "See."

"Hug a logger and you'll never go back to hugging trees!" proclaimed a Kelsey Bay bumper sticker. There, in the mist-laden valleys of north Vancouver Island where every year it rains as much as a logger stands tall, survives a lineage of flannel-collared woodsmen who go back to great-grandfathers drawing on nineteen-foot crosscut saws. Lars, pushing sixty-six, ran one of the few independent crews left in an otherwise multinational, corporate-owned woods.

Lars's hardy crew of six had been felling, bucking, skidding, and loading logs since sunrise to take advantage of the long summer hours. As we jounced up the packed-stone road in his pickup, Lars's blue plaid arm traced the hillside.

"We dynamited rock from the cliff here and crushed it for the road. Soil's mucky, so we cut and laid down logs first. The bed has to be strong to carry eighty-thousand-pound logging trucks."

"How'd you learn all this?"

"Oh, I guess it runs in the blood. My father logged with draft horses."

"Really, they used horses?" I said, eager and all ears.

Lars teased, "You mean hay-burners, that's what you call Clydesdales. Before horses, the camps used bulls."

"Bulls?"

"Shod oxen. They were strong pullers, skookum and steady, but horses were smarter, faster, and more agile in the woods."

I nodded, recognizing the truth in Lars's words. My older brother and sister raised horses for a time. My father would have agreed. "Horses," I could hear him saying, "are doubly smart, because they keep teenagers out of mischief."

"Long before trucks and skidders like Doug's, teams of four to twelve horses towed each turn of logs from the forest to the beach," explained Lars. "Of course, you couldn't expect a horse to yard logs through the rough terrain of a cut forest. So back then, the fellas built a corduroy or skid road. It was kinda like a railroad, only no rails, just crosswise ties. Logs were chained end to end like train cars. Each set or turn moved along behind the horse team on a cut groove. A 'teamster' guided the horses, and a 'greaser' smeared crude oil on the logs for lubrication. I heard one old timer used whale oil. Imagine that."

"I bet it was slick."

"Yeah, maybe too slick. Skid roads were always built on low inclines, or else you'd have one helluva time slowing the logs down. Once the load pulled parallel to the beach, fellas used peaveys—a tool with a spike at one end and a free-swinging hook to roll them into the water. Then they herded them into a bullpen. What you might call a booming ground—a floating corral enclosed by boom sticks for sorting the logs according to species, sectioning them into rafts for towing to the mills. MacMillan-Bloedel has a big booming ground right below us."

Outside Lars's window, four hundred feet down, Salmon Bay stretched like a corrugated blue fan. Couldn't see the booming ground for the fir trees, and I guessed that was a good sign.

The truck jitterbugged sideways over a washboard turn. Lars noticed that I was gripping the vinyl seat and quickly lightened his boot on the gas. Stuffed out of reach in the seat crack, safety belts weren't an option. And truthfully, I preferred to vibrate up mountain untethered, ready to spring out the window if we rolled. Lars pulled a dusty cassette tape from the glove box and plugged it in—Johann Strauss's *Emperor Waltz*. A breeze washed through the pickup's open windows smelling like Christmas with a pungent infusion of cedar, hemlock, and fir . . . punctuated by mud and diesel.

In 1792, Captain George Vancouver wrote in his ship's log, "The country now before us presented a most luxuriant landscape. The whole had the appearance of a continued forest extending as far as the eye could reach."

Call it the "Rain Forest Coast," "Pacific Mediterranean," or, as one historian fancied, "Long-log Country." By any name it adds up to one thing: BIG trees. Herein is the God-given recipe for growing behemoth Douglas firs: Prevailing westerlies laden with vapor from the warm Japanese current drop their burden on the cold shoulders of the coast mountains. Consequently, the forest drips puddliciously in winter and bakes in summer. It was, and still is, a land nurturing secreted pockets of thousand-year-old trees.

Lumber barons such as W. P. Sayward, J. H. Bloedel, H. R. MacMillan, and now corporations such as MacMillan-Bloedel, Crown Pacific, Western Forest Products, and B.C. Forest Products, grew their fortunes off this green gold—the lush softwoods that dominate that rugged coast. Douglas fir is king of the lumber industry. It's strong, resistant to decay, easy to work, and has a straight grain. It's perfect wood for lumber, pulp, or luxurious veneers. It's also relatively lightweight, making it well suited for shipping. According to Lars, it carries the heftiest price tag and has done so for the past century.

"On a good day," explained Lars, "we get six truckloads. On a poor day, four. One load of mixed logs brings $3700 Canadian. But if it's all fir, $4500."

Not one member of the orange-vested crew, boot-deep in mud and shoulder-high in felled fir trunks, would have said logging is easy living. In fact, felling trees to create the lumber, toilet paper, toothpicks, and book pages we thrive on is dangerous work. When a twenty-ton fir plummets 120 feet at fifty feet a second and gets caught on another tree—all hell breaks loose. Even a cautious feller is liable to get knocked in the head by ripping branches—widow makers they're called.

Lars eased the truck onto the roadside where three men squatted hunched over an orange power saw. They waved when they saw Lars. Out of respect, he introduced me first to the head feller, Glen, then to Terry and Luke, two more fellers. Glen tilted back his orange hardhat and wiped the sweat from his freckled forehead. With arms muscular as fir limbs, an oil stained, blue work shirt, and suspenders stamped with the white letters SAW SHOP, it wasn't surprising that his handshake was a firm squeeze.

"This is my fortieth year," Glen told me, "I've been fortunate I've never had a broken bone. Not many make it to forty without some serious limp."

"Glen, what are ya, sixty?" asked Lars.

"-one," said Glen, pushing a wreath of thinning silver hair back with a gloved hand. His other hand lightly clutched a twenty-pound chainsaw as easily as one might grip a Kevlar fishing pole.

"Glen's one of the best fellers around," extolled Lars. "Had a big fir, we thought it would smash, but he laid a couple little ones down and dropped the big one on 'em."

Glen shook his head, smiling with a combination of embarrassment and pleasure from Lars's admiration. But within seconds he was back to earth, down on one knee cradling the saw in his oil-blackened hands, tinkering again with the toothed chain.

Douglas Fir Branch and Cone
Pseudotsuga menziesii

Long ago, legend says, a great fire scorched the great Northwest forests. All the animals ran or flew away. Except the mice. To escape the high flames they raced up the fir trunks and jumped into the cones, where their tails and back legs can still be seen.

"Do saws break often?" I asked the other two twentyish fellers, Terry and Luke, who, it turned out, grew up in the valley. "We're 'valley boys,'" they joked.

Terry, a part-time logger, pig farmer, and fisher, answered, "Saws break all the time. Gotta be workin' on 'em all the time."

Glen nodded in agreement, smiling up at us from his dismembered chainsaw. "What I did was, there's a floating sprocket and I missed it. Well, it's not every day I'm being watched by a pretty lady."

I laughed with the guys and swished a hand at the compliment like I was shooing away a fly.

"So what's it like running a powersaw all day long?" I asked to no one in particular.

"You put on your earmuffs and you can't hear anything but your brain ticking," chortled Luke.

Glen won out over his saw—for a while anyway. He swiped a glove at his dirt-caked knee, replaced the orange hardhat, then waved an oily hand toward the clearing where Doug's skidder was clanging uphill, dragging sixty-foot tree lengths. The orange Timber Jack bumped along stirring up an eternal scribble of dust and exhaust. The valley boys called Doug's skidder "the fogger" because "it keeps away the skeeters."

"I'm gonna lay 'em across the skid road," Glen nodded to us.

To gain better vantage of Glen's tree felling, Lars and I walked downslope following the skidder's mud ruts. Our toes jammed against the ends of our boots with each step. We heard the telltale *whir-gig* of Glen's saw as he cut a deep notch into a tall fir. I clambered onto a stump. Lars leaned against the corrugated bark.

"That one he's felling," said Lars, pointing to the crown of jiggling boughs on a second-growth fir "is 110 feet."

In past times a 110-foot fir would have barely qualified as a stripling adolescent—having achieved only a third to a half of its potential height. When mature, Pacific Douglas firs rank among earth's most Goliathan trees. Some measure more than three hundred feet tall and fifteen feet in diameter. Scientists theorize that this tendency toward gigantism is the result of uninterrupted millennia of genetic evolution. During the Ice Age, for instance, Pacific Douglas fir survived by retreating down north-south coastal mountain corridors to a less chilly climate. Northern tree species from eastern North America, Asia, and Europe, however, were blocked by east-west mountains. They essentially got mowed over, tossed into the genetic deep freezer.

Nootka Sound is on the west coast of Vancouver Island. When Captain James Cook sailed into Friendly Cove there in 1778, the world was forever changed. Cook's bedraggled ships, the *Discovery* and the *Resolution,* were en route from New Zealand and the Sandwich Islands. Among the brass-buttoned crew standing at the rails anxiously eyeing Chief Maquinna's village of smoking longhouses was the lad George Vancouver.

Captain Cook's ambitious "to-do" list included befriending Chief

Maquinna, trading swords and brass buttons for food supplies, caulking the ships and replacing rotting ship spars, and brewing up a cure for scurvy—vitamin C-rich spruce-tree beer. Everything was to be made shipshape in one month before hoisting sails for Alaska. Consequently, Cook's crew became the first white men to log on Vancouver Island.

Pacific Douglas fir would become the timbery face that launched a thousand ships, literally, in the form of one-hundred-foot octagonal ship spars from the New World. Rave timber reports penned by Cook and later captain-explorers John Meares and George Vancouver read like a billboard to his majesty's overseas entrepreneurs.

In the century to come, a shrewd commander of British Pacific forces would ship a load of Douglas fir spars to the Portsmouth naval yards for comparison with four-star Baltic timber. If the wood proved worthy, it guaranteed investors a shot at the world's ship-building market. Not surprisingly, the tests resolved once and for all that British Columbia fir was far superior even to trees from Latvia—then touted as the strongest, tallest spars on earth. Within decades covetous investors and loggers poured into the Pacific Northwest from England, Norway, Finland, Sweden, and eastern Canada.

Spar camps mushroomed from the Fraser to the Columbia Rivers. Fellers wielding broadaxes measuring sixteen inches at the face would choose the straightest fir—often two hundred feet tall with nary a branch for the first hundred feet. Balanced on spring boards chinked into the trunk about six feet off the ground, these early Paul Bunyans would *saw-shh saw-shh* or *chop-chop-chop* all day long until one leviathan finally crashed down. Notches from the spring boards still can be seen in huge old stumps throughout the Pacific Northwest. At the camp, the spar shapers would whap off the bark and hew the wood into an even taper. The completed spars were dispatched on ships that sailed as far afield as China, Europe, South America, and Australia.

"Long Life Giver" is the Kwakwala name given to great trees. The First People harvested cedar, spruce, fir, and hemlock to fashion an infinite number of vital items: rain capes, hats, skirts, sleeping mats, baskets, cradles, ropes, torches, totem poles, spears, tree-climbing equipment, smoke houses, dance masks, rattles, ceremonial drums, spirit whistles, animal traps, fish hooks, fish spreaders, canoe bailers, paddles, burial boxes, and mortuary poles.

For thousands of moons before Cook cut ship spars in Nootka Sound, the ancestors of the ochre-faced people who greeted Cook had carved their lives around trees. Taking anything from the forest, the First People knew, required reciprocity, in words or in gifts.

A coastal Salish woman placed a miniature basket among the tree's roots before gathering its bark. A Kwakiutl man who wished to cut a tree for a canoe or a house post prayed to the tree before felling it: "Do not fall too heavily, else you, Great Supernatural One, might break on the ground." Coast Salish woodworkers who possessed the power called "su'win" spoke to a tree by name and told it which direction to fall so it would not shatter.

After visiting Chief Maquinna's village, Cook wrote copious notes on Nootka woodcraft. To dispel the rain, Cook observed, the people donned a "strong straw [actually spruce root] hat which is shaped like a flowerpot and is as good a covering for the head as can possibly be invented." Wearing otter, bear, and wolf cloaks "with sometimes the addition of Coarse Mat over all, they sit in their Canoes in the heaviest rain as unconcerned as we can under the best of cover . . . ."

Cook tasted smoked salmon from wood drying racks and spit-roasted venison. He wrote in amazement of another commonplace culinary art involving trees.

"Boiling is performed in a wooden Trough like an oblong box, by putting red hot stones into the liquor, a heap of which always compose the fire hearth, they put them in and out of the pot with a kind of wooden tongs. In this manner they boil all kinds of meat and make Soups, which even a European would relish . . . ."

Underneath the leaning 110-foot fir, Glen's hardhat tipped back as he looked into the spoked branches far up the trunk.

"He is trying to judge the wind and angle of the tree," explained Lars.

"From where we are upslope, it's easy to see the lean. But he's in a blinder spot."

Glen's saw started up again. *Whir-gggggg, whir-ggggg*. He was working a second and a third fir tree. Suddenly, there was a soft crackling like fir needles pitched into a bonfire, then an explosion of sound—a lightning crack—as the heartwood shattered and bark fell away like a discarded overcoat. There was a *whoosh* as the thirty-ton tree dropped so fast its crown lagged behind—bent back like a bow.

Whoosh. I quickly scanned the slope for Glen who had jumped out of the way at the first splintering. The first fir landed on a neighboring fir and both fell onto a third tree whose splintering was just beginning. The whole cutting ended with a *WHUUUUFFF!* as the three firs hit the mountain.

Glen stood in the clearing raising cupped hands together like an Olympic athlete: "Yeaaaaay!" The wind blew the citrus of broken fir needles up the mountain.

I squatted on the stump, both exhilarated and dumbfounded, feeling my part in this enormous energy of give and take. I felt the tree's passing. *Thank you, fir.* I held my notebook firmly in my hands to record my thoughts. I had this paper I was writing on. I had that mountain I was looking at. That tree in my hands that fell long ago to make this writing possible.

Someday someone's house would rise where I stood on a stump. A woman or man would look out from their window through this opening on the mountain. But they maybe would not know what preceded them. I was thankful to Lars for being aware of the cycle. Mountain, chainsaw, tree. Chainsaw cuts tree. Tree falls on mountain. Paper unfolds in my hands. Rock, scissors, paper. It's an age-old circle that begs remembering.

Rock, scissors, bone. Later in the evening Doug told me that he's been running a skidder for fifteen years. Driving a two-ton tractor up and down a mountain of rock and loose mud while dragging precious tons of felled trees is tricky business. It's easy to roll or get mired. All the while, the vibration of the engine and *ca-chunking* of the load makes it feel like you're riding a bucking bronco for a living. When Doug was forty-eight, a doctor cut and removed four discs from his back, then slit open his suntanned neck and inserted bone chips between each vertebrae.

"Basically, I'm getting jangled to death," he told me.

Mountain, metal, rubber. "Worse yet," complained Doug, "the rocky slope is eating up the skidder's tires too durn fast. They're eight thousand dollars per set of four and should last me three years. I'll tell you, I think it's too steep for a skidder. Lars should be using a spar pole."

With the grace of a dancer, Glen walked down the felled fir tree swinging the saw in one hand.

I turned to Lars, "So what is Glen doing now?"

"He's pacing the tree. For bigger trees he's got a tape measure on his belt with an automatic rewind because those big trees have to be cut exactly."

Glen finished the pace and began dropping branches with his saw. Soon the three fir trees resembled telephone poles with a ragged bark cloak. Doug backed the 130-horse Timber Jack down the rocky skid road and hooked a cable to the trees. To keep the cable from dragging and getting abraded, it was threaded through an arch shaped like a huge pelvic bone on the back of the skidder.

I pointed to the stump I stood on. "What's the size of this one, two feet?" I guessed.

"Sixteen inches. You don't count the bark," Lars explained.

Doug's skidder rumbled up slope in a blue fog. When it cleared the top, Doug, Glen, and I followed along, climbing up over waffle-wheel indents.

I left Lars and Glen to go watch the log loader. But I was regarded with some skepticism by the operator who, upon seeing my notebook, asked suspiciously, "You aren't working for the feds or the department of environment are ya?" I opened the pages to sketches of birds, flowers, shells, and landscapes, and watched his transformation. "An artist," he grunted.

Two hours after we began our visit "up the mountain," Lars and I warmly shook good-byes to a chain of ungloved hands.

Riding down the steep road, he told me, "The guys on the mountain think you're a hero, you know."

"Me?" I laughed. "Oh, I don't know. Logging's dangerous, one of the most dangerous jobs of all. Out on the water, I only have waves slamming into me."

Lars smiled a quiet, knowing smile. I flashed back to a moment earlier in the morning when I first met the fellers. As if he were my proud father, Lars had exclaimed to Glen, Terry, and Luke: "Can you believe she's paddling all the way from Alaska in a kayak?" The same kind of smile had crossed his lips when I was sitting on the stump in the clearing telling how my Dad taught me to weld so I could pay for college. "Somehow, it seems fathers have a much closer relationship to their daughters," he'd commented. And I wondered if Lars had a daughter too.

Strauss was playing again. A red-shafted flicker waltzed through the clearing above the road. As its wings burst open, a melon-orange fan rose up. When the fan snapped shut, an ashen creature went into free fall. It arced and dropped, arced and dropped toward the uncut trees, white tail patch disappearing like a snowball in summertime. It moved as if aware of the *Emperor Waltz*.

"There's an eagle over there. A nest. We aren't cutting nearby."

I told Lars I was relieved that his operation wasn't a knock-'em-all-down-and-carry-away-the-eagles affair.

He laughed. "I like the animals, too."

"Lucy in the Sky with Diamonds" bayed from a tape player on the porch where Margarite sunbathed in a flowered swimsuit top. Seeing us approach, she grabbed her blouse and was still buttoning as she ran down the stairs. A menagerie of animals tromped after her: Maxwell, half lab, half pit bull with a steam shovel jaw; Molly McButter, half poodle, half golden retriever; and a cinnamon-striped, deaf cat. Margarite told me she used to have five cats at her own home—a rustic cabin up the valley with no electricity or running water. Once while she was away the river flooded the cabin up to the stovetop. Only recently did she reluctantly arrange for telephone service. The cats, she was certain, were eaten by cougars.

She gave us a hug and asked teasingly, "Do you know what a mistress calls her lover?"

"No idea."

"A paramour. Thorough love. Anglo-French for illicit lover. A philanderer is a man who loves women."

In the afternoon, Margarite's landlord and friend Mr. Duncan came by to drop some rubber balls off for the dogs. The last two had floated away on the tide and Max had to be content finding small rocks for us to throw.

Doug came down from the mountain at 5:10 P.M.

"Can't beat the ten-minute commute," he laughed as he lit a cigarette.

Over tea at the kitchen table, he mentioned that his hands were so callused he could push a pin a quarter inch into his finger and not feel pain.

"Don't make for very good hands to hold," he sighed sadly. And I sensed there was something more, yet felt privileged just to hold these words. But after a moment Doug spoke candidly of his family and home life.

"I'm a faultless provider," he said. "Spend most of my time working to provide a home for my wife and kids." Perhaps he works too much, he admitted. His wife had asked him to leave for a while.

"The kids, of course, want things to be different." No, counseling wasn't an option for his wife. "We eat dinner together, now and then."

Doug hoped they'd mend, but wasn't sure when. Once he got up to fill our tea cups, dug into his wallet, and handed me his business card.

"Drop a line. Tell me if you made it."

That night we ate beef stew, leftover pork chops, chocolate cake, and amaretto cherry ice cream. My eyes stung from the dryness of the house heat. With Margarite ensconced in a bubble bath, I helped Lars clear the dishes.

"Margarite's stomach is feeling queasy," he casually mentioned, then added rather unexpectedly, "She's a strong woman . . . had to be the way she lost her husband."

I set a handful of silverware in the sink and turned to listen.

"Her husband was a trucker. Margarite sometimes rode in the cab. A few years back, the truck rolled down a mountainside, and he was killed. Margarite was cut up pretty badly, with all the glass and things, but she managed to crawl away and flag down help."

"Wow. That's *really* sad, Lars."

"Yeah, makes you glad for each day."

"That's for damn sure. You know, I lost my mother when a semi-truck hit our VW."

"That's why you're so close to your Dad?"

"Yep, Dad's girl."

Around 9 P.M., the phone rang. It was my friend Bob Lyons from Lopez Island, Washington, who had circumnavigated Vancouver Island the summer before. I'd called him to get some firsthand advice on kayaking through Seymour Narrows, my third "threshold," which was coming up next, timed to correspond with a "half moon, slack tide." He was kind enough to return my anxious phone call.

"Hug the left bank. There's a nice campsite. From that side, there are two ways you can do it. You can portage over a small earth dam between Fink Bay and Maud Island—it's all rock, but not too steep, about forty feet. Then you can drop over the other side. Or you can keep going around Maud Island if there's still time in the slack."

Before the conversation ended, Bob emphasized, "Go at the end of the ebb. And check that there's a *small* exchange." His tone sounded dead serious, but wholly supportive. Then he chuckled, as if sensing my nervousness. "Don't worry. Piece of cake."

I laughed back, unconvinced, "Yeah, hope it's a double-chocolate cream torte."

By 10 P.M. I could barely stay awake. Crouched in the guest bedroom, I wrapped the spray skirt's leaky nylon top with ten coils of silver duct tape. The next day I'd look like the Tin Man pushing off from the Emerald City. Margarite gleefully brought me a ziplock bag stuffed with boiled potatoes, a pint of yogurt, and a mysterious paper bag.

"Don't worry, I asked Lars if it was all right," she laughed, lifting out the satin-covered box with Chinese healing balls.

Morning came too quickly at 5 A.M. Down at the beach, the air tasted thick and salty. The kayak lay dew-pearled while the wharf lights shone frost-ily in the haze. I was stuffing the kayak's hatches with gear as the marine radio gave the 5:45 A.M. weather report.

Johnstone Strait: small craft warnings. West winds 5-15 knots becoming northwest 25 knots by evening. Outlook moderate to strong northwesterlies.

Strangely enough, I was getting used to hearing "Johnstone Strait, small craft warnings," and paddling anyhow. As long as the wind was out of the northwest, it blew me south toward home. Given the twenty-five-knot wind forecast, however, I vowed to leave right away and take advantage of a calm morning.

Doug had already headed up the mountain, and Lars would soon follow, but first he came down to lift the stern while I carried the bow. Margarite's eye caught the red cloth rose knotted to the bow's toggle and beamed. "Now that's a woman's boat!"

After hugs, Lars gave me a shove and I floated free. The water was mill-pond still, and the horizon diffuse and soft as cottonwood gone to seed. I paddled over a seemingly endless silhouette of Vancouver Island mountains toward a brightening, gilded sky. Margarite waved from the wharf, camera around her neck. She wore Lars's yellow wool sweater, the same one that she'd loaned me the day before.

"I want a photo of you out there with all those big mountains. How small you look, strong woman!"

A pallor of blue wood smoke hovered over the valley like a huge winged heron. Below the smoke, a forklift shuffled logs at the MacMillan-Bloedel site. *Tink, tink!*—it was so amazingly still—*tink! tink!*—up on the ridge I could hear Glen's axe pounding a metal wedge into a saw cut.

I turned around to find that Margarite had become a small yellow dot on a wood-colored line. Behind her perched a tiny white house, and behind that the forest rose thickly to a jagged scar of red earth—the logging operation.

That morning I didn't feel much like Kelsey Bay's heroine. My mind was uneasy watching a boiling dark seam of water one hundred yards off the light in Race Passage where a dozen trawlers bobbed with their spreaders out like insects ready for lift off.

I pointed the bow toward a white trawler drifting on the current with diesel smoke chugging out the chimney.

"What, Steven?" I heard a gentle voice ask from the deck of a nearby boat. All at once, I realized how the presence of another woman out here, a fisher or a paramour, made me feel that I wasn't alone on this rugged, mountain-fenced strait. Two days ago at dusk I had paddled into a little logging community and knocked on an unknown door. Like Hansel and Gretel, my curiosity was piqued by the little goodies adorning the house. Instead of being locked in a cage and my finger checked for fat each day, however, I was taken in as family. I was stuffed with stews and pork chops, cake and ice cream, wine and garden taters, and begged to stay another day.

I was beginning to see how a sense of "home" isn't conjured so much by a particular geography, defined by house walls, property lines, or loran-exact latitudes and longitudes. Rather, the feeling of "being at home" grows out of an openness of the heart. That morning, drifting away from Sayward and Kelsey Bay, I felt loved beyond boundary by people who had been complete strangers two days before. Even though I couldn't say exactly where I was headed, I was already at home. Right there. Right then. And that night I hoped to find home again wherever and with whomever I was with, including myself alone.

12 Half Moon, Slack Tide

Cal and Janice Sherman of High River, Alberta, fancy themselves the adoptive parents of the Inside Passage's few-and-far-between long-distance sea kayakers. Each summer the retired couple parks a motorhome at a campground on the banks of Little Bear Bay. Winters, they wheel south to Baja, Mexico, chasing the migratory gray whales, ospreys, calliope hummingbirds, and snowbird tourists.

Unaware of my impending hosts and their gracious intentions, I was sprinting across the mouth of Little Bear Bay headed for the Rock Point government wharf when a glint of aluminum flashed from the dark shore. I figured it was a car windshield catching the last sunlight. The twinkle was Cal's aluminum skiff. I paid it no mind.

I was focused on getting to Rock Point before sundown. I had a date with the slack tide in Seymour Narrows the next afternoon. Seymour Narrows is fabled for capsizing boats in turbulent upwellings, then sucking victims into giant whirlpools. It would be a half moon and the least amount of tidal exchange all month. I didn't want to miss it. Rock Point's government wharf set me three miles closer to my third "threshold."

Halfway across Little Bear, my belly panged with ferocious hunger. It was inconsequential that I'd tanked up on almonds, dried fruit, and a peanut butter granola bar just an hour ago. I needed food NOW! Paddling twenty to twenty-five miles a day, my appetite's gauge was like that. Burning calories for fuel, I could flag from reserves to empty in no time. My watch read 5:15 P.M., late enough to turn in. So I raised the binoculars to survey the far shore for a camp.

I was astonished to see a village of trailers. Perhaps a Bible camp? A private RV campground? It was a tempting mayhem of kids chasing about, moms and dads sitting in lawn chairs with fishing poles bent to the sea, canoes, a couple of power boats. At the same time, I wondered if I wouldn't feel overwhelmed. Maybe I should just keep on to Rock Point or eddy out at some little hole-in-the-wall beach and sleep alone. But I'd been alone all day. I was timbering toward mayhem.

About the same moment, Roy, Cal's accomplice, was pulling the starter rope on Cal's outboard. I saw the aluminum bow and two fishers in broad-brim hats motoring out the bay.

I waved.

"Say, is this a private campground or is it public?" I asked hopefully.

"Puhhh-blik," announced the bow man, nodding his straw hat for emphasis.

Ruddy-cheeked and lanky, he appeared as though he'd spent some leisure time south of the U.S. border, soaking up Mexico's rays and an easy-come, Jimmy Buffett attitude. Smiling, surveying the kayak bow to stern, neither man said another word.

"I'm Jennifer."

"This is Cal," said the steersman, prompting his friend in the straw hat. "He's the campground host."

Fancy that, I thought, the fisher I waved down just happens to be the host, too! Of course, I didn't know this was a repeating plot.

"We could see your paddle blades flashin' from way 'cross the bay, eh?"

"Roy (that's Cal's neighbor and friend who grew up on the banks of Little Bear, back when it harbored a float of company homes for logging families) had been lookin' through that there scope," his wife told me later, pointing to a tripod on the grass.

"He was expecting a guy and decided it was a long-haired hippie. Then Cal took a gander and said, 'That's not a hippie! It's a woman, and a good-lookin' one at that!'"

We all snickered over that confession later at the picnic table set with checkered tablecloth, corncob forks, and a crocheted napkin holder—all the homey accessories of an old-fashioned picnic with my grandparents.

Out on the water, Roy asked "Where you from? We get a few kayakers through now and then. Long-distance ones, that is. Are you one of those?"

I laughed and nodded.

"Great! Would you like to join my wife and me for dinner? We'll swap you home cooking for stories . . ."

Their invitation was unbelievable! It caught me entirely by surprise.

" . . . but I have this date with the slack tide in Seymour Narrows tomorrow afternoon," I told them worriedly. "I've been planning it for days. Rock Point's government wharf is closer . . . ."

"Rock Point isn't a government wharf anymore," warned Roy. "It's private now," piped in Cal. "They'll charge you seven dollars to take the kayak out and twelve more just to camp!" He shook his head in disgust. "But you can stay here for free."

I sensed that Cal and Roy, the welcome wagon for kayakers, were my newest allies. My rumbling stomach cast the unanimous vote.

At the campsite picnic table, we sat down to fresh sweet corn, green salad, baked potatoes in aluminum foil, barbecued steak from the grill, and home-baked bread from an island across the strait.

This habit of being good Samaritans to kayakers had a long history, I learned. One kayaker came through in a pedal-powered boat. Another lonely fellow coming down from Alaska loved the cooking and company so much he stayed for a week. But not everyone they motored out to was invited in.

"There was this guy in dreads . . . ." explained Roy.

We talked of how to make yummy, aluminum-wrapped grilled potatoes: "Slice 'em thin. Add a dab of margarine. Pepper 'n' salt. Wrap 'em in foil—just one wrap, two and they won't get done fast enough—put over the grill," recited Janice, Cal's wife.

"Janice overcooked 'em the other day. They were sticking to the foil, but nice and crispy. Now she always overcooks 'em," said Cal, smiling at his cherub-faced wife looking proud in her lawn chair.

Janice, it turned out, was the queen of home crafts. Her gallery was the motorhome. She crocheted blankets and tiny earrings. She twisted copper wire into faux bonsai trees, curled the branches, and then glued gemstones on for leaves. She needlepointed napkin holders. I bought a pair of dream-catcher earrings. She laughed, delighted to make a sale and tucked them into the tiniest ziplock in the world.

Soon we were all telling stories in the trailer over vanilla ice cream topped with gobs of radioactive-yellow lemon meringue pie filling and chocolate marshmallow cookies. When Cal and Janice heard I guided winter whale-watching kayak trips in Baja, Mexico, Cal asked, "Where?" They both responded with a double-chinned chuckle. Janice handed me a stack of photos and said, "Then you'll recognize these places."

Sure enough. Flipping through the photos, I discovered my beloved Baja haunts—the crumbling, candy-striped lighthouse at the sleepy fishing village of Bahia de los Angeles on the Sea of Cortez; a field of blue lupine skirting a cinder cone mountain on Isla Coronado; and a wiry osprey nest balanced atop a sea arch on Isla La Ventana.

I couldn't quite believe my great fortune again! I had hoped for new friends. And there they were. Earlier that morning, bolting through tide rips south of Kelsey Bay in Race Passage—with Margarite watching in the distance from the government wharf—I'd conceded I wouldn't mind clean sheets all the way down. But mostly, I'd hankered for another home-cooked dinner. The thought seemed ludicrous, if not a smidgen greedy. Why push my luck?

But now I believed my hope went out ahead of me. It traversed the miles like a hungry seawolf. Long before I would come riding up to Cal and Janice's, I sensed something good cooking down coast. I could feel it. Taste it. Visions are like that. They precede you.

Scary visions can precede you too, unfortunately.

The night before I was to paddle the terrifying Narrows, I lay tucked in crisp sheets in a spare bunk in Cal and Janice's trailer poring over charts and the *Sailing Directions, British Columbia Coast (South Portion)*. Since 1875, 114 people had drowned from shipping mishaps in this constricted, two-mile-long, dogleg kink in Discovery Passage. It is the only inside route deep enough for coastal ship traffic headed to Alaska. Likely one third of the tidal water in the Strait of Georgia races through this keyhole that locals named "the Graveyard."

Paging through the *Marine Atlas*, I was reminded of a scene in Johnstone Strait. A city-size cruise ship had been hanging out in mid-channel for an hour. I talked with some orca whale monitors in a Zodiac.

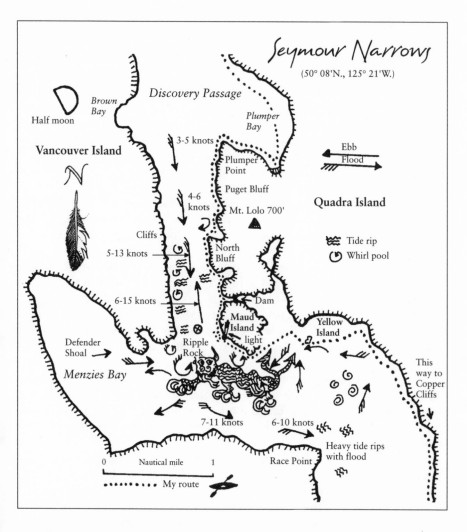

Seymour Narrows
(50° 08'N., 125° 21'W.)

Discovery Passage

Brown Bay

Half moon

Plumper Bay

Vancouver Island

3-5 knots

Plumper Point

Ebb

Flood

Puget Bluff

4-6 knots

Mt. Lolo 700'

Quadra Island

Cliffs

North Bluff

5-13 knots

Tide rip

Whirl pool

6-15 knots

Dam

Maud Island light

Yellow Island

Defender Shoal

Ripple Rock

This way to Copper Cliffs

Menzies Bay

7-11 knots

6-10 knots

Heavy tide rips with flood

0   Nautical mile   1

Race Point

.... My route

The Aussie steersman corrected me, "No, mate. That cruise ship isn't wait-ing for whales. When they're ahead of schedule they pause for slack or flood tide so the water's against them. They have better control. Or else they might go careening into the cliffs or another boat, eh? I ain't kidding you . . . even the orcas wait."

It didn't help my peace of mind that Cal had seen monstrous whirl-pools near slack tide. He was motoring through in his aluminum skiff when "a black hole just opened up . . . I could look down inside. It was a steep-walled funnel that carried things to who knows where. Scariest thing I've ever seen." He gunned the motor for all it was worth and narrowly escaped the sucking rim.

Sea monsters have haunted the Narrows since remembered time. Chief Henry Assu of Cape Mudge, Quadra Island, recalled that his people named the place "'u'stoy" because dangerous sea monsters were often sighted in the turbulent waters there.

"One of these monsters," he explained, "always emerged around Maud Island. It must have been fifty feet across and always, above its body, which looked like a great skate, there were little birds swirling round and round on the water. Everybody stayed away for fear of being dragged in and pulled under the water."

Sailing Directions shows two photos snapped during Seymour's full-tilt flood and ebb tides. It looks like a white-water river bolting through the mountains. It's no wonder Maud Island is where the sea monster waited in ambush. During both tides, a long fin of white turbulent waves—probably fifty feet across just as Chief Assu remembered—jets off Maud's southern tip and straight across the Narrows. Though I couldn't see birds in the aerial photos, I imagined the ferocious upwelling of currents made for a seafood smorgasbord of confused herring.

But Maud Island isn't the only obstacle that stirs the Narrows' cauldron. An even bigger monster lurks in the four-hundred-foot depths: an underwater mountain. I'd seen a diagram of it in Jim Gibb's sobering book *Perils at Sea* (a great read for humbling you before an ocean journey). The mountain's jagged summit, casually named "Ripple Rock" or "Ol' Rip," juts up mid-channel like a sea monster's forked tail. Before 1958, the tail reached to within ten feet of low-tide water.

Geologists believe the depth of Ol' Rip was even less in former days, especially if you figure sea levels have risen since the Ice Age's great meltdown. Legends tell of Native men standing brazenly atop the highest pinnacle with seawater rushing around their hips. The vibration of the water jiggled their cheeks.

It's amazing Captain George Vancouver made it through Seymour Narrows without so much as a scuff in 1792. His passage in *A Voyage of Discovery* offers the first written record:

"The tide, setting to the southward through this confined passage, rushes with such immense impetuosity as to produce the appearance of falls considerably high."

Of course, Vancouver piloted the *Discovery* through the passage entirely on sail power. His skill is doubly admirable considering he maneuvered his brig along the more treacherous west side of Ripple Rock. Today, most boats take the east side.

Since Vancouver's voyage, the statistics for ship damage due to Ol' Rip are staggering. At least twenty-five ships and barges and more than 120 smaller vessels—pleasure boats, tugs, fishing boats, skiffs, and such—have been damaged or sunk from grazing the massive rock or foundering in the turbulent waters. Who's to know how many dugout canoes spilled over in earlier times?

A mastermind plan to destroy Ripple Rock was begun in 1953 after a previous scheme failed. Using a drill, engineers dug a coyote tunnel under the passage. At Maud Island, a 570-foot shaft was cut to below the sea floor. Next, a nearly half-mile-long horizontal tunnel was excavated out to the base of the basalt pinnacle. Up, up into the rock mountain went two more vertical shafts. Each one had side arms with finger-like holes that were gingerly stuffed with 1375 tons of dynamite.

The New York Times reported on April 5, 1958, Easter weekend, that Dr. Victor Dolmage, the master engineer, fired the plunger from a bunker on Quadra Island, 2400 feet from Ripple Rock. None of the scientists and explosives experts hunkered elbow to elbow with Dolmage knew for certain the blast's outcome. The engineers calculated that the blasting agent, called nitramex 2H, had to shatter 370,000 tons of rock and move almost 320,000 tons of water to accomplish its purpose. The Royal Canadian Mounted Police blockaded the passage and roads for three miles in all directions keeping cars, boats, and planes at a distance. People feared a tidal wave, earth tremors, and a hail of rocky debris.

At 9:31 A.M., Ol' Rip blew sky-high in a massive, colorful, eight-hundred-foot plume of pulverized rock and ocean spray. Rock hailed down over both sides of the Narrows. An earth tremor shook Vancouver Island. Ten minutes later, a tidal wave engulfing both shores receded. The explosion was detected 2400 miles away. After thirty-one months of labor, the pinnacle dropped from ten feet beneath the low-tide waters to forty-seven feet down. One of the most dreaded hazards on the Pacific Rim became history in a matter of seconds.

With Ripple Rock decapitated, you'd think mariners could navigate in peace. Not so. The current Sailing Directions gives these sobering warnings:

"Caution: Small vessels have been capsized with loss of life while navigating Seymour Narrows even near slack water and in reasonable weather conditions . . . All crew members should be alert and ready to cope with any emergency."

My courage went into a tailspin. I read on.

"Tidal streams . . . attain 16 knots . . . The duration of slack water can be as much as twelve or fifteen minutes. . . . On the flood, along the east shore, rips and eddies start north of North Bluff and extend in an almost straight line down to Maud Island light. The rips extend due south of the light to about the middle of the channel, where they meet the rips and eddies from the west shore and culminate in large whirls and eddies. . . . Maximum strength of the stream can be expected in the vicinity of Maud Island."

It only made sense that the mythic sea monster would dwell where the fastest current lies—Maud Island.

There are places in nature so full of danger and raw, physical power that they live in two worlds at once. First, they dwell in the elemental and ordinary world of the senses. Second, they occupy an ethereal, mythic realm. Long ago, the old people said these were the same world. But things have happened—I'm not sure exactly what. But I suspect that dynamite, combustion engines, Coast Pilots, NOAA charts, even VHF weather radios, computerized tide and current tables, and satellite-based Global Positioning Systems that can tell a mariner her whereabouts to within a rock's throw have something to do with the change. The mythic realm of sea travel has shrunk. Over the centuries, Sisiutl, the terrifying water monster, has reared her two-headed, serpent body less and less often along this coast. The giant, many-armed devilfish no longer grabs at canoe bows as they pass around turbulent points.

Chief Henry Assu of Cape Mudge wondered if those monsters didn't go off to some other sea. I wondered this: Where will they go when they run out of mythic space—and mythic minds? I'm just as afraid they'll go the way of the longhouse and shaman's soul-catcher, forsaken for other modern comforts and conveniences, like tract homes and antidepressants. Who could blame any of us for wanting to be rid of the chilly dampness and downward-spiraling, dark-moon thoughts?

Nonetheless, experience tells me that mythic creatures still lurk near solo travelers drifting in wild places. They have no problem finding me in my dark tent. Even tucked between warm sheets in a spare bunk in Cal and Janice's trailer, I could feel them slithering and hissing in Seymour Narrows miles away. In fact, I've noticed that solitude has a way of inviting monsters—perhaps for the best. Monsters make a traveler more cautious.

One need only recall the ancient maps of oceany places, whose uncharted perimeters snorted with sea dragons and sirens beckoning sailors off the rim of the visible world, to know what I mean. Seymour Narrows had that kind of grip on me. Staring at the narrow gooseneck of Seymour Narrows on page 32 of the atlas, I wondered about changing my route.

My finger hemmed and hawed eight miles north of the Narrows at the junction of Okisollo Channel and Discovery Passage. Should I turn east and opt for this alternate route south? Only catch was—the optional route is flecked with rapids as well. One . . . two . . . *three*! Granted, they were shorter rapids. Maybe smaller. But it seemed ridiculous to compare the jaw strength of the great white shark with that of the grizzly bear. Both catch prey equally well.

Smaller rapids are nothing to get cocky over. They are still rapids, still dangerous. I mean, they could drown you if you weren't cautious. And, because there were three rapids in a row, the optional route would call for extended strategy. Wait and go, then sprint ahead. Stop, wait, sprint again. Lickety-split. Hit the slack for each one.

Looking at the chart, I knew it would be tricky, perhaps impossible, to kayak nonstop through three courses of slack-tide rapids in one go. I slid my finger back to Seymour Narrows. Less than half a mile wide, the two-mile stretch was stippled with more whirlpools, tide rips, and eleven- to fifteen-knot current flags than I'd seen marked on the entire Inside Passage so far. Why not choose one huge rapid area? One big bang and it'd be over.

Taking my leave early, I rounded Little Bear Point in silky seas. Far behind me in the north, the blue mountains I paddled by the day before slid out of view behind the point. A weasel loped down a basalt-gray cliff and into Rock Bay—a russet arrow aiming for low-tide critters. It was in this fateful bay, long ago, that Fool (later, Fool the shaman) beached his dugout canoe and loaded two abandoned bentwood boxes heaped with clothing and food. The mysterious gift, tainted with smallpox, wiped out his entire family ten days later.

I floated a little sprig of cedar in the water. I prayed for family and friends afar. *May we all enjoy a long, full, safe journey.*

Crossing west to east from Chatham Light to Sonora Island, I counted forty-three boats, one tug, and one freighter. Three quarters of these were fishing and trolling for salmon along Sonora Island's western cliffs. I was so focused on the moon's voluptuous clock, I'd forgotten it was a weekend. Navigating zigzag through the fishing fleet, blue clouds of diesel exhaust and rooster-tail boat wakes made me nauseous. Overhead, above the cloudless, blue strait, mustard-gold air stained the sky. Pollution, I sighed, from the umpteen boats traveling this thoroughfare and from the pulp mill at Campbell River.

At the mouth of Okisollo Channel, I again debated for an hour and a half while I floated and snacked, read over the current table, and checked the route via chart, trying to judge if I still might go the long way around. My indecisiveness drove me nuts. Eventually I decided, again, to head to Seymour Narrows. The jostling of the kayak in soft waves had nearly rocked me to sleep.

In the next eight miles, two different skiffs motored up to my kayak to tell me to turn around. The conversations went something like this:

"EXCUSE ME, ARE YOU LOST?"

"WHAT?" I turned toward a skiff that held two or three fishers. The steersman cut the engine to reduce the rumbling.

Our eyes met.

Gee, it's a woman! I saw that deer-in-the-headlights look dawning across their faces.

"Do you know where you're going, Miss?"

"Yes. Thanks for your concern. I'm kayaking through Seymour Narrows. I've planned this for weeks . . . Slack tide, half moon," I said, gesturing to the cut moon overhead.

They looked at me like I was speaking pig Latin. *Eymour-say Arrows-nay? Es-yay I-yay ow-knay!*

I smiled and waved. They motored off shaking their capped heads.

Two miles to go. I gave an African trill and paddled off toward Seymour Narrows like an excited banshee. For some beautiful reason I was giddy to have a date with the slack before the flood tide at 4 P.M., goofy that I could look up and see the half moon. After days of worry, the sea looked delicious. Maybe everything was going to turn out fine.

High above in the cloudless blue, a V of geese followed the passage south. I flew with them, singing out to the water, to the narrowing salt river:

> *The river she is flowing,*
> *Flowing and growing.*
> *The river she is flowing*
> *Down to the sea.*

A one-knot current pushed softly against *Yemaya*'s hull. The words carried us forward. Water held me in her arms, kept me moving.

> *Mother carry me,*
> *Your child I will always be,*
> *Mother carry me*
> *Down to the sea.*

I felt the full, muscular stroke of the paddle, the push on shaft and blade growing stronger with the singing. White Pegasus wings opened beneath the bow with each down-crashing into waves. Paddling Pegasus! I loved it! Flying above the waters as if Pegasus were beneath! What I'd give to have wings.

Looking down into transparent water, I saw amber kelp leaves fluttering far below. And I realized, I *am* flying. Right over the heads of my long-haired, beautiful sisters. Golden tendrils billowed up. I could almost touch them. Rapunzels of the sea.

I stopped and sketched a picture of *Yemaya*'s bow with its cloth rose and spare paddle blades strapped onto the bow. Half moon above.

At 4:29 P.M. I arrived at Plumper Bay a quarter-mile above Seymour Narrows. Half moon over clear-cut. If ever I puzzled over whether a half moon is waxing or waning, I remember what a sage young girl told me on a teen kayak trip I guided one summer:

"Just imagine the small letters 'd' and 'b.' Each letter's bottom half makes a right- or left-facing half circle. Place the half moon in the half circle. If it fits in the 'd' it's diminishing. If it fits in the 'b' it's growing bigger."

I like that kind of knowing. It's old wisdom coming from a young mouth.

The half moon over Seymour was getting bigger.

The last of the ebb tide was getting smaller. Seymour was still emptying. The flood was late, according to the tide and current table's predictions. But it was right on time given the bigger cycles I couldn't necessarily see. High pressure systems and strong winds can hold up a tide for hours.

No problem. I didn't mind bucking a little current. I preferred it to being *whooshed* along from behind out of control.

I saw four power lines half a mile ahead crossing from the western cliffs. They marked the middle of Seymour Narrows. A float plane flying north passed above them. The Brown's Bay marina, one mile across the passage, glinted sun off a tin roof.

I needed to pee and took a pit stop at Plumper Bay. When I returned to the boat, I dropped cedar in the saltwater. Prayed for a safe passage.

Nearing Plumper Point a seal *ka-plooshed* and surfaced behind me. This was it. The passage I'd been dreading and tasting—academically. Here came the real saltshaker.

But as I was leaving Plumper Bay, one last skiff sputtered close by. It was a couple, a woman and man trolling lines.

"You paddling through?" asked the woman.

I nodded.

"Then you're a *brave* woman!" she said beaming.

I shook my head. "No, I'm a chickenheart. That's why I'm going through at slack."

We laughed. Raising one hand high, she wished me well. I disappeared around Plumper Point into the Narrows. I bloodhounded the kelp below Mount Lolo and Puget Cliff. Thrums of waves mumbled under the hollow ledges. They sounded like elders talking. I was as alert as a salmon, pushing against ebb current.

A half-mile ahead, North Bluff leaned out like a Roman nose sniffing for danger. That was where the passage narrowed. Steep basalt cliffs rose on both sides. I was coming in through the broad, stone funnel. Riffles of white frothed in mid-channel off North Bluff. Did more kelp grow there? I was counting on kelp to hold down the turbulence.

Seven Bonaparte's gulls—pink legs, black crescent on white face— hitch-hiked on a huge log bobbing north. I thought again of the shaman spirits, which ride logs, but in the form of birds. Red nori seaweed hung in rumpled sheets from the Puget Cliffs. I stopped momentarily to pluck and munch some down for good luck. Was it superstition? No, I realized, I'm asking the plant for its resilience through this passage. It crunched and tasted of minerals and salt. Drying and resurrecting with each tide, holding fast in battering waves, nori lives on through the late summer. I wanted to live on—to be resurrected.

It was just a short distance now to North Bluff. Ebb tide was still streaming against me. Slack tide hadn't begun. Wondered when slack would be. Relaxed tense arms and fingers. Breathed. Believed all would be more than well. And so far it had been. Water streamed past outside the kelp line like a river. I worked along in the quieter zone.

"Thank you for your protective fence," I told the kelp ushering me around North Bluff. The current felt hard, fast, and relentless. It made me toil at the pace of a limpet snail. I don't mind this mundaneness, I told myself. I prefer it. Let me be bored, Goddess, please.

I counted two tiny indents to Maud Island on the chart. A dam was inside the second one. I remembered kayaker Bob Lyon's calming and reassuring words: "If it's really rough, portage over the dam to the bay on the other side of Maud Island."

I came even with the thirty-foot earthen dam. Took a break. Inside the divot, kelp gyrated in great circles. High power lines looped overhead. Red-and-white navigation balls, strung like chunky beads, marked the wires for float planes following the channel. I pushed on down the pass, which was still narrowing.

The half moon looked like a white china cup spilling over Race Point a mile and a half distant.

Maud Light was saluting ahead, a red-and-white pillar standing at attention inside the kelp. The water was so amazingly still beneath the light that the reflection hung long. What a relief it was to see a calm reflection. A smattering of rock islands surrounding Maud's light signaled shallows.

I was almost even with Ripple Rock and the dogleg kink in the passage. I looked right. Out in mid-channel, some forty-seven feet down, the great serpent tail orchestrated the whirlpools. Could I have swum it? Wouldn't have wanted to find out. That day, nearing slack tide, the worst area was only a chattering riffle. It eased my mind.

Coming up channel were six big boats—a couple of sixty-foot purse seiners and four yachts, forty-plus-footers. I sized up their wakes. They didn't look good.

It quickly dawned on me that shallows and shelves were an idiot place to wallow because waves surge higher as they bottom out. I cranked hard ahead. But the hull dragged along. Current was pouring invisibly against me at two knots. I creaked forward slowly, evenly, at the speed of a submerged log.

The first seiner drew toward my side of the Narrows, east of Ripple Rock like the *Sailing Directions* recommends. It roared along frightfully close to shore and to me. The wake was rolling away like a herd of galloping horses, all white—a curling, frothing stampede thirty yards away.

I wished the captain would SLOW DOWN!

Thanks! I yelled.

Who could hear me over the roar? Who even knew I was there? All eyes were watching the channel for BIG boats.

With cliffs to the left, I had no way to escape the wake. I was still in the shallows when I wheeled around to face the spuming wall. Behind the first charge rolled two more compact charges, one after another. I bolted for them. Running at what you fear counts most when it comes to boat wakes. It's best to cut them at a fierce forty-five-degree angle, force against force. I needed speed and momentum to cut through so I wouldn't be tossed aside—or over!

Twenty feet away, the hurdle roared and rose from two feet up to three feet to meet me. I was sprinting forward at that point, but viscerally aware I was three feet tall from hull to hat.

The icy wall hit the bow . . . *WHUMPH!* . . . paddle . . . *SOOSH!* . . . chest . . . *WHAM!* Froth fizzed down face and neck. *Yemaya*'s bow dropped down HARD! Whitewater wings flared up on either side. Flying? No, SLAMMING— TWO, THREE, FOUR, FIVE, SIX times—once for each boat wake. I turned around fast to get back toward shore. Waves were still smashing into Maud's cliffs and back through the sets, tossing me everywhere! What a pileup! I was drenched. Shaken. But still upright.

I pumped past Maud Island with waves drumming beneath. Thank Goddess. Thank *Yemaya*. I was beyond the worst.

I bore southeast, dogging Quadra Island's forested shore and bucking more current. More boat wakes. But the wakes were manageable. I was safely out of the dogleg canyon of Seymour Narrows. Discovery Passage stretched a mile and a half wide again. Wakes had room to roam. Greatly relieved, but still trembling, I told myself, "You're in the home stretch."

How utterly confounding. After all my research and sweat it wasn't the monster whirlpools, tide rips, over falls, or even Ol' Rip I had to be wary of, but the damn boat wakes hitting the shallows off Maud Island Light.

Chief Assu's ancestors were right—monsters do dwell off Maud Island. They come without warning, leaving white turbulent tails. The *Sailing Directions* doesn't mention these kayak-pertinent details. Nor does it mention that more monsters bolt through during slack tide than any other fifteen minutes of the day.

Tree frogs sang *dee-jee-EEP* from the woods on Quadra Island. Two kingfishers rattled through the air. One flew explosively, chasing the other who was fleeing—banking, again and again—to avoid being nailed. Two marbled murrelets corked up twenty feet in front of the bow. Their black-and-white-swirled tuxedos flashed gold in the last light. *Kerploosh!* Black tails fanned and disappeared.

The sun guttered over Discovery Passage like a candle flickering out. Everything—the forest, cliffs, waves, rock, and dewy kayak—pulsed with golden light. I drifted beneath the Copper Cliffs where mineralized waterfalls streak the slope. Reflected sunlight quivered like a laser show—an aurora borealis on the cliff rock. Gold over copper green and clamshell white. Waterfalls of color.

Three miles south of Seymour Narrows, I rounded the Copper Cliffs, kayak hull glowing like red-shafted flicker feathers from the sundown sky's canvas.

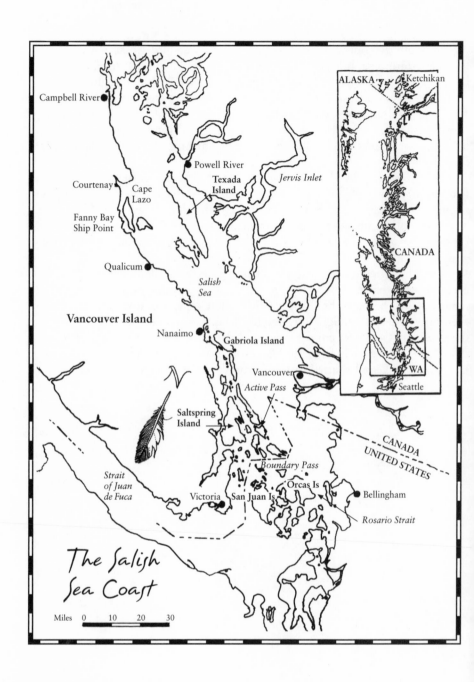

Campbell River

Powell River

Courtenay
Cape
Lazo

Texada
Island

Jervis Inlet

Fanny Bay
Ship Point

Qualicum

*Salish
Sea*

Vancouver Island

Nanaimo

Gabriola Island

Vancouver
Active Pass

Saltspring
Island

Boundary Pass

*Strait
of Juan
de Fuca*

Victoria   San Juan Is

Orcas Is

Bellingham

Rosario Strait

CANADA
UNITED STATES

ALASKA   Ketchikan

CANADA

WA
Seattle

*The Salish
Sea Coast*

Miles   0   10   20   30

Part 5

The Salish Sea Coast: Strait of Georgia and San Juan Islands

Late Summer, 158 miles, 16 days

*And I thought over again
My small adventures
As with a shore-wind I drifted out
In my kayak
And thought I was in danger,
My fears,
Those small ones
That I thought so big
For all the vital things
I had to get and to reach.
And yet, there is only
One great thing,
The only thing:
To live to see in huts and on journeys
The great day that dawns,
and the light that fills the world.*

—Translated from Inuit by Knud Rasmussen

13   The Black-Mouth King

A Salishan legend from Bella Coola, recorded by Franz Boas in 1897, tells how a young boy stowed away in a canoe bound for the Salmon Country. The canoe headed west, and passed through wondrous terrain. *First came the country of the Smelt where the coast gave off an overpowering stench. Next the place of the Herrings where fish scales fell in great numbers like snow. Then the village of the Eulachon, where everything was smothered in grease. At last they came to a large, beautiful prairie where a huge sun shone in the sky. It was the home of the Salmon People.*

In their village were six great longhouses. In the first house lived the Spring Salmon, in the second the Sockeye Salmon, in the next dwellings the Humpback salmon, the Calico Salmon, the Dog Salmon, and the Cohos. Children chased about and played on the beach. The stowaway was hungry, so the people in the first longhouse told him to carry two children down to the river and throw them into the water. A male and female salmon appeared in the shallows where he had thrown the children.

"You must take care to preserve the intestines and the bones," warned the elders. After roasting and eating the salmon, the boy was told to carefully return these to the exact spot where he threw the children into the river. He did so, and as he walked back to the longhouse, he heard the children trailing behind him. The girl held a hand over one eye. The boy hobbled. The people searched the ground where the boy had been sitting and eating. They discovered the eye and a missing bone. When the boy threw all the pieces into the water again, the children became whole.

The Salish, like the Nootka, Kwakiutl, Tsimshian, and Tlingit, understood that the Salmon People journeyed far away from their beautiful country to beyond the ocean horizon so that they could be sacrificed then returned to the ocean again. It was an ongoing cycle of life. The salmon came of their own will. They were not simply fish, but people who themselves had souls. It was essential to pay them respect.

The first salmon caught each season by Northwest Coast peoples was treated as an honored guest, like a king or chief visiting the village. After catching the first chinook salmon, a Sliammon fisher from the northern Strait of Georgia (Salish Sea) would hold it aloft and speak to the fish. He praised it for coming to fill the bellies of his people. When so honored, salmon often were not called by their ordinary names but by their mythic names. The Bella Coola Salishan name for dog salmon is "sisia'ltoa," or "fair weather." The

Tyee • Chinook • King • Black Mouth

slimmest and most streamlined salmon, the sockeye, was called "very long." The silver salmon's mythic name translates to "making itself beautiful." After praying to the fish, the fisherman would send a messenger to the village to announce the feast of the first salmon. After a communal meal of boiled fish, all the bones were gathered together and tossed into the ocean, so the fish could be reborn.

Every year, the Salmon People agreed to give their flesh as long as certain taboos and ceremonies were upheld. These might be as simple as a prayer, or the placing of the first salmon on a special cedar mat and dabbing it with eagle down. Whatever the gesture, it was steeped in humility and gratitude. Reciprocity was part of the early ways of all the People. Salmon People must be treated with utmost reverence. If they were pleased with the gifts their scouts or salmon chief and his wife received, then they would flood the fish weirs and traps and brighten the rivers with their shining canoes.

The Spring Salmon had the fastest canoe. The canoe of the Sockeye Salmon came next. The people in the canoe of the Calico Salmon were laughing all the time.

Paddling under a mile-wide bruise of smoke trailing from pulp mill stacks in Campbell River, I wanted to hold my breath. I longed to make a U-turn and skedaddle back to the rich country of Queen Charlotte Sound. I wanted to follow the salmon to its pristine home.

Spilling along Vancouver Island's eastern shore, four-story condominiums with patio decks and lawn chairs replaced the open beaches of the north. Telephone and electric lines adorned the uplands. There were more buildings and fewer trees. Everywhere the air clanged with human-generated sound. Combustion engines, tires whizzing over asphalt, the blast of a train whistle, doors slamming, the *deet-deet-deet* of a truck backing up.

On Island Highway, which parallels the shore, a steady stream of campers, trucks, vans, and cars zoomed by in metallic green, red, blue, and silver. Every tenth vehicle seemed to trail a fiberglass fishing boat or aluminum skiff. It was fishing derby time. Offshore, where I paddled, dozens upon dozens of recreational fisher folk trolled lines from rented skiffs. I dodged them, hearing their *sputt-a-put* engine songs. Now and then I could make out crickets humming over the muffle of traffic. A raft of Bonaparte's gulls floated by tail first, their heads steered north into the wind. A loon rose up into the air shaking its cape of moons, then dove as two skiffs sped over top.

What a startling contrast to the wilder desolate islands, the slant of fjords and mountains of the north. So few people dared to live beyond the sea monster in the Narrows. Perhaps the monster has another purpose now, like keeping the north less populated.

Paddling out of Discovery Passage and into the Salish Sea, I saw a palm-size fin tracking in the water ahead of me. Up jumped a salmon, dazzling as anything I have ever seen! The great wall of fish hovered in the air at head level for just a moment, as if frozen in mid-leap. It sailed horizontally against the snowcapped mountains rising blue and white across the strait. My eye snapped its shutter as the huge fish flew by seemingly in slow motion: open mouth, shining sleeve of silver, speckled back, glorious tail fan with coal dots. It astonished me breathless as it splashed back into the sea.

"THANK YOU salmon!" I cried out, after it disappeared.

Yemaya and I shared the broad ribbon of the Salish Sea with untold fleets of commerce and leisure boats. Two tugboats chugged south hauling loads. The first towed three red barges heaped with wood chips. The second tug pulled two barges with a crane and caterpillar tractor. From *Yemaya's* low vantage point, international freighters, fishing boats, sailboats, barges, and yachts appeared and vanished over the far horizon like airplanes on an infinite blue tarmac.

I was so culture shocked, I just kept paddling until it was dark and I was too exhausted to stay upright in the kayak anymore. That's how I found Kitty Coleman Provincial Park. A diamond in the rough—it wasn't even on the British Columbia Provincial Parks Map I carried. At $5.50 per site, no running water, no electricity, it is popular with the "Geritol ward," as hosts Judy and Irv fondly called it. Irv, a brawny, fiftyish logger by trade with a spring in his gait and an infectious laugh, insisted on loading my whole kayak and caboodle into his truck, then shuttling me to a camp spot.

"I'm taking you to a private clearing hedged by ocean spray and honeysuckle. Campground's full, eh? You'll be safe right next to our trailer."

After I staked out the tent, Judy howled out the trailer's window, "How 'bout a salmon sandwich and a nightcap?"

The trailer was just big enough for three if I sat in a folding chair by the door. Judy sat at the Formica table knitting purple trim on a cotton facecloth. As she watched me and chatted away, her suntanned hands worked confidently with the needles as if they had eyes of their own. She looked light of frame but strong as ironwood.

"How's that salmon? Want more? Last summer we canned 150 pounds of salmon, clams, and sea cucumbers. Ye gads, took us weeks."

"How do people find this place?"

"Word of mouth. Mostly, old-timers comin' back every summer," said Irv. He was hunched in a chair at the foot of their bed with a schipperke dog panting at his knee. The black, furry muff reminded me of a bear cub.

"Kitty's not listed on the B.C. Provincial Parks maps. Hope it never is," said Judy.

"How'd you get so lucky?"

"Isn't flashy enough."

"Judy and I like that, of course."

I enjoyed hearing Irv and Judy finish each other's sentences. It kept their stories as lively as a game of hackysack.

"We were raised in the bush—in Nitinat and like Nitinat, Kitty's kind of short on amenities . . . ."

"Who was Kitty anyway?"

"Farmer Coleman's mistress," said Judy.

"In 1918, at the end of the first World War," explained Irv, "Five thousand vets had no place to live, so Farmer Coleman put tents and cabins along his beach. He'd visit Kitty here on the sly . . . married her after his wife died. The government took over in 1965. It's in the bylaws. It must be kept in a natural state. Can't cut anything."

Irv and Judy told me they got married at nineteen and fifteen. Irv's been a logger, fisher, and . . . well . . . just about everything. Judy's dad, turns out, welded like mine did.

"My dad's dream was to come fishing here every summer. Last year, he pulled in a BIG ol' king. Right out there in the Strait of Georgia." She tapped her knitting needles on the dark window glass.

Three loud raps at the trailer door derailed Judy's story. The schipperke sprang toward the door.

"Excuse me, but this happens." said Irv. "Folks call on us at all hours."

Underneath the porch light stood a buxom, white-haired woman with an angry scowl. She was stuffed in a yellow Helly Hansen rain coat and waved her fillet knife angrily in the air as she spoke.

"You know a guy drives around in a white van? Kinda talks with an accent?"

"Yeah?"

"Anyhow, he's fishing over his limit! Two chinooks—that's supposed to be all you get! I was just at the fish cleaning table. We was both cutting up our fish. I said, 'Nice fish' to the two in his bucket, then looked over and there was a third lying there!

"I says, 'And that's an illegal one you got there!'

"He glares and says, 'Is not!'

"I leaned closer, 'That's a chinook! Look at that tail, it's silver . . . look at them spots,' I says. 'They're small and round, not big and oval.'

"And he says, 'Is not. That's a pink.'

"It weren't no pink. No, siree! I been fishing sixty-five years and I know the difference 'tween a chinook and a pink.

"Then you know what he did?—" She didn't wait for us to respond.

"When I wasn't looking, he cut the fish in three chunks. I saw him pitch something out onto the rocks on the dark beach. It was the third chinook! I found it with my flashlight a few minutes ago. Had a black mouth, too. Just like chinooks do."

"Well, pinkity dinkity!" said Judy.

"You can go down there and look. It's still there." She pointed to the water with her fillet knife and gave Irv a nod. She waited for him to jump up.

"Well, I wouldn't have much to stand on," Irv explained, shuffling in his chair, "as I didn't see it myself."

The woman huffed. "Fellow should have his license torn up!"

"I agree. Darn shame. I'll be watching him from now on. Promise."

Satisfied enough, she left. And the schipperke returned to Irv's knee.

"I like her!" smiled Judy. "She's got piss and vinegar!" And with that she picked up on her dad's fishing story without missing a stitch.

"After we netted the king, Dad asked for a fish photo. You know, to show his cronies. I grabbed the camera. He held up the king, smiled this 'I've-got-the-whole-world-in-my-hands' grin, and keeled over from a heart attack!"

"Jeez! Right then?" I gasped.

"With the fish hardly a breath gone."

Irv sighed a deep breath himself. "But Dad died happy, I'll give him that."

"He's buried right out there, too," said Judy, knitting her needles in rapid satisfaction. "Almost wasn't though," she added, like there was more to tell.

"Oh?"

"Well, I've this older brother in Victoria. You know, Big Brother always gets what he wants. He insisted Dad's ashes be buried in his back yard. Utterly ridiculous! In the middle of the city for God's sake! Dad wanted to be spread here, off the coast at Kitty.

"So, I fixed that. I went to the coroner's to pick up Dad's ashes. I looked in the box, and I got an idea. I'd make a trade. I dug around in the barbecue grill and got some different ashes, added in some burnt chicken bones. Irv and I joined Big Brother at the memorial in Victoria. Planted a tree . . . everything. We all took turns putting in a handful of Dad's ashes. Cried a few crocodile tears. Of course, we'd already buried Dad in the Georgia Strait . . . with the salmon, where he belonged.

"Yup, Dad sure loved fishing these waters!"

For lunch the next day, I reached into a jacket pocket for one of Judy's salmon sandwiches. Drifting and munching, I thought of the fisher who hacked the chinook in three chunks and threw it on the beach. Long ago, indigenous people enforced strict taboos during the salmon runs. They feared any offense might chase the salmon out of the river. Children were forbidden to play with the entrails. Young women in their first "moontime" and people who had been in contact with the dying could not touch salmon. They were ritualistically impure. Salmon were carried one per hand from a canoe to the beach, not heaped carelessly in a basket. First salmon should never be sold, or the hearts might be devoured by a dog. A fisherman must not brag of how many he hooked, netted, or speared. After eating salmon, a person must drink fresh water so that the fish may be revived and swim home again gladly.

At Union Bay, *Yemaya* drifted over the still reflection of ashen storm clouds in twelve shades of nasty gray. Setting paddle across cockpit, I bent my head forward and touched chin to chest. Ahhh . . . to stretch the neck and back muscles! My forearms hurt and my left shoulder felt ratcheted tight in its cuff. Over nine hours in the seat with only a few pee breaks in between and still nine miles to the next campground at Deep Bay.

Out of sheer escapism, I plumbed my gaze beyond the cloud reflections and into the emerald depths. What a magnificent sight! Thousands of ghostly white jellyfish pulsed in the dark universe of Union Bay. Moon jellyfish, *Aurelia aurita*. Clouds beneath the clouds. Far off, a train whistle blew and the *ring-ding-ding* of the railroad crossing gate sharpened the twilight air. But below— floating in the bay like so many translucent silk parachutes . . . closing into tear drops, opening into parasols . . . closing . . . unfolding . . . fringed edges waving with each beat—dwelled another world and rhythm entirely.

Each medusa looked no larger than a grapefruit. They propelled themselves with a cardiac-beat rhythm. *Bah-boohhm. Bah-boohhm.* Like a human heart, jellyfish never rest. At the mercy of currents, tides, storms, and calms, they keep on beating.

"Ghost hearts," I said aloud. I felt startled by my own words. I remembered Judy's father, whose ashes swirled through the Strait of Georgia. I remembered the butchered chinook salmon. Is this what the ocean's dead become? Thousands of ghost hearts? Beating, beating in the great mother sea's amniotic waters?

Darkness fell at Ship Point, four miles short of Deep Bay campground. A tiny constellation of lights glimmered in the south across Baynes Sound, where I guessed the campground lay. I didn't like the idea of night navigation, especially across a three-mile-wide bay with potential motorboat traffic. I considered duct taping two glow sticks to the paddles for visibility and igniting the strobe light on my flotation vest. Strong tidal current, a growing head wind, and twenty-seven miles had utterly exhausted my spirit. It would exhaust everything I had left to push another four miles. Lassitude is not a good companion with which to begin an open crossing. On forested Ship Point, a gray and white, floodlit sign caught my weary eyes:

SHIP POINT BEACH HOUSE

David and Lorinda, the proprietors, weren't so keen on my erecting a tent on their bed and breakfast's beach, but they kindly offered me a vastly discounted rate for the "Teddy Bear Room." In a weakened state, I was easily bent to making exorbitant splurges. I dug out my Visa card, hoping it still worked. I gobbled the Belgian chocolates on the bed stand, showered with pink teddy bear soap, and collapsed in a vacuous cloud of pillows and comforters. Rain cracked against the dark window glass. Wind pummeled the north-facing wall. A half-dozen teddy bears kept storm watch. I was in over my head and happy as a mermaid in sea foam.

Over tea and orange soufflé pancakes with lemon cheese croissants, David and Lorinda told me a delightful story about salmon and community ingenuity. A short ways north, the Oyster River rolled off Mount Adrian and Alexandra Peak into the Salish Sea.

"Chinooks, cohos, and pinks spawn in the Oyster. Mostly pinks, though," said Lorinda. "A bunch of ol' hippies started a hatchery, but there was no money, of course. We helped raise fifteen thousand dollars."

"Ted at Campbell River Lodge was the brain behind it," explained David. "'Our Way,' a group of handicapped adults and kids, carved fifty-five hundred wood salmon and painted them fluorescent orange. We sold salmon tickets for ten dollars a piece. Didn't sell all the tickets, but we released all fifty-five hundred at a little logging bridge near Campbell River."

I imagined a joyful cascade of carved orange fish pouring down the Oyster River.

"They floated for about forty-five minutes in a big pack while we all drank beer and waited," said David.

"Of course, then we had to collect them all again! We strung fifty at a time on a wire run through the eye holes. It was quite a bit of fun."

"But you mustn't leave Ship Point without visiting our local artist and neighbor, George Sawchuk," pleaded Lorinda. "His forest gallery is across the dike in the woods. You, Jennifer, would especially appreciate George's work."

I followed the beach to the last house before the dike then crossed the earth dam to George Sawchuk's woods. Storm clouds thrummed along the Big Island's front range and threatened to let loose their fury. But far above, a field of blue sky called their bluff. Where the dike reached the forest, the air turned cool. Cedars and firs dripped with last night's rain. The path narrowed. A spider's gossamer broke across my lips. This morning, I would be the first visitor in George Sawchuk's forest gallery. I wondered what I'd find.

At the first cross path, a rusted street sign read: "Brown Rd and Browngate Rd." It seemed odd to find a city sign planted in the middle of a woods, even though I'd been forewarned.

"Turn left at the street sign, cross a wood footbridge, and you'll be in the gallery," Lorinda had instructed. Twenty paces in from the sign, a bench turned my eyes toward a large cedar tree with a tiny window carved in its trunk. Behind the glass lay a cache of unshelled walnuts. A metal arrow, appearing to pass through a hemlock tree, pointed down the trail.

The next sculpture sat atop a stump. It reminded me of a dollhouse with its shingled roof, green-painted walls, and bare lightbulb hanging underneath. Written on the gable were the words "HOME FOR A STONE." Inside squatted a cheery yellow stone. I couldn't help but think the stone looked happy in its little house. I gave it a pat on its yellow head.

Deeper in the forest, carved wood books with hinges dangled from tree trunks on delicate chains. I opened a book hanging from a cedar and read the quote: "One must not allow himself to become so heavenly minded that he ceases to be of any earthly use."

I laughed. The Ship Point folks were right. I liked George's work—and his sense of humor. A western hemlock tree's text read: "Go placidly amid the noise and haste and remember what peace there may be in silence." —*Desiderata*. A book fixed to a stump opened to "Religion inhibits the inner self."

Something flashed in the upper tree branches. George had cut little mirrors so they fit perfectly in carved niches. Perhaps to help us reflect on our relationship to the natural world? Later I discovered a mirror tucked into a tree trunk behind a shelf with a shiny red apple on a plate. I peered over the apple at my face in the mirror.

"What tempts you?" George seemed to ask.

More stones were elevated on podiums throughout the woods, as if delivering a silent requiem to ears that would only listen. One tree was plugged with an intravenous bag filled with red liquid, as if nursing the tree back to health. Or, perhaps, it was drawing blood from the tree? George left possibilities open-ended, like a question mark. Some sculptures didn't need interpreting. They were parables in and of themselves.

At a wetland mud hole a wood sign read: "Water for Sale." A fishing lure hung from the board inviting "buyers." Angling out from the forest's edge, a fishing pole dangled a salmon skeleton carved of wood. Behind it, the tree was fitted with a water spigot mouth and hot and cold handle eyes. A sign tacked to the trunk read: "Ministry of Environment." At the wetland's railing, I opened a wood book chained to a pulpit. It said:

> The sellers of water
> prostitute not only
> their own souls,
> they are also
> prostituting the
> very soil and
> birthright of our
> nation.
> One who treats water
> as a commodity has the
> mentality of a hen
> house floor.

Two different sculpture trails looped around the forest. I pushed along, anxious to see George's next piece. It was a five-foot wood cross with an arrow piercing it. From the horizontal beam hung a dozen red fishing lures with metal crosses in the place of treble hooks. Was the cross trolling for souls? The arrow spearing the head board suggested Native resistance to Christian religion. I thought of Blunden Harbor and the potlatch goods seized by government agents. I thought of the tragedy of ten thousand years of Northwest Native culture crushed not only by religious arrogance but greed for this graced land and her wealth of natural resources.

After just a few minutes of wandering the wooded gallery, I realized this was truly a sacred grove filled with totems of modern-day culture. These were trees as scripture, sculpture, and modern testament.

Through the thinning woods I could see George's yard, vegetable garden, and bungalow house. Classical music drifted from speakers in the trees. George, at least I guessed it was George, was walking a power mower back and forth across the side lawn. Gray-haired, large in frame but slightly stooped, dressed in cotton slacks and a wool sweater, he approached his late sixties. I waved, but George didn't see me for the forest. Why badger him with questions, after all? I'd come to his gallery and gotten his gifts. I turned and headed back toward Ship Point, passing a hand-lettered sign nailed to a mossy tree trunk. It read:

GEORGE SAWCHUK'S SCULPTURE GARDEN
STARTED IN 1988 FOR SELF
EMPLOYMENT.

PLEASE FEEL FREE TO
WALK THROUGH AND
INTERPRET AS YOU WILL.
ALL WE ASK IS RESPECT.

I left Ship Point so late that I had traversed only eleven miles before the sky over the Beaufort Range and Mount Arrowsmith on Vancouver Island trailed the brilliant salmon cirrus clouds of sunset. At the mouth of the Qualicum River I rounded a spit and paddled a slalom course around mid-channel marker poles. Gravel banks rose steeply on each side. A dozen trailers cozied together above the south bank. Rainbow wind socks whirled a cheery welcome. A man with a plaid work shirt and sport fishing cap tinkered irritably with a boat motor at the river's edge. He gruffly directed me to the opposite shore, a deserted field owned and run by the Qualicum Tribe.

"*That's* the campground. These are *private* sites," he scowled.

Four blue, portable outhouses, a couple of picnic tables, two trailers, and an orange tarp lashed between some distant fir trees were my only neighbors. I wasn't sure with whom or where to register, so I simply walked far away from the cyclone fence barring Island Highway and dropped my tent. I was relieved to find only grass and a sea wall for company. Crickets and ocean waves drowned the late day traffic.

Jogging along the highway under a deepening magenta sky, swinging arms in circles, I had two wishes for the night: stretch out the kinks and find cheap seafood. A mile down the road, the Sea Lion Restaurant offered just the ticket. Their roadside placard advertised "Pan-fried oysters $5.99." They didn't tell you each oyster was as big as a kid's tennis shoe and took six bites. I ate my fill of four and stowed the leftovers in the kayak's front hatch. No worry here about bears. They'd been chased and hunted from these shores long ago by townsfolk and civilization. Now, I wished a great big blacky could come sniffing along. A wild bear would be a hopeful omen for Mother Nature on the beaches of southeast Vancouver Island.

Under my headlamp beam, squatting on the bank of the Qualicum River, I splashed the salt off my face and arms. Two fishers hoisting a giant king salmon crunched up the beach with flashlights, heading for the camp. The fish looked as big as two aluminum cookie sheets.

"Wow! That's a beautiful fish! If I ever hooked one of those it would tow me home!" I said, admiring the salmon.

Brian, a good-natured, bearish man, had the kind of laugh that shook his shoulders and jiggled his belly.

"Are you the kayaker? This fish would tow you to Nanaimo. I'm Brian, this is Harvey. Where you from?"

"Jennifer." We all shook hands. "Bellingham, Washington."

"You carrying a fishing pole?"

"A hand line."

They looked skeptical. "Sounds like work. Catch anything?"

"Nope. Mostly I've been eating sea urchins."

"Sea urchins! Yich! We eat better—even when we DON'T catch fish!" Harvey kidded.

"We're just headed to camp for dinner . . . have enough food for a small army. Want to join us for salmon?"

"Oh golly, I was stowing my leftovers from the Sea Lion Restaurant when you walked up!"

His belly shook again—like a sea lion, I thought. "We cook better salmon than any RESSS-tau-RANT!" And, you know, I figured he was right.

"When?"

"Now!"

"But I'm still full!"

"Well, if you change your mind, or stomach, we're at the Halloween-orange tarp," Brian laughed.

They were nice guys, like teasing older brothers. But somehow I wasn't comfortable eating dinner after dark with two men I didn't know. So I climbed into my tent and flossed my teeth. All the while berating myself for saying no. Gee, Jen, how else do you meet interesting people? These are family men. One's a fishing guide! You could learn something!

I unzipped the tent, exhaled my fear, and strode toward the orange tarp backlit by a Coleman lantern.

"What you need is an eight-and-a-half-foot fiberglass rod—graphite is too brittle for you . . . pulling it in and out of the kayak—and a Shimano reel," Brian advised me, cracking an egg into a bowl of cream on a counter he'd built off the picnic table.

"What kind of line?"

"Berkley would do."

"Can you tell me the different salmon runs again? Each fish has several names, and I get them mixed up."

"Basically, there are five kinds of salmon, eh? Not including the steelhead. They do have multiple names—which is darn confusing. Springs are running now. That's what we caught. Named so because the biggest runs come in spring. But they spawn in fall too."

"Ever hear of chinook winds—warm, wet sea air that rushes through in spring?" He pushed his hand across the garlic-scented steam rising from a skillet on the Coleman four-burner stove.

"Sure, they cause all sorts of havoc in the Cascades. Big snow melts, river floods." Brian nodded, as he emptied a pack of spices into the fry pan.

"Chinook is another name for the springs because they often occur together. And because the fish's tongue, mouth, and gums are black, it's also known as 'black mouth.' Down in the states they call it the 'king' because it's the biggest. One female returned to the Qualicum River hatchery here weighing—what was it, Harvey?—thirty-two kilograms. Those big chinooks are called tyees."

"Yeah, some tyee—around seventy pounds! Did you go visit the hatchery yet?" asked Harvey.

"No, is it far? Walking time, I mean." I had learned to clarify this.

"Mile maybe. Twenty minutes. Qualicum Tribe runs it. Same group that owns the campground. It's worth the walk. You can swing by in the morning."

I nodded. "Say, how big was that king you caught today? It looked as long as my leg!"

"Maybe forty pounds."

Brian checked another pot, and dropped in succulent sweet corn. "Hope you're workin' up an appetite."

"I'm trying. The oysters are going down fast watching this Galloping Gourmet show."

Brian waved the comment off. "I love eating as much as fishing. Anyhow, then there are the dogs or chums. They run in fall. Dogs grow those big canines."

Harvey held his thumb and forefinger three-quarters of an inch apart. "They get teeth this big. They are the ugly ones. Aggressive, too."

"A dog salmon charged two friends who were strolling along a spawning stream at a park near my house. Just territorial, I guess. It lurched right out on to the river bank," I said.

"That's a mad dog!" Brian's belly and shoulders shook again. "Bet that surprised the heck out of them. A dog charged my waders once."

"Care for some cheap German wine?" asked Harvey, pulling a bottle of Liebfraumilch from the cooler.

"Got any cheap water?"

He handed me a stainless steel mug. "Hot or cold?"

"Hot, if you have it."

"Will soon," he said pouring water from a thermos. "Peppermint tea or Lipton's?"

"Peppermint, or I'll be counting salmon all night! Anyhow, three species down. What else, sockeye?"

"Or reds. During spawning they've got the bright red bodies and green heads. Think of Christmas socks. Then come the coho or silvers. We sport fishers are big fans. They're strong, agile jumpers."

"So what's left, the pink?"

"Yep. Another fall spawner. They've got the hooked nose and humpback, so the nickname 'humpy.' Mushy in the flesh, but the most abundant. Oily and good for smoking. The smallest. Two kilograms, or five pounds. And dinner's served!" Brian handed me a plate with corn, a beautiful tangerine filet of salmon with garlic cream sauce, and sliced peaches. "There's another corn in the pot for you," he said preparing two more plates.

"No, for you. I'll get too full."

"More salmon too," he kidded, winking at Harvey.

"You think I've an appetite like a mastodon?"

"Yes. And you need it! We don't!" He patted his belly.

I asked Brian what a fishing guide earns.

"Forty-five dollars an hour. And I just love to see people have fun out there!"

"And he always catches fish," said Harvey. "Others see us with fish and get mad sometimes," he snickered.

Finally a bag of scones was flushed out from the shadows.

"Oh boy! Local bakery, and they're blueberry," announced Brian.

"Let's get the jam!" said Harvey.

A little Ball jar with blueberry jam written neatly on its lid appeared. I felt the nice presence of a wife, who hadn't been mentioned. Kind of a customary exemption, I guessed, among mixed strangers.

When I left the camp, they sent me away with more scones and asked if I wanted a morning wake-up call.

"What time?"

"6 A.M."

"Nope, I'll still be counting salmon then."

At the blue-and-white sign reading "Big Qualicum Fish Hatchery," I turned west off Island Highway. I walked down the paved road, steering my feet as if they were car wheels, following the signs and painted arrows to "Parking." In the spiffy asphalt parking lot more signs read "Don't leave valuables in car" and "Salmonid Enhancement Program," with a stylized salmon drawn in graceful ovoids and curves. I paused in front of another sign that read "Visitor Hours 8 A.M. to 4 P.M." and pushed the jacket sleeve from my wrist: 7:57 A.M. Whew!

The first building housed a scale model of the hatchery. The table-size model began at the Salish Sea and included the river estuary where I camped, as well as the visitor center buildings. Then it climbed up the green-painted hills and under a railroad trestle to an artificial spawning channel for chum salmon.

As if to make the multi-level, painted diorama more realistic, "swimming" up the blue-painted Qualicum River was a half-inch-long pill bug. Another dozen bugs lay dead in stiff, gray crescents, as if spawned out in the turns and eddies. Up past the determined pill bug, the river valley continued climbing to mountain-flanked Horne Lake and a towering concrete incubation building, valve house, and gate shaft. At the valve house, water shot out one of two concrete tunnels and into the river to prevent drought. It was an amazing prospect.

A few paces from the hatchery model building stood a curious table with a lidded, white plastic bucket labeled "Head Depot Bucket." Beside it lay a box of fish tags and a sharpened pencil. I lifted the lid and found one fish head with its black mouth agape. The tag, which was strung through one gill, read "Chinook (Spring). It was caught by: Ben of Nanaimo. Length: 24-1/2. Place caught: Ocean."

A poster notified anglers of the purpose and locations of "Head Depots."

"Hatchery fish are recognized by the missing adipose fin [small fleshy fin on back immediately in front of tail]. Anglers catching and keeping hatchery steelhead are requested to remove the head and deposit it at any of the locations listed below.

"Participating anglers are eligible for draws for five $50 cash prizes and one $500 prize . . . Any entry not containing the tiny coded wire tag internally affixed to the steelhead's nose before it left the hatchery will not be accepted . . . The information on tags recovered from hatchery fish will assist fishery managers in improving and expanding programs designed to produce more steelhead in Vancouver Island streams."

But the head I'd found in the bucket was a chinook, not a steelhead. If I was confused, maybe Ben of Nanaimo was confused, too. But I read on and got my answer.

"Same goes for salmon and trout. Check to see if it is missing the adipose fin. It signals the presence of a coded wire tag in the fish's nose cartilage . . . ."

Leaving the "Head Depot" and making my way to the fish-viewing area, I imagined buckets full of fish heads set outside tackle shops and hatcheries up and down the coast from Port Alberni to Nanaimo like gruesome booty after a battle. I understood their purpose and agreed with the scientific reasons; nonetheless, it was a haunting image.

I walked down a dozen steps into the fish-viewing area. It was a subterranean room of poured concrete with six windows open to the Qualicum River channel. The air felt cool as river stone. Somewhere, something was dripping, and it echoed through the cavern, giving me the impression that I had limited time before the river won it back.

Through the glass, the river water was smoky jade. Two fish, each about two feet long, waved their leopard-spotted bodies in the river current. Their mouths and gill covers opened and shut rhythmically with each breath. I tried to breathe with them for a few counts—one, open . . . two, close . . . .

A Native man with a black mustache and gold neck chain hopped down the stairs like he'd been there a hundred times before. "Those are springs . . . jack springs," he said, pointing at the two fish in the window.

Jack springs was a new term for me. So I asked, "How can you tell?"

"Their size is small and they have spots on the tail."

Sure enough, dozens of round freckles covered the tail fan. It was just as the spunky fisher at Kitty Coleman Provincial Park had described.

"You learn by catching and holding them. Late October, we start milking fish for eggs. You get to hold a lot of fish then. Eight hundred to a thousand of 'em."

"Wow, that's really cool. How do you milk a salmon?" I pictured a milking barn and milkers squeezing salmon like cow's teats. I was way off.

"A female salmon's ripe when her belly's soft. Then the eggs are real loose in the skein . . . the egg sack. If you can squeeze a few out, she's ready. After you kill her, you slit open the belly and put the eggs in a bucket." He pantomimed cutting open a fish, pulling out the eggs. "Then you take a male salmon . . . he's dripping with sperm . . . a few long milks over the bucket fertilizes the female's eggs. You wait a few minutes, add a little water, and put them in incubators."

I couldn't help but think nature was being stripped of her mysteries and jewels. I thanked the man for helping me see behind the hatchery walls and turned toward the viewing window.

A singular wall of silver wallowed by the glass. It was brilliant as moonlight on water, longer than the display window at three feet in length and one foot high. Its motions were slower, more graceful than the petite, swift-tailed jacks who had darted off—*zip! zip!*—into the misty river current as soon as they appeared. Here was the chief! The king of chinookdom.

The regal king drifted past like one great procession of F-I-I-I-I-S-S-S-S-H-H-H in a trailing silver robe. His tail fan of opalescent jewels swished like the wings of a speckled butterfly lifting the robe's end. I pressed my hands and face to the glass. Its silver eye and black pupil rolled back and looked at me. The king turned. He approached the window as if to address my thoughts: "Hey, beautiful one, what a long journey you've made!"

With one inch of glass between us, it seemed a miracle to find the tyee here. After seemingly insurmountable obstacles, the king had returned to his castle, the Qualicum. I tried to fathom the odds against him, the astounding acts of nature one salmon takes part in to reach its river home.

Five to seven years ago, his mother would have navigated up this very stream, heavy with eggs. Were she a wild salmon, she would have dislodged enough fist-size cobbles with violent pumps of her tail to fit a king-size mattress—9 by 6 feet. It would be so enormous that a biologist could survey it from a helicopter! The three to seven thousand harvest moon eggs she spewed into her nest would be safe and snug in their aerated, cobblestone bed, so long as no farmers diverted the river water for crops and no clear-cut logging, road building, or land slides happened up river. Any one of these catastrophes, including one careless stomp of a fisher, could wash down a suffocating blanket of silt and snuff the eggs in a wink.

In the wild, one in 1,500 king salmon eggs survive to be spawning adults. Gorging on mayflies and caddis fly larvae, this alert fry-king survived in part because the Qualicum River has not been straightened by channelization, nor the trees cut, nor fallen branches hauled out. Hiding in log jams, he escaped the hungry herons, fish, and seals. After as many as two years, he graduated from estuary high school into a smolt among waving eel grass banners, but with far fewer of his brothers and sisters for company than at birth. He is fortunate that no shortsighted profiteer diked the estuary for farmland or industrial flats.

I tried to imagine the moment this salmon teen streaked (or idled) out to the Strait in his bright silver Ferrari! Like one metallic muscle, the ocean warrior may have navigated north through Seymour Narrows, Johnstone Strait, and Queen Charlotte Sound, then shot west two or three time zones into the Pacific, and finally up to the Gulf of Alaska—and back! Swimming day and night for five to seven years! By luck or instinct, he dodged oil spills, illegal drift nets, commercial fishing boats, sport fishing boats, orcas, sea lions, and the devastations of El Niño.

Behind the window glass, the road-weary king's coal-black nose showed a white nick from who knows what kind of scrape. Its mouth opened and closed an inch from my nose. Were I a minnow in the ocean, I'd be swimming for my life if this guy's shadow crossed my path. In one flash, I'd be woofed right down its cave-dark mouth and ushered through the one-way ticker gate of its black, barbed tongue. Somewhere back in time, a part of me had not given up the shiver. But for this life anyway, I was higher in the food chain.

A salmon's heart feels like a small, wet plum. I knew from cutting open a salmon—a gift from a passing fisher—in Johnstone Strait a week before. I had dropped the fish in a plastic bread bag, smiled at my good fortune, and paddled south. When the bag flexed between my legs, I realized the fish was still alive. A half-mile from shore, I decided to kill it right then. I severed the spine with a three-inch Swiss army knife, blood trickling across my knuckles.

If I could do it all over, I would let it go, though it may have been too near death to survive. Instead, I cut off the head. I worked the blade from the top of the head down around the gills. I gave the head back to the sea with a thank you. It floated lifeless, then sank slowly into the jade green water and disappeared. I inserted the knife through the anus hole and cut upward. I lifted out the sperm sacks, two long, flimsy, flesh-colored strips. Out of curiosity, I cut the stomach open. It was corrugated inside and two little copepods fell out on my finger tip. I could see their small dots of eyes. The liver lay like a shiny, burgundy streamer. The heart was obvious. It was big as my thumb pad and still pulsing when I removed it from the salmon's body. I lowered it gently into the sea, again with thanks, and tipped my hand over. The salmon heart sank into the depths, estranged from its body but still beating.

14 Talking Stones

The first night south of Nanaimo I went to sleep on Gabriola Island, not far from a smoldering fire ring. An hour had passed since the last coals collapsed into ash. Shivering in the sleeping bag, I thought of forcing fifty sit-ups to stoke the internal fire. Then it occurred to me that if I did just one sit-up in order to nab a fire-scorched rock, I'd have a petrified hot-water bottle!

By lying on my side I could make just enough room in the bag for the two of us. The stone radiated warmth like a sleeping animal. Given this stranger's delicious heat, and how it tucked effortlessly between belly and bent knees, I soon felt as if it were a living, breathing creature with ears to hear my thoughts.

"You feel wonderful," I said. "Thanks for keeping me warm."

It felt perfectly natural to talk to a stone. And yet my bedfellow had, for all practical purposes, no ears, eyes, or mouth. It was, after all, just a rock. A granite rock, I think.

It struck me then what indifferent, if not odious, boundaries we strike between the living and the dead. Stones are lifeless. Trees are verdant. A branch shaken loose from a living tree falls instantly dead. We tweeze one creation from another, granting some a throne in the halls of the quick and others a death sentence. When it comes to having souls, we get even more persnickety. Humans have them, trees don't.

That's not how the First Nations saw things. For instance, according to anthropologist James Teit, the Interior Salish believed that "all animals and everything that grows, such as trees and herbs, and even rocks, fire, and water . . . have souls, since they were people during the mythological age."

As for me, I'm a lunatic if it isn't so, talking as I do to the ocean, moon, otters, sea urchins, and *Yemaya*. That very night on Gabriola Island I decided that rocks, even if they aren't furred, horned, or leafy, are as alive as anything else.

I felt so happy for this change of heart, and for the rock's companionship, that

I sank deep into the ocean of dreams. At daybreak, the stone was cool as granite, but seemed strangely more alive than the night before.

After packing up camp I headed south to hitch a ride on the ebb tide churning through False Narrows. Harbor seals lounged and belched on exposed rocks garnished with sea lettuce. An arctic loon in a coal tuxedo ferried a thousand moons on its back. Washed by sunlit air, my arms and shoulders felt delightful on that warm morning. I unhooked the spray skirt to expose my legs to the warmth. I set the paddle down and watched the kayak ride sidecar on the streaming current. Perhaps, it was a good omen—sleeping with a stone. After all, I had come to Gabriola Island to pay homage to petroglyphs.

Years ago, during my first visit to Gabriola on a weekend kayak trip, a local islander, trusting my intent, had shown me the way to the "Talking Eagle." It perched above a small valley and overlooked the ocean below. Now, excited at the prospect, I tied the kayak to a boulder at the island's edge, crossed a quiet road, and dashed up the hill.

A great spine of sandstone winds through the forest there like a petrified serpent. Cedar, Douglas fir, large-leaf maple, and madrona trees rise up at the base, as if to conceal its presence. Throughout the sloped landscape, boulders the size of ancient sea chests have broken loose and tumbled down, resting beside sword ferns and fir stumps.

The path through the boulders was as narrow and faint as a deer trail. Other than the pathway, there were no signs. And once away from the water, the woods seemed insanely quiet. My memory hazy, I was not sure where to begin looking. Not, that is, until I felt an eye watching me and turned to see the "Talking Eagle." It roosts sideways above a dark fissure and stands nearly as high as my shoulders.

Deeply carved wing and tail feathers imbue the "Talking Eagle" with magnificent strength. Strangely, the bent legs and clawed feet imply both human and bird forms, as if this were a person in bird attire squatting on the earth with elongated, clawed toes. The agape bill and snake-like tongue appear frozen in mid-speech. The eagle's eye is a perfectly executed human iris, a circle floating inside an almond lid. Not surprisingly, it resembles the style seen in Northwest Native masks today. Except that this eye has an uncanny ability to defy geologic taboo. Like a haunted gargoyle, it tracked my whereabouts as I slipped past to view the other carved boulders.

Though I didn't know it at the time, these primal images dust the entire Northwest coastline. Pecked into basalt, sandstone, and, less often, granite, their whereabouts (and whatabouts) is shrouded by centuries, if not millennia, of secrecy and forgetfulness. Few will venture to say who carved them. At Fort Rupert, Franz Boas was told by Native informants that petroglyphs were put here "before animals were turned into men." Likewise, the Tlingit told the anthropologist E. L. Keithahn that the carvings came from "a time before time." T. L. McIlwraith, an anthropologist who visited the Bella Coola rock sites, learned that "the meaning of the designs is not known to any of the present inhabitants." Bear in mind that many of these ethnographers combed the coast more than a century ago.

Even with the aid of present-day scientific tools, dating petroglyphs is elusive business. Pegging the geologic epoch of the rock is one thing, but dating the incision on its surface is quite a different matter. We can only say they have survived a long time. Carbon 14 dates from the bottom layer of archaeological sites at The Dalles, Oregon, show humans have lived there since at least 8000 B.C. Further north, people are known to have inhabited the village of Namu since 5850 B.C. and Ground Hog Bay village at Glacier Bay, Alaska, since 8230 B.C. Closer afield, logging equipment recently scraped a foot of soil from the surface of some Nanaimo area petroglyphs. Scientists guessed the soil layer to be one thousand years old.

Most of the petroglyphs on Gabriola Island and elsewhere in the Northwest were discovered quite by accident. A road, cleared to bedrock, reveals a monster-figure watching from under a bandage of moss. An island family, remodeling a deck, spies a sawdust outline filling the grooves on a petroglyph boulder underneath the newly sawn boards. Loggers, fed up with a rock that snarls their log booms, push the nuisance to shore only to discover Vancouver Island's "Rain Maker" petroglyph. Island kids walking to school ogle at childlike drawings in the rain-filled squiggles of some bedrock cleared for a new garage. How many others are hidden in the intricacies of the coast?

Beyond "Talking Eagle," a tablet of rock displayed a menagerie of watchful eyes. A bear-eared figure with unblinking orbs raises its arms pitifully from a half-buried stone. Atop a fractured rock, a heart-shaped face reveals two eyebrows and a Cyclops eye. Across the way, a large boulder with a concave corner conceals a female figure peering upward, her vagina placed where the rock naturally indents. Similar female figures stand sentry along a stone wall as big as a garden shed. Their alert eyes, O-shaped mouths, generous bellies, and dilated vaginas suggest women nearing childbirth. As a whole, the images present a haunting canvas that begs for explanation.

Why are women, who carry the doorway to new life, honored on these stones? What tongue did the bird speak to its maker?

But I had hardly a moment to ponder these questions when a sudden wind whooshed up the valley. Fir branches rose and fell as if tethered to a puppeteer's invisible strings. Worried about the loosely anchored kayak, I returned down slope to tie a second stern line off to a tree. A blue truck slowed to a stop as I recrossed the road to go back to the rocks. I wondered if I'd get knuckled for trespassing. But after informing the curious couple that I was on a long solo kayak trip and looking for petroglyphs, they offered to give me a lift down island to ferret out a second area called simply the Church Site. It was unearthed in 1976 by islanders Mary and Ted Bentley. More than sixty etchings fleck this half-acre tablet of basalt in a grassy glen as large as a gymnasium. Surrounded by tall trees and silence, this site felt even more remote than the first.

Years ago, kayaking in Kyuquot Sound on the pummeled outer coast of Vancouver Island, I brushed across an islet made almost entirely of 150-million-year-old fossils. Atop an uneven crust of petrified mussels, the dusky blue valves of Pacific Mussels, their modern successors, opened and closed. Epochs had come and washed away, yet each species had lived here once, straining plankton from the same sea. It was like seeing past and present in one lucid stroke.

That's what I love about petroglyphs. At the Church Site I could plant my feet in front of a wolfish beast with a down-curved tongue pecked into the forest's basalt floor and know that I was standing in perhaps the exact spot where another had stood who felt something profound enough to carve it in stone. If I closed my eyes, I could almost hear the *tink* of hammer-stone on rock. When I opened my eyes, the enigmatic soul of an unknown carver stared out through a wolf's almond eye. The Tlingits spoke of eyes as symbols of spirit. The Kwakiutl tell of the spirit in the stone. Who were the spirits who made these petroglyphs, and why?

The only ones who know for certain are long gone. We have only the early records of explorers, anthropologists and their Native informants, as well as modern petroglyph aficionados. Today's First Nation peoples, still linked in blood and spirit to these ancestral stones, may not know the exact origin of the petroglyphs, but they are their guardians and staunch protectors. They, too, apply meanings that are sacred and often secret. And rightly so.

By doing a little side reading, I learned that some petroglyphs are thought to have been carved to influence the weather. In *Rock Art of the North American Indian,* Campbell Grant writes, "At the Twana reservation in Washington, there was a carved Thunderbird on a basaltic rock . . . if the rock was shaken, it would cause rain because the Thunderbird was angry." In the Klamath River area, the Shasta carved long parallel scratches in stone to make the snow fall. To stop a snowstorm a mark was struck counter to the parallel lines. Dry weather came after covering the rock with a ground aromatic root.

Some glyphs seem to recount an entire Homeric journey. In southeast Alaska, one such carving carries the tune of the creation. George T. Emmons, a nineteenth-century anthropologist, was led to this story stone by an elder Tlingit.

"In 1888, while hunting in one of the deep bays that indent the western coast," writes Emmons in a 1908 edition of *American Anthropologist,* "I met a very old Native who claimed the locality by hereditary right . . . [The petroglyph] was near the mouth of a stream, at the edge of the woods, a short distance above the high-tide mark. Hereabouts, at least a century back, was a small village of which nothing remains . . . . We could remove the obstructions from but one of the three faces, which was completely covered with . . . five principal figures. The grooved lines were almost obliterated in places by weathering, giving evidence of considerable age . . . My guide interpreted the design, not perhaps from his own ideas, but rather from what he had been told by those who had gone before . . . ."

It was the most ancient of all stories:

In the beginning, all was chaos. Ocean and rock enveloped in darkness. All the elements were jealously guarded by a few powerful spirits: Hoon, the north wind, Kun-nook, keeper of fresh water, and Una kgna nink, "where the sunlight comes from." Yehlh, a sympathetic spirit, disguised himself as Raven in order to filch a tongue of fire from Sun and bring daylight to Earth. Later,

Yehlh outwitted Kun-nook by ferrying a beak of contraband water about the world, letting fall here and there drops that swelled into rivers and lakes. Likewise Raven wrestled the howling winds into submission. Each elemental gift he shared with humans.

Other rock drawings describe less mythic historic events such as property sacrificed at potlatches; a war near Hoonah, Alaska, where the design is said to be painted with the blood of the warriors; a ceremonial killing of a Nanaimo slave during a Hamatsa ceremony at Fort Rupert; and, in Alaska, a slave who saved a village from starvation by constructing a lengthy caribou fence for catching animals. Others spell out fishing and hunting boundaries and rights.

The coming of Europeans is also recorded in stone. I have walked the shores of Cape Alava at Wedding Rocks on Washington's Olympic Peninsula where a perfect replica of a tall ship in full sail scoots among the polished beach boulders. Further north, at Clo-oose on Vancouver Island, is an exact signature of the Hudson Bay Company steamship *Beaver* with paddle wheels spinning and black clouds fuming.

At the Church Site, a large, finned sea monster with a double eye and huge head swims across the sandstone toward sunrise. The terrifying muzzle opens to reveal an armor of teeth and lolling tongue. Bella Coola shamans called upon sea serpents such as the mythic Sisiutl to aid them with supernatural power. Franz Boas said the sea serpent is one of the most potent means of curing disease. A person could catch a Sisiutl only by throwing sand on it, wrapping it in white cedar bark, and slicing it open with a holly leaf.

On closer look, inside the petroglyph serpent's dorsal fin sprouted a branch of pecked lines. Ribs striated the chest. It was as if I was looking at a skeleton of the animal and at the same time seeing the outline. Appropriately called X-ray art, this style is not unique to Gabriola Island, nor the Pacific Northwest for that matter. The earliest X-ray art appears in bone engravings carved thirteen thousand years ago in southern France. It is found in rock pictures in the arctic art of Norway made as long ago as 6000 B.C. No matter the locale, X-ray art goes hand in hammer-stone with shamanism. It's no wonder that Gabriola Island is believed to have been an ancient training ground for shamans.

Walking about the Church Site I found a whale-like beast lumbering across the dark basalt, its two-foot-tall dorsal fin rising from an unfinished torso showing seven ribs. Not far away, a frog-like figure of a man, complete with genitalia, squatted with arms raised skyward, as if about to jump. He also wears a head plume. Headdresses and plumes were thought to symbolize supernatural power. North of the leaping man swam three salmon incised with bones and spinal cords. One salmon nosed up to the outstretched hand of a human who seemed to be petting its snout. Is this figure a shaman, I wondered? Two more salmon harbored by the moss of the nearby forest.

Certainly not all petroglyphs were pecked by shamans. But there are certain characteristics that have become associated with a shaman's unique world view. In *Shamanism, the Beginnings of Art,* Andreas Lommel explains that worldwide among hunting peoples, pictures showing an animal's bones, lungs, or heart are probably based on the conviction that a "whole animal can be brought back to life from certain vitally important parts." Early hunting cultures believed that through art they could guide nature in a way that favored them. Animals portrayed with the X-ray style, says Lommel, "are neither living nor dead, but spirit animals . . . the soul from which the real animals are forever reborn."

E. L. Keithahn, a turn of the century anthropologist familiar with Native myths, wove a fascinating theory about petroglyphs and their influence on salmon runs. Keithahn noticed carvings were abundant at the mouths of salmon streams even when the rock was a curmudgeon to hammer-stone. Curiously, the petroglyphs always faced the sea. Many were washed by waves or completely submerged at high tide.

Keithahn knew that salmon was life to the Native peoples. "Failure of the annual salmon run meant nothing short of starvation." Indigenous peoples the world over pleaded to higher powers to grant full hoppers, fine weather, healthy children, and long lives. It only made sense that people would call upon supernatural means to prevent a failure in the salmon run and, better still, to ensure a large run. These mythic designs, he reasoned, "were never meant to be read by man." Instead, they were "carved on the rocks for the sole benefit of the Chief of the Salmon People." Placating the chief, "who had power to send his 'people' wherever he willed or deny them to those who offended him," is thought to have been the vital function of these glyphs.

Moreover, and here's a key link, a Haida elder told Keithahn that the salmon stream petroglyphs, like the Thunderbird stone, were made to bring rain. Downpours translated to fish, Keithahn reasoned, "since salmon often school-up in saltwater and wait for a heavy rain before ascending the streams to spawn." Two centuries ago, sockeye, coho, chum, kings, and humpies rushed up river by the millions, rippling the surface like a great storm. In the Northwest, it literally rained salmon.

On the fingertip of Jack's Point, a natural breakwater jutting north from the Nanaimo River, nestled a spectacular stone so packed with fish images you could just as well have been staring into a glass display window at the Seattle Aquarium. Dog salmon, coho, humpback salmon, a king salmon, and a flounder all swiveled across the rock's face pulled along by a streaming current of pecked lines. Long ago, legend says, a shaman brushed the original designs in ocher. He later hammered them into eternity to communicate with his daughter, who was transformed into a dog salmon. Succeeding shamans lit fires at the stone's base and set out offerings to ensure the return of the daughter and the Salmon People.

Spirit fish in the rock. It is a beautiful concept. These lively images surge from the stone and carry a message of reverence, faith, and interconnection.

I want to kneel down and pray to them to be the fiercest guardians of their kind.

15 Symphony of Trees

Every night for three nights after departing Gabriola, I dreamed of stones. I woke on beaches of polished stone. I found stones hidden in the soft cradle between toes. All day I paddled through islands made of basalt, granite, and sandstone: De Coursey, Wallace Group, Saltspring, Galliano, Pender. I straddled stones at lunch, leaving offerings of peanut butter and bagel crumbs. And when I couldn't land because of steep shorelines, I peed on stones, balancing with one foot on a rock outcrop, one leg in the cockpit, holding equally to both.

But most distressing was how I felt. Heavy as stone, stone cold, stone serious when I imagined crossing Boundary Pass. Boundary as in the Canadian–U.S. border. Border as in a four-mile-wide swath of no-man or -woman's water. A shifting field of white waves, fierce tidal rips, and six-knot currents. A commuter highway for international freighters. And I was not in the fast lane. Here was the fourth and final "threshold."

I was camped for the night at the pebbled shoulder, like a frightened animal giving pause before running from one side of the interstate to the other. I did not want to flip out there. Or collide with a steel-hulled freighter. I didn't want to swim for my life through a jouncing tide rip chasing a runaway horse. Though I knew it was unlikely, in my daymares I feared my kayak would break in half and sink like a brittle gourd spilling seed.

I needed to pull myself together. Tomorrow was the day.

The next morning, I laid the charts out on the beach gravel, opened the tide and current table, and cracked the *Coast Pilot*. I read the warnings.

In crossing Boundary Pass from the east end, Saturna Island to Patos Island, a distance of three miles, "*the tidal currents are particularly strong and dangerous between Patos Island and East Point on Saturna Island, B.C. . . . East of Rosenfeld Rock, overfalls and dangerous tide rips . . . The duration of slack at both HW and LW is 10 to 12 minutes.*"

Crossing Boundary Pass at the middle, headed toward Waldron Island, a distance of five miles (give or take a mile depending on current drift), the news was equally daunting. "*The tidal currents have a velocity of 2 to 5 knots, and heavy swirls and tide rips, especially with an adverse wind, form off the N point of Waldron Island and between Waldron and Patos Islands. The rips are generally heaviest with the ebb current . . . There is no true slack.*"

Crossing Boundary Pass at the west end, a paddle of two and a half miles, would encounter "severe tide rips" off Turn Point, Stuart Island. *The ebb may attain a velocity of 6 knots during large tides.*" I read the warnings a second time just to get it right, to assure myself I understood my Miranda rights before getting handcuffed into this stunt.

I had the right to remain silent on this beach and not launch. I had the right to hitchhike to North Pender and take a ferry home. I had the right to procrastinate, to be wild with fear, to plead insanity, or, maybe, to get across Boundary Pass by the skin of my kayak with all my marbles intact. Maybe.

No matter how I tried to leave, I just couldn't face the thought of crossing. At last, overcome with procrastination anxiety, I started skipping stones. *Plip-plip-plip-ploosh! Plip-plip-ploosh!* Then I got an idea.

"Hey. Anyone here want to go to the U.S.A.?" I shouted down the empty beach.

Surprisingly, one little stone seemed to shout out from the masses. "Me! Take me!"

I picked it up. A plum-smooth black stone.

"You really ready?" I asked the stone.

Okay then, next stop: America.

It was as simple as that. I put the stone in my pocket and became a taxi driver with a purpose. Most important, I was not alone. The bold-hearted stone and I pushed off with a *yi-yi-yi-yi* trill. And I aimed our slow-mo taxi at south Waldron Island's fir cowlick five miles away.

Any traffic out there? I looked both ways. Nothing west. East? Nope. Zephyr wind out of the south. Tides near slack. Boundary Pass was a plate of rippled, azure glass. Nonetheless, a shiver washed through my back and legs. Just for practice, I tucked into the roll position to help my body remember. I sat up, gripped the paddle shaft and pushed south with an even cadence. An iron seam had welded itself around the shape of my wild spirit. It was the shape of mountains, the height of Orion's bow. It was the width of Boundary Pass and beyond. Some might call it a don't-mess-with-me assuredness. I called it juice. Fire in the soul. It got me where I needed to go. America.

Two miles and forty minutes later, far away at the channel's furthermost bend, I spied a large square shape, white above, dark below. From its size, I imagined this freighter loomed several stories tall. Smoke trails blew back from the roof top. Bobbing up and down, looking through binoculars, I couldn't see the white and dark square any better. I tucked the binoculars back into my flotation vest. I kept moving, measuring, triangulating, to see if we'd meet. How fast was the steel hulk bearing down? Fifteen knots? I was punching along at three. He'd be seven miles away as he steered into the east entrance of the pass. Should I sprint? Should I wait? Or turn around?

I was slightly on his starboard side. I could tell because the white wall of the rear wheelhouse was visible to starboard only. I thought, "It'd be nice to radio him. Can he see me? Silly question. I'm a matchstick on his radar screen." I was a sprinting matchstick. The port and starboard walls of the wheelhouse were both visible—we were head-on now. What if he didn't see me? I imagined my kayak crunching like a butterfly under his sledgehammer bow. I held one end of the paddle blades in my hand and waved it back and forth in big arcs. He was still pointed straight on me. I knew he was too big to change course. I drew my paddle blades deep and hauled myself forward again, this time tightening my grip and paddling so hard my sternum ached. Three minutes passed. I could hardly catch my breath, but I began to see more of the white wall on the ship's port side. I was three hundred feet to port of him as he churned past, bow pushing a white beard of froth.

Breathe! Breathe! I told myself. But the puffs of air I heard were louder than my own exhalations. *Pooffff! Poofffff!* Dolphins! A pod of dolphins erupted beside the boat. They circled back around, exhaling clouds of spray. *Poofff! Poofffff!*

Breathe! Yes, *breathe!* Yes! We were breathing together. The dolphins and me. What a welcome committee! A five-dolphin salute! I was in the United States again! The stone and I survived!

Paddling toward the San Juan Islands, the islands of home, I realized I was crossing the boundaries of my internal journey, entering the last stretch of this

750-mile solo trip. At 10,785 feet, Komo Kulshan (Mount Baker) peered over the eastern horizon like a gargantuan barnacle. Years earlier, I experienced the immensity of that beautiful volcano's presence by standing on the summit and looking west at sunrise. Kulshan's triangular blue shadow cloaked farms, rivers, and towns. It spanned several counties and reached across two nations—west into America's San Juan Islands and north to Canada's Gulf Islands. It's no wonder the Salish name translates as Great White Watcher. I felt watched by a snowy god.

Fifteen miles east lay Bellingham. My thoughts drifted to friends who were likely hard at work on that weekday afternoon. Some were typing at keyboards, administering health care at low-income clinics, or teaching high schoolers and college coeds inside four-walled classrooms. I wondered, "Do I want to be home?"

How would I make the transition from having a wide open sky for a light source, the moon and tide as timekeepers, and the animals and plants as teachers, to a home bereft of wind, birdsong, even the absence of fearsome bears and wolves? I felt lost and uncertain. Indecision muddled my brain. What to do? I was almost home. My route reflected the ambiguity in my heart. Floating aimlessly across the last two miles, I eventually washed up on John's Island.

I grew tired, sleepy really . . . could hardly keep . . . my eyes open . . . as if I was un . . . der . . . a spell. For maybe forty minutes I napped—deeply. When I woke, the tidewater was a foot from my ankles and holding steady. I felt rested. Even happy! I stretched. I remembered the stone I brought with me from Canada. Delivering it to the beach, I felt lighter, relieved.

But I was also restless. I couldn't sit still. I pushed off again, aiming on Orcas Island's Point Doughty. There's a Department of Natural Resources campsite on the point's rugged tip. I would camp there. Paddling down President's Channel, I was still indecisive. Perhaps I should have aimed on Jones Island State Park and gone west around Orcas Island? Why was I dithering?

There is a Salish myth stirred up from these very waters that might explain the weird, wavering energy I felt. Back when Beaver was the size of Grizzly Bear, Komo Kulshan's wife wandered from the Cascade Crest, down the Nooksack River, and into President's Channel. She had turned her snowy back on Komo Kulshan because her spirit had been broken by his jealous first wife, Mount Rainier. Pregnant, uncertain where to go, she stood in the channel while whirlpools swirled about her giant hips. She was a big MOUNTAIN of a woman! Dugout canoes were spilling over in the current. The Creator saw what was happening. "Lie down, please, you must lie down," he said. "The people are drowning on account of you." The mountainous woman lay down and snored herself to sleep. She became Spieden Island. Smaller Sentinel Island is her child.

I'd given birth to something or someone, but I didn't know what or who.

The next morning, having slept in a dry, cozy camp in the lee of a fir tree on solitary Point Doughty, the building winds excited me. They heaved oxygen into my soaring spirit. A storm was blowing in. Funny how things come full circle. At the start of my Inside Passage journey, I was initiated by a storm, and now I would be ushered out by one.

But I was a different kind of traveler now. The same unpredictable, wild energy that blew holy terror into my soul in southeast Alaska now intrigued me with profound possibility in the islands of home. Over two springs and two summers, my courage and competence in storms had grown like the rings of an old fir tree. I was stronger in my heartwood and exterior. I was crustier, even a little sassier.

Anything seemed likely after so much time alone—even flying—on that terrifically windy day. By terrifically, I mean winds galloping thirty knots plus. Blows that were shape-changing Rosario Strait into smoking spindrift, whipping the surface into wild horses rearing waves over Parker Reef. It was the kind of wind that made me eternally grateful for a protected beach below camp. There, behind a silver beach log, I'd nested and triple-hitched the kayak out of reach of the waves.

Winds like those inspired me into singing praise for terra firma, for all rooted things—praise for the way rooted beings take a stand. Seeing a storm-blown fir, ten times my height, swaying but not breaking, made me wish to learn something from its ways. Leaning into the wind that stormy afternoon, leaning like I meant it—rooted feet, strong trunk, jacket filleted out to snag the gusts—I wanted to discover a new way to fly.

Standing on the open grassland of the point, head thrown skyward watching the forest's pitching tree crowns, I, too, was soon pitching. My muse was a forty-foot red alder, forked and etched black against a clamshell sky. I began to weave and sway my trunk to the alder's slow rhythm. Because I stood a few leaps upwind from the alder, the wind bucked into the alder first, then me. This seconds-long delay set up a lovely sequence. The stovepipe-size trunk took a moment to get its great straw rocking, so the tree was already dancing by the time the wind heaved into me. Wind gusts roaring up President Channel hurled into me like a heavy wool blanket. My body tipped back, then eased forward as wind rubbed past. So this is how the rooted dance?

I felt so exhilarated, so happy for a lively companion, that I hugged the scraggly three-story tree. The pinto-spotted bark of the alder felt cool against my cheek. Leaning into the tree's base, staring straight up its capillary-filled trunk, was when I heard it. I heard the river roaring beneath the crust of bark. It was as strange and sudden and unexpected as that. A river inside a tree!

I pressed my ear closer and cupped my free ear from the crush of wind. Inside the tree, rushing, whooshing energy passed through the wood, as if there was no wood at all. As if, when I closed my eyes, this was not a tree, but a glacier-melt river. A hundred yards from the saltchuck of storm-bucked seas, my arms wrapped the alder's trunk like a lover. Time melted back to an old memory—I had just wiggled loose of my blue jeans, underwear, tee shirt, and left them on the riverbank. I was stumbling barefoot across the cobble-strewn riverbed into the numbing blur of the North Cascade River. Cobblestones of seemingly every color—rose, teal, olive, umber, evergreen, white—galloped in place, knuckled my ankles.

I had come to the river to see wild salmon, to follow the thread of a dream where my legs fused with silver shingles and lungs opened like fringed fans. In that glorious dream, my body arched through jade pools whose current smelled of musky leaf litter and ironlike tree tannin. I had smelled home. And now, in my waking life, I wanted to become a salmon.

Naked, I thrust myself beneath the shallow rapids and grabbed tight to one large stone. I held firmly, bearing the icy drumroll of current, just as I imagined a caddis midgeon gripped a pebble to keep from washing away. I had come to experience, for one glorious, throbbing minute, what a salmon might hear in its river of birth—water falling in a hundred places at once, singing like a thousand choirs of river angels. I had come to hear the river sing.

The river in the Point Doughty alder trunk didn't ring and chime so much as it chucked and groaned like river cobbles clucking in place. It was the sound of rocks becoming round. The alder swayed a big circle. I hugged it hard. Wind energy poured from the sky country to the roots beneath my feet. I tried to imagine what the vole, nuzzling its long pink snout into unseen roots, heard now—a symphony of trees?

The alder had become a conduit for the wind's silent voice. People always talk about the sound of the wind. But the wind is silent. Voiceless. What we hear are the instruments of the wind—the surfaces, hollows, dips, and edges that wind trills over and through. Henry Wadsworth Longfellow knew about this difference when he wrote, "I hear the wind up in the trees playing celestial symphonies, I see the branches downward bent, like the fingers of some great instrument."

I leapt and pushed through the forest to press my ear against the corrugated bark of a western hemlock. Ah, so different—wispy, higher threads of notes. And the red cedar rising from salal held inside its shaggy trunk a longer, sustained drone, almost inaudible unless I waited for a strong-armed blast that could rock the two-foot trunk into a slightly perceptible sway.

Then I heard a curious whine. It was coming from up in the canopy of branches. Following the notes with my ear, I ferreted out two creased-bark maples. The limb of one tree was rubbing against the limb of its neighbor. One had become a fiddle, the other a bow. To check the sound closer, I pushed my ear into a dished-out plate in the silver bark. It cupped my ear like a cool palm.

The first notes shrieked like a stubborn nail withdrawn by a hammer's crook from a board. Then a second note rose up—a low groan ending with a high, sustained thread. Then, silence. Next a full-throated humming transformed into a whine and dove into a resinous groan.

"Humpback whale trees," I laughed out loud, smiling up the trunks. Perhaps here were two trees that longed to be whales. They sang to the ocean of sky from their home, deep-rooted in earth.

It was as if these trees—like the river, like the ocean—were a hollow conduit for sound waves. I once read that finback whales use an oceanic trough and low-frequency humming to communicate to fellow finbacks swimming hundreds of miles away. It is an astounding feat. How could I doubt that a vole, nuzzled in an earthen pocket of the trees roots, could hear the windstorm's song?

Years ago I posted a treasured quote on my cabin wall. Andrew Joe of the Skagit sensed an endless curve for human understanding and potential when he said, "When we can understand the animals we will know the change is halfway; when we can talk to the forest, we will know that time has come." He voiced something our Native ancestors, shamans, Saint Francis, and those who live close to the earth have always understood. Just as human spirit can be touched by the spirit of place, place and the creatures in it can reach their roots and paws, hooves and flippers infinitely into the human heart. If the sky country could sing to a vole, and a whale to its own nation, why couldn't a country of trees speak to me?

A story I was told said yes, it was possible.

In the North Cascades of Washington, up the Nooksack's South Fork drainage, there lived a stand of four- to eight-hundred-year-old red cedar trees slated for milling. Jewell Praying Wolf James, a human with a heart of ancient cedar, heard them calling. Lummi Native, earth steward, activist, he gave them his voice. Jewell tried through all the traditional routes—state and federal government, and, at last, protest—to take the teeth out of the saw. No words could halt the plans. Grief sandbagged his spirit. At last, he visited the trees one last time. To say goodbye.

As he often did, he carried with him a hand-carved cedar flute. He walked slowly to the grove. Underneath Grandfather Cedar, he sat down. Words of sorrow wept from his lips. He had tried to do everything he could think of. And there was nothing more he could do. He was brokenhearted.

The grandfather and grandmother trees listened. They took pity. When at last they spoke, they filled Jewell's heart with a sweet, sorrowful song. He lifted the flute to his lips and played. Fluid notes lifted from the flute like birds. The cedars were pleased.

That's not the end, though.

Weeks later Jewell addressed a large gathering as a guest speaker. He told his story. Afterward, he raised the cedar flute to the microphone and played the song the cedars had whispered. The notes rose from the cedar flute into the auditorium like a wind lowing over cedar boughs. The song settled in the hearts of the people. Unfolded like a prayer. Some were moved in wonderful ways. One couple took Jewell aside. They knew friends of the U.S. president. Perhaps money could be donated for buying the earth back. Certainly something should be done.

With the threesome forming a foundation, a series of meetings ensued. Out of this, the land was purchased through private donations. The grandfathers and grandmothers kept on talking. Whispering among themselves. Talking to the faraway stars, the returning rains, the young salmon rising from the rivers each spring. Inside the cedar flute their voice lingered like a prayer.

What have we lost by not listening? I wondered. Out here, with no human

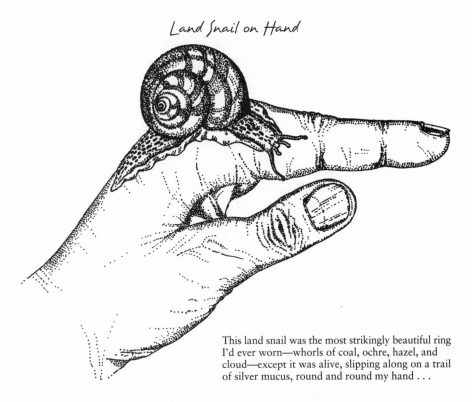

Land Snail on Hand

This land snail was the most strikingly beautiful ring I'd ever worn—whorls of coal, ochre, hazel, and cloud—except it was alive, slipping along on a trail of silver mucus, round and round my hand . . .

companions, my heart longed to speak with some *thing*. Before I left on my solo journey, people often asked, "Won't you get lonely? How can you handle so much solitude?" Now I knew the answer.

It is this: We must talk with many things. Seals and eagles. Water and wind. Columbine flowers and spruce trees. Land snails and lichens. By broadening our idea of companions, we discover we don't so much experience solitude, as multitude.

The Nooksack South Fork groves were saved. Here along the Salish Sea coast and Olympic Crest, however, the seemingly endless trees that the people of the Lummi Nation knew—one of which my father and we four kids couldn't encircle in 1964—are fewer than before. In their place are second-, third-, even fourth-growth fir, cedar, and hemlock, interspersed or replaced entirely with dairy farms, orchards, paper and pulp mills, oil refineries, aluminum smelters, resorts, and housing developments built from thin-grained, ancient cedar. Yet an undeniable presence ghosted me as I walked through the woods on Point Doughty. Crisscrossing the forest on foot, it was as if I suddenly brushed through the spirit of a grandmother cedar rising from the forest duff. An invisible old-growth tree standing silent and watchful under the cool maritime sky.

I turned back and passed again through this strange, invisible energy. My outstretched arms reached hard for a nugget of something tangible, yet touched nothing—no fibrous bark, no tear stain of wood sap or sawman's foot grooves.

Rather, it was as if the legacy lived on, not as artifact or stump, but as an invisible still-life of energy. A vertical memory. A phantom conduit that stubbornly remained, despite time's passing, between earth and sky. It was a nonverbal dialog begun and continuing seventy-five, one hundred, one hundred and fifty years later.

The trees told me the time had come to listen. After seventy days on the Great Mother ocean, cast loosely over two springs and two summers, I now heard voices where once I had found only wind.

Off the coast of Lummi Island, there is a stone tumbled there long ago by the feet of glaciers. It is a granitic, glacial erratic stone, to be exact. The origin, considered by itself, is magnificent enough. But this stone can see. It is a visionary being. In its wave-smoothed surface, two eyes and a mouth have been staring out to sea for eight hundred years. It is a petroglyph. It is sacred. *It is sacred.* I say that because we must take care of the stone. It is the salmon's and the wind's. It is the Lummi people's heritage.

Long ago, the Old Ones took seaweed and ceremoniously placed it on the stone to call the west wind, to summon the salmon. The stone also marked the northern terminus of a Native village. At that time the great rock faced out to sea. Now it is underwater. Now the stone's oval eyes are filled with the sea— and sometimes, at low tide, the soft rains.

I paused by the bathtub-size stone in my kayak. I touched the water from its eyes to my own. I touched the water from its lips to my lips. I was home. *I am home!* Tears rolled down my face. I trembled with humility and gratitude.

Qwa-cha-set is the Lummi word associated with this enduring stone face. When a dancer is going to break the ice to go in, to purify himself, and everyone says, "Oh, man . . . oh man . . . it's cold in there!" that dancer's frame of mind is Qwa-cha-set. Fear mires the brain, stampedes inside the heart, but the dancer still plunges in, no matter.

How often this journey was like that. Time and again fear surged its Medusa head. Horrendous and unbidden, it threatened to snuff me in my tracks. I had to run toward it, hug it to my chest, and receive its gift of humility. Plunging in, no matter, that's how I got from Alaska to here.

And still I get frightened. Fear, like faith, love, and hope, is an endless human cycling. I just know a little better how to deal with my own. This ocean-voyaging boat, with its shabby but still fragrant wreath of cedar on the stern and a cloth rose on the bow, successfully made a full-circle journey home. I floated away from the rock, crumbled cedar into the sea—cedar that grew in the forests of home. Its brittle, sun-bleached, salt-washed leaves still retained the volatile oils of evergreen pitch. They smelled of endurance.

After crossing Hale Passage, I hauled the kayak out for the last time on the Lummi Reservation's sandy beach. A Lummi youngster wandered over.

"Where did you come from?" he asked.

"Alaska. Over two springs and two summers."

"You see any whales?"

"Yeah, lots of whales . . . orcas, minkes, grays."

"Real close?"

"I could see their eyes sometimes."

"Where do you live?"

"Bellingham part of the time, Mexico in the winter, and the San Juan Islands in the summer."

He shook his head. I could tell I had lost him on this one.

"I lived here all my life," he smiled.

Bibliography

Anderson, Bern. *Surveyor of the Sea: The Life and Voyages of Captain George Vancouver.* Seattle: University of Washington Press, 1960.

Assu, Harry, and Joy Inglis. *Assu of Cape Mudge: Recollections of a Coastal Indian Chief.* Vancouver: University of British Columbia Press, 1989.

Batdorf, Carol. *The Feast is Rich: A Guide to Traditional Coast Salish Indian Food Gathering and Preparation.* Bellingham, Wash.: Whatcom Museum of History and Art, 1980.

Bentley, Mary, and Ted Bentley. *Gabriola: Petroglyph Island.* Victoria, B.C. Canada: Sono Nis Press, 1981.

Boas, Franz. *Geographical Names of the Kwakiutl Indians.* New York: Columbia University Press, 1934.

———*The Religion of the Kwakiutl Indians, Part II—Translations.* New York: Columbia University Press, 1930.

———*The Mythology of the Bella Coola Indians.* Memoirs of the American Museum of Natural History, vol. 2. November 1898.

Brown, Gary. *The Great Bear Almanac.* New York: Lyons & Burford, 1993.

Duff, Wilson. *The Indian History of British Columbia: The Impact of the White Man.* Victoria, B.C.: Royal British Columbia Museum, 1997.

Durshka, Ken. *Working in the Woods: A History of Logging the West Coast.* Madeira Park, B.C., Canada: Harbour Publishing, 1992.

Elmendorf, William W. *Twana Narratives: Native Historical Accounts of a Coast Salish Culture.* Seattle: University of Washington Press, 1993.

Emmons, George T. "Petroglyphs of Southeast Alaska." *American Anthropologist,* vol. 10, no. 2, 1908.

Fisheries and Oceans, Canada. *Sailing Directions, British Columbia Coast (South Portion). Volume 1, Fifteenth Edition.* Sidney, B.C.: Canadian Hydrographic Service, 1990.

———*Sailing Directions, British Columbia Coast (North Portion). Volume 2, Twelfth Edition.* Sidney, B.C.: Canadian Hydrographic Service, 1991.

Guberlet, Muriel Lewin. *Seaweeds at Ebb Tide.* Seattle: University of Washington Press, 1956.

Gunther, Erna. *Ethnobotany of Western Washington: The Knowledge and Use of Indigenous Plants of Native Americans.* Seattle: University of Washington Press, 1977.

Herrero, Stephen. *Bear Attacks: Their Causes and Avoidance.* New York: Lyons & Burford, 1985.

Hill, Beth, and Ray Hill. *Indian Petroglyphs of the Pacific Northwest.* Seattle, University of Washington Press, 1974.

Inglis, Joy. *Spirit in the Stone.* Victoria, B.C., Canada: Horsdal and Schubart Publishers Ltd., 1998.

Jonaitis, Aldona, editor. *Chiefly Feasts: The Enduring Kwakiutl Potlatch.* New York: American Museum of Natural History; and Seattle: University of Washington Press, 1991.

Jones, Mary Lou, Steven L. Swartz, and Stephen Leatherwood, editors. *The Gray Whale: Eschrichtius Robustus.* Orlando, Florida: Academic Press, 1984.

Keithahn, E. L. "The Secret of the Petroglyphs." *Alaska Sportsman*, March 1937.

Kennedy, Dorothy, and Randy Bouchard. *Sliammon Life, Sliammon Lands.* Vancouver, B.C. Canada: Talon Books, 1983.

Morris, Frank, and W. R. Heath. *Marine Atlas. Vol. 1, Olympia to Malcolm Island, 1990 Edition.* Renton, Washington: Bayless Enterprises, 1990.

——*Marine Atlas. Vol. 2, Port Hardy to Skagway, 1990 Edition.* Renton, Washington: Bayless Enterprises, 1990.

Scammon, Charles Melville. *The Marine Mammals of the North-Western Coast of North America. Together with an Account of the American Whale Fishery.* San Francisco, Cal.: John H. Carmany and Company, and G. P. Putnam's Sons, 1874 and New York: Dover Publications, Inc., 1968.

Schufield, Janice J. *Discovering Wild Plants: Alaska, Western Canada, the Northwest.* Seattle: Alaska Northwest Books, 1989.

Stewart, Hilary. *Cedar: Tree of Life to the Northwest Coast Indians.* Vancouver/Toronto: Douglas & McIntyre; and Seattle: University of Washington Press, 1984.

——*Indian Fishing: Early Methods on the Northwest Coast.* Seattle: University of Washington Press, 1977.

Swanton, John R. "Tlingit Myths & Texts." *Smithsonian Institution, Bureau of American Ethnology, Bulletin 39.* Washington, D.C.: Government Printing Office, 1909.

Teit, James. *The Jessup North Pacific Expedition. IV. The Thompson Indians of British Columbia,* American Museum of Natural History, vol. II. New York, April 1900.

U'mista Cultural Center. *U'mista Cultural Center* (brochure). Alert Bay, B.C., Canada.

Vancouver, George. *A voyage of discovery to the North Pacific ocean and round the world: in which the coast of north-west America has been carefully examined and surveyed.* London: Printed for G.G. & J. Robinson, 1798. (2d. edition London: printed for J. Stockdale, 1801.)

Young, Cameron. *The Forests of British Columbia.* North Vancouver, Canada: Whitecap Books, 1985.

About the Author

Jennifer Hahn grew up in Wisconsin, where she was raised by her wanderlust father. A love of outdoor adventure was born during summers tromping about Alaska, Canada, Mexico, Central America, and Europe with her family—four pubescent kids and a widowed welding teacher. She has worked as a welder, ski instructor, editorial assistant for *Audubon* magazine, illustrator, and tour leader in the Galapagos Islands. She is the founder of Elakah! Kayak Tours (1990) and has guided extensively in Washington, Alaska, and Mexico. She lives with her potter husband and a fleet of kayaks in Bellingham, Washington.

Barbara Savage Miles from Nowhere Memorial Award
The *Barbara Savage Miles from Nowhere Memorial Award*, given biennially to an unpublished adventure narrative, is made in honor of author Barbara Savage, who was killed in a cycling accident near her home in Santa Barbara, California. Ms. Savage's husband, Larry, helped create the award by donating royalties from his wife's book, *Miles from Nowhere*, a book based on their 23,000-mile round-the-world bicycle trip. Candidates for the award are book-length stories conveying the risks, joys, hardships, disappointments, triumphs, moments of humor, and accidents of fate that are invariably part of a personal outdoor adventure. Previous winners include *Where The Pavement Ends* by Erika Warmbrunn and *American Discoveries: Scouting the First Coast-to-Coast Recreational Trail* by Ellen Dudley and Eric Seaborg.

For more information, contact: *The Barbara Savage Miles from Nowhere Memorial Award*, The Mountaineers Books, 1001 SW Klickitat Way, Suite 201, Seattle, WA 98134; (206) 223-6303.

THE MOUNTAINEERS, founded in 1906, is a nonprofit outdoor activity and conservation club, whose mission is "to explore, study, preserve, and enjoy the natural beauty of the outdoors . . . ." Based in Seattle, Washington, the club is now the third-largest such organization in the United States, with 15,000 members and five branches throughout Washington State.

The Mountaineers sponsors both classes and year-round outdoor activities in the Pacific Northwest, which include hiking, mountain climbing, ski-touring, snowshoeing, bicycling, camping, kayaking and canoeing, nature study, sailing, and adventure travel. The club's conservation division supports environmental causes through educational activities, sponsoring legislation, and presenting informational programs. All club activities are led by skilled, experienced volunteers, who are dedicated to promoting safe and responsible enjoyment and preservation of the outdoors.

If you would like to participate in these organized outdoor activities or the club's programs, consider a membership in The Mountaineers. For information and an application, write or call The Mountaineers, Club Headquarters, 300 Third Avenue West, Seattle, Washington 98119; 206-284-6310.

The Mountaineers Books, an active, nonprofit publishing program of the club, produces guidebooks, instructional texts, historical works, natural history guides, and works on environmental conservation. All books produced by The Mountaineers fulfill the club's mission.

Send or call for our catalog of more than 450 outdoor titles:

The Mountaineers Books
1001 SW Klickitat Way, Suite 201
Seattle, WA 98134
800-553-4453
mbooks@mountaineers.org
www.mountaineersbooks.org

The Mountaineers Books is proud to be a corporate sponsor of Leave No Trace, whose mission is to promote and inspire responsible outdoor recreation through education, research, and partnerships. The Leave No Trace program is focused specifically on human-powered (non-motorized) recreation.

Leave No Trace strives to educate visitors about the nature of their recreational impacts, as well as offer techniques to prevent and minimize such impacts. Leave No Trace is best understood as an educational and ethical program, not as a set of rules and regulations.

For more information, visit *www.lnt.org*, or call 800-332-4100.

Other titles you might enjoy from The Mountaineers Books:

MILES FROM NOWHERE: A Round-the-World Bicycle Adventure, *Barbara Savage*. A funny, honest, and poignant account of the Savages' two-year, 23,000-mile, 25-country bicycle tour and the people, cultures, and personal challenges along the way.

WHERE THE PAVEMENT ENDS: One Woman's Bicycle Trip Through Mongolia, China & Vietnam, *Erika Warmbrunn*. Winner of the 2000 Barbara Savage *Miles from Nowhere* Memorial Award, this is Warmbrunn's story of her eight-month, 8000-kilometer trek deep into Asia and the people and landscapes she encountered on the journey.

JOURNEY ON THE CREST: Walking 2,600 Miles from Mexico to Canada, *Cindy Ross*. A compelling narrative of a young woman's journey on the rugged Pacific Crest Trail.

ESCAPE ROUTES: Further Adventure Writings of David Roberts, *David Roberts*. From rafting down an uncharted river in Ethiopia to exploring ancient cliff dwellings of the mysterious Anasazi to tracking climber Jeff Lowe on a new route on the Eiger, Roberts' adventures span the globe.

IN THE ZONE: Epic Survival Stories from the Mountaineering World, *Peter Potterfield*. True-life accounts of three climbers who faced the ultimate challenge in passionate pursuit of their sport.

FRAGILE EDGE: A Personal Portrait of Loss on Everest, *Maria Coffey*. Coffey tells the story of her love affair with elite high-altitude mountaineer Joe Tasker, who left to fulfill his dream on Everest—and never returned home.

KAYAK ROUTES OF THE PACIFIC NORTHWEST COAST, *Peter McGee*. Everything you need to know about kayaking routes and camping sites from Puget Sound to the Queen Charlotte Islands.

KAYAKING PUGET SOUND, THE SAN JUANS, and GULF ISLANDS: 50 Trips on the Northwest's Inland Waters, 2nd Edition, *Randel Washburne; R. Carey Gersten, editor*. Updated guide to exploring the scenic shorelines of one of the world's most popular kayaking destinations.

WASHINGTON WHITEWATER: The 34 Best Whitewater Rivers, *Douglass A. North*. From the Spokane River in Eastern Washington to the Elwha River on the Olympic Peninsula, detailed route descriptions include mile-by-mile river maps, matching river logs, and information on water-level curves.

PADDLE ROUTES OF WESTERN WASHINGTON: 50 Flatwater Trips for Canoe and Kayak, 2nd Edition, *Verne Huser*. The best 50 routes in western Washington rated Class II+ or below, with fully detailed trip descriptions and maps.